KATHERINE PARR

About the Author

Dr Donald Matzat has been a pastor in the Lutheran Church for over fifty years. He graduated from the Lutheran Seminary in St. Louis in 1965 and was granted an honorary Doctor of Divinity Degree by Concordia Theological Seminary in Fort Wayne, Indiana in 1998. Don has authored numerous books including his best-selling *Christ-Esteem*. In 2017, Don adapted Katherine Parr's *The Lamentation of a Sinner*. This is probably the first time this treatise has been made available as a standalone volume since 1562. It remains the only available edition. Don continues to serve as a part-time pastor at Immanuel Lutheran Church in Wentzville, Missouri.

KATHERINE PARR

OPPORTUNIST, QUEEN, REFORMER

A THEOLOGICAL PERSPECTIVE

DON MATZAT

AMBERLEY

Dedicated to
Lady Elizabeth Ashcombe
of Sudeley Castle in Gloucestershire, England,
for her commitment to keep alive the
memory of the remarkable
Queen Katherine Parr

This edition published 2023

Amberley Publishing
The Hill, Stroud
Gloucestershire, GL5 4EP

www.amberley-books.com

Copyright © Don Matzat, 2020, 2023

The right of Don Matzat to be identified as
the Author of this work has been asserted in
accordance with the Copyright, Designs and
Patents Act 1988.

ISBN 978 1 3981 1545 3 (paperback)
ISBN 978 1 4456 9687 4 (ebook)

All rights reserved. No part of this book may
be reprinted or reproduced or utilised in any
form or by any electronic, mechanical or other
means, now known or hereafter invented,
including photocopying and recording, or in any
information storage or retrieval system, without
the permission in writing from the Publishers.

British Library Cataloguing in Publication Data.
A catalogue record for this book is available
from the British Library.

Typesetting by Aura Technology and Software
Services, India. Printed in India.

CONTENTS

TIMELINE

	Pope Leo X excommunicates Martin Luther
	Henry publishes 'Defence of the Seven Sacraments'; Pope titles him 'Defender of the Faith'
1525	Luther and Erasmus debate the issue of free will
1526	Katherine Parr marries Lord Borough
	William Tyndale publishes first English New Testament
1527	Henry VIII seeks annulment of his marriage to Catherine of Aragon
1528	Lord Borough dies
1529	Katherine's mother, Maude (Greene) Parr, dies
1533	Thomas Cranmer becomes Archbishop of Canterbury
	Henry marries Anne Boleyn
	Princess Elizabeth born
1534	Act of Supremacy declares Henry Supreme Head of the Church of England; Treasons Act makes rejection of Act of Supremacy high treason and punishable by death; Church of England separates from Rome, initiating English Reformation
	Katherine Parr marries John Neville, 3rd Lord Latimer
1536	Anne Boleyn executed on 19 May; Henry marries Jane Seymour eleven days later
	John Calvin publishes the first edition of the *Institutes of the Christian Religion*
1536–37	Pilgrimage of Grace; Katherine Parr taken hostage at Snape Castle
1537	Prince Edward born; Queen Jane Seymour dies in childbirth
1539	The Great Bible, the first official English translation, published
1540	Henry VIII marries Anne of Cleves in January, but annuls marriage on 9 July
	Henry VIII marries Catherine Howard on 28 July
1542	Catherine Howard executed for adultery
1543	Lord Latimer dies
	Thomas Seymour begins courtship with Katherine Parr
	Katherine Parr and King Henry VIII marry on 12 July

1544 Queen Katherine becomes regent while Henry goes to war in France

1545 Katherine publishes *Prayers or Meditations*, the first book published by a woman in England under her own name

1546 Anne Askew tortured and burned at the stake for heresy
Queen Katherine and her court suspected of holding Lutheran views by Stephen Gardiner and Thomas Wriothesley

1547 King Henry VIII dies on 28 January; Edward VI becomes king; Edward Seymour designated Protector
Thomas Seymour, brother of Edward, secretly marries Catherine Parr in April
The Lamentation of a Sinner published 5 November

1548 Second edition of *The Lamentation of a Sinner* published in March
In May, Elizabeth leaves the household of Thomas and Katherine and moves into Hertfordshire to take up residence with Sir Anthony Denny and his wife, Joan
In June, Katherine, six months pregnant, together with Lady Jane Grey, moves to Sudeley Castle
In September, Katherine gives birth to daughter Mary and dies in childbirth; Lady Jane Grey is official mourner

1549 Thomas Seymour executed for treason

1553 Edward VI dies; Lady Jane Grey becomes queen and is deposed after nine days; Mary becomes queen and reverses Reformation policies

1558 Mary dies; Elizabeth becomes queen and Parliament passes *Act of Toleration*; Elizabeth reigns for forty-five years and dies without an heir

1603 James VI and I crowned King of England; end of Tudor dynasty

INTRODUCTION

As a pastor in the Lutheran Church for over fifty years, my interest has always been in systematic theology – the critical evaluation of Christian concepts – with a particular interest in the doctrines that emerged in the sixteenth-century Reformation, especially justification by faith. I do not claim to be an historian. My initial interest in Queen Katherine Parr, the sixth and final wife of King Henry VIII of England, was theological not historical. I discovered a Wikipedia reference to a treatise she had published in 1547 titled *The Lamentation of a Sinner*. The article stated that her work contained an unusual degree of self-debasement that would not have been appropriate for the monarch's wife and promoted the key Lutheran concept of justification by faith alone. My interest was piqued.

In considering the sixteenth-century English society in which Queen Katherine had written her treatise, it became immediately evident that history and theology were inseparably linked. It was not possible to read *The Lamentation of a Sinner* without considering the historical context in which it was written, and the history was fascinating. In 1543, King Henry desired an annulment of his marriage of twenty-four years to Catherine of Aragon. When Pope Clement VII rejected Henry's appeal, Henry rejected Pope Clement and declared himself to be head of the Church of England. Henry was now faced with the daunting task of determining the practices, piety and content of the new Church.

Theological definitions took centre stage. He imposed uniformity, beheading those who rejected his supremacy over the Church and burning at the stake those who taught doctrines contrary to his decrees.

Initially England remained Roman Catholic with all the attendant sacraments, rites, rituals, superstitions, bells and smells associated with the same, but two 'champions' of reform appeared on the stage: Desiderius Erasmus, the 'prince of the humanists', and Martin Luther, a German reformer. The reform touted by Erasmus involved the internal rejection of the superstitions and meaningless rites and rituals of Catholicism and a return to the simple *philosophy of Christ* as presented in Scripture. Luther, on the other hand, was determined to blow the whole Romanish system out of the water.

Henry, having been tutored by a noted humanist, had no difficulty initiating the Erasmian reform despite the opposition of Catholic traditionalists and a northern uprising that was soon crushed. However, embracing Luther was a different matter. Much discussion did take place between Henry and German reformers, but the English king could not embrace justification by faith and thereby deny the salvific efficacy of good works. This 'fly in the ointment' was no small matter since justification was the central Protestant doctrine. In his history of the English Reformation, A. G. Dickens writes regarding justification, 'We gravely underestimate this doctrine if we think of it as yet one more theological proposition added to the multitude. Once understood it developed an intimate power to alter both the inner lives and the religious habits of the millions who came to accept its message.'[1] In spite of the opposition of her husband the king, Queen Katherine embraced justification.

Justification by faith, taught in the Bible by the Apostle Paul primarily in his epistles to the Romans and Galatians, was the central teaching of the Protestant Reformation. As it is not possible to understand the character of Martin Luther without understanding the teaching of justification, the same is true of Katherine Parr. The teaching is quite simple. In fact, children can understand it. Jesus, the perfectly righteous Son of God, paid the just consequences of our sin by shedding his blood on the cross and gave to us his perfect righteousness. Martin Luther wrote that if you get justification wrong you get everything wrong, and all Christian doctrine is lost at the same time.[2] This is not some mere picayune doctrinal distinction but answers the practical universally relevant question of how it is possible for a flawed human being to stand before a perfectly holy and righteous God. Every person who believes in the existence of God and the reality of life after death must acknowledge that such an encounter is an ultimate reality. As one British hymnist put it, 'My hope is built on nothing less than Jesus' blood and righteousness.'[3]

This is a highly controversial teaching since as a prelude it requires the repudiation of all self-goodness, a frontal assault on good works and human pride. If perchance an average person, when confronted with moral failure and the Law and judgment of God, confesses his sins and receives in faith his forgiveness and justification, this would be significant but not monumental. For such an application of the Law of God and Gospel of Jesus Christ is the norm whereby an unbeliever becomes a Christian. But for a queen of England, having attained such a lofty status, to publicly tell her story and engage in an unusual degree of self-abasement that is not appropriate for a monarch's wife and embrace the truth of justification by faith was both courageous and scandalous. In his book *The Queen and the Heretic,* Derek Wilson writes, 'Like innumerable Christians who have experienced a dramatic conversion, Catherine felt the need to tell the world about it'[4] – even if it meant incurring the wrath of her violent husband.

I had to read *The Lamentation of a Sinner*, but it was nowhere to be found, even though it was obviously old enough to be in the public domain.

In searching for books written about the life and writings of Katherine Parr, I discovered a massive work titled *Katherine Parr: Complete Works and Correspondence*, edited by Dr Janel Mueller, Distinguished Service Professor and Dean Emerita, English and Humanities, the University of Chicago. It contained the treatise.

I ordered the book, anticipated its arrival and read the treatise with great joy. I was not disappointed. It was remarkable that this woman, Katherine Parr, a queen of England, would so publicly debase herself to find her holiness before God in the person of Jesus Christ. I was very impressed by her theological understanding. I felt compelled to self-publish this treatise as a small, standalone volume. Since Dr Mueller had worked with an original 1547 edition of *The Lamentation*, she had updated the ancient English used by Queen Katherine into an Elizabethan style or, if you will, 'King James speak'. I wanted to take it a step further, and hopefully put it into English the average person might readily understand.

The problem was, Dr Mueller's adaptation was a derivative work and therefore copyrighted, so I required her permission to do so. I went to the University of Chicago website and found their faculty roster, including the name of Dr Janel Mueller and her email address. I wrote to her, sharing my intention. I honestly did not expect a response, but I was wrong. She graciously gave me permission to adapt her version of *The Lamentation* and commented, 'You have my best wishes as you continue your retirement projects.'

I since discovered a 2009 anthology by Brandon G. Withrow, *Katherine Parr: A Guided Tour of the Life and Thought of a Reformation Queen*, which contained a 1548 edition of *The Lamentation* taken from volume three of an 1842 anonymous work titled *The British Reformers*. In his foreword to the book, Dr Paul Zahl, speaking of *The Lamentation*, writes, 'A few years ago, I tried to acquire a copy of this book. The only source where it appeared was a nineteenth-century edition of *The British Reformers*.'[5]

On the Internet I found a public domain volume of *The British Reformers* containing the 1548 edition, which was somewhat different from the 1547 edition adapted by Dr Mueller – it contained chapter headings. According to the colophon at the end of the 1547 edition, the treatise was published on the fifth day of November in 1547, ten months after the death of King

Henry and nine months before the death of Queen Katherine. *The British Reformers* proposed a different scenario. The anonymous author writes, 'But the most valuable of her writings was "Queen Catherine Parr's *Lamentation of a Sinner*, bewailing the ignorance of her blind life". This was published after her decease by Lord Burleigh (William Cecil), who found it among her papers, and it is reprinted in the present collection.'[6]

Since the 1547 edition of *The Lamentation* contains the prefatory letter of William Cecil, it is obvious that the reference in *The British Reformers* was in error. Perhaps the author of the 1842 *British Reformers* was only familiar with the 1548 edition and annotated Cecil's preface with the sentimental assumption that he had found it among her papers and published it after her death. My adaptation of *The Lamentation*, included in this volume (see chapter 11), is based upon the earliest 1547 edition.[7] In order to distinguish the various themes presented by Queen Katherine, however, I have chosen to include the chapter headings that were a part of the 1548 edition.

Katherine wrote *The Lamentation* in 1546 while her husband King Henry was still alive. She praises him in her treatise as a new Moses who is freeing his people from the domination of Pharaoh, referring to Henry's break with Rome and rejection of Papal authority. Given the fact that Katherine praises Henry in the present tense, I do think it is possible she intended to make the work public before Henry's death but that the burning of the 'gospeller' Anne Askew and heresy hunting of Stephen Gardiner, Thomas Wriothesley and Richard Rich dissuaded her from doing so. If her promotion of Luther's teaching on justification by faith – which King Henry strenuously rejected – had become public, she could have been convicted of heresy and burned at the stake. C. J. Sansom, the author of the bestselling detective Matthew Shardlake series, develops this theme of danger and intrigue in his 2014 novel *Lamentation*. In the story, Queen Katherine had written *The Lamentation* in secret; no one had seen it. She had hidden it away, but somehow someone stole it from her private possessions. In the story, Katherine says, 'And if it finds its way to the King's hand, then likely I am dead and others too.'[8] Shardlake is hired to recover the document before it falls into the wrong hands.

I self-published this intriguing, controversial, scandalous treatise by Queen Katherine Parr, *The Lamentation of a Sinner*, in September of 2017, adding a brief historical context. From what I have been able to determine, this might have been the first time this treatise was made available as a standalone work, rather than being a part of a larger anthology, since perhaps 1562. It remains the only available edition of *The Lamentation of a Sinner*. Why no publisher has not released this little volume for wider circulation remains a mystery.

In her 2011 biography of Queen Katherine, Dr Linda Porter is unduly critical of Queen Katherine's treatise. She states that *The Lamentation of a Sinner* 'has not stood the test of time'. Her assessment is obviously accurate since it is an obscure work. The question is, why? Porter suggests it is due to the quality of the work, stating, 'It is neither great literature nor compelling religious writing. No one but a specialist in the period would sit down to read it today. By turns rambling, repetitive and derivative, it is heavily based on St Paul's teachings and epistles.' Dr Porter goes on to say that Katherine Parr was 'no theologian'.[9]

I strongly take issue with Dr Porter's assessment. As one who has studied the theology of the Reformation for over fifty years, I found Queen Katherine Parr to be an excellent theologian. A skilled theologian establishes their positions with precision based on primary sources. Since all theology is derived from the primary source of the Bible, Katherine Parr cites nearly one hundred biblical references to support her claims. The bulk of Christian theology is derived from the teaching and epistles of St Paul. It is incongruous for Dr Porter to claim that Katherine Parr is no theologian while criticising her work because 'it is heavily based on St Paul's teachings and epistles'.

Others would disagree with her assessment. In her biography of Queen Katherine, Elizabeth Norton refers to it as 'a remarkable document'.[10] In her 1853 work on the lives of the Queens of England, Agnes Strickland writes, 'Her celebrated work, *The Lamentation of a Sinner*, is one of the finest specimens of English composition of that period. It is a treatise on morality and the imperfections of human nature.'[11] Alison Weir in her *Six Wives of Henry VIII* says that the treatise was highly praised by scholars everywhere, thus sustaining Katherine's reputation as a woman of learning.[12] Susan James writes that *The Lamentation* was 'dedicated to stirring people up and enkindling their devotion. In it, the passionate outpouring of her religious fervour found a unique and final voice.'[13] Janel Mueller describes *The Lamentation* as 'one of the rarer literary achievements of the earlier Reformation in England'.[14] She further states, 'In fervent first-person locutions, his self-identified wife, a Queen of England, abjects herself for her blind, foolish embrace of worldly wisdom. She then evokes her exaltation in love and gratitude when Scripture – what she calls "the boke of the crucifix" – opened her eyes and heart to justifying faith in Christ's redemptive death.'[15]

Conyers Read, regarded as one of the foremost Tudor historians, wrote of *The Lamentation* in his biography of William Cecil, 'This pamphlet deserves more attention than it has received. It was evidently popular enough to justify a second edition the following year.' He goes on to praise the work, stating that Queen Katherine believed that Christ was the only Messiah, therefore rejecting the adoration of the Virgin and the Saints; the Gospel, not human inventions, was the only sure proof of the Bible; and that justification by faith is no derogation of good works, as many claimed, 'for out of that faith spring all good works'.[16]

While Martin Luther's discovery of justification fuelled the Reformation, the importance of Katherine Parr's discovery of the same truth in sixteenth-century England is largely ignored. The eighteenth-century revivalist John Wesley was familiar with the writings of the English reformers of the sixteenth century, but there is no evidence to suggest that he was familiar with the writings of Katherine Parr. In 1797, William Wilberforce in his book *Real Christianity* called England back to authentic

Christianity, yet he makes no reference to the sixteenth-century work of a former queen of England written for the same purpose. *The Lamentation of a Sinner* seemed to be unknown.

Derek Wilson points out that 'this spiritual autobiography had a shorter shelf life than her earlier devotional writings. *Prayers or Meditations* went through thirteen editions in the sixteenth century.'[17] While Katherine's *Prayers or Meditations* – a work presenting the notion that through spiritual disciplines one might attain favour with God – remained popular in the sixteenth century, *The Lamentation* – her conversion narrative presenting the alternative, that faith in the righteousness of Christ is the sinner's only hope – faded into obscurity. Without citing a reference, Wilson further suggests that *The Lamentation* remained popular, particularly with dissenters during the Civil War period. Its candour and emotionalism certainly chimed with seventeenth-century pietism and Wesleyan religious introspection. It provided a classic conversion narrative for use by preachers and evangelists, who could point out that even queens had climbed the ladder of repentance and faith.[18] I doubt whether this is true.

Janel Mueller says that Katherine Parr's *Lamentation* is the earliest published instance of the conversion narrative, a genre that would become central in English Nonconformity a century and a half later.[19] While the genre of 'conversion narratives' was popular with the Puritan Nonconformists, there is nothing to indicate that the same was specifically true of Katherine Parr's *Lamentation*.

Not only did *The Lamentation of a Sinner* lapse into obscurity, the same is true of the entire life of Queen Katherine. In an article that appeared in the *Huntington Library Quarterly* in 1960, C. Fenno Hoffman Jr quotes from Agnes Strickland's 1853 work *Lives of the Queens of England*. In his footnotes, Hoffman states, 'Miss Strickland's work still remains the only extended biography of Catherine Parr.'[20] It is somewhat incongruous to think that no one undertook the task of writing a biography of Queen Katherine for three hundred years following her death. Linda Porter writes that Katherine Parr was 'one of our best but least known queens'.[21]

But times have changed. Since about 2009, a wealth of biographical books has been published defining the life and historical significance of Queen Katherine Parr. Most of the biographers are women (Susan James, Janel Mueller, Elizabeth Norton, Linda Porter) who appear to be writing from a feminist viewpoint, and for good reason. Katherine Parr was an amazing woman who deserves to be elevated as a feminist ideal. My biography of Queen Katherine, written from a theological perspective, presents her life in a new light, taking issue with many of the observations and conjectures of the previous biographers. Defining Queen Katherine Parr as an opportunist who became a reformer upon discovering justification by faith is a controversial perspective.

In addition to offering a biography of Queen Katherine I have also included the 1547 edition of *The Lamentation of a Sinner*. For those who may have an interest in examining the theology of Queen Katherine within the context of the Protestant Reformation, I have added an appendix, comparing her teachings from *The Lamentation of a Sinner* with the theologians of the Reformation, particularly Martin Luther, Philip Melanchthon and John Calvin, and offering relevant personal experience and observations. Queen Katherine's understanding of the key points of Christian doctrine, especially the relationship between self-accusation and the discovery of justification by faith; her lamenting of the spiritual conditions of her day; and her desire for every person professing to be a Christian to come to know the truth are as relevant today as they were in the sixteenth century.

A couple of points of clarification: In sixteenth-century England there seems to have been a limited 'name pool'. People tended to name their children after a relative or famous person, so there are numerous people with the same first name. This can be confusing. Some biographers speak of Catherine Parr while others Katherine Parr. Her official signature was 'Kateryn the Quene, KP'. I have chosen to refer to her as Katherine to distinguish her from the other Catherines. When I quote from sources that identify her as 'Catherine' rather than 'Katherine', I have made no change.

Throughout the text I use the term 'Lutheran'. This is not intended to identify the specific church body or denomination by that name or the teachings of said church body but the work and teachings of Martin Luther. All Protestant denominations embrace the primary tenets of the Lutheran Reformation but not all identify themselves as 'Lutheran'. I will often refer to the 'Lutheran Reformation' to distinguish it from the concurrent reformation of Erasmus, a distinction most biographers of Katherine Parr fail to make.

The obscurity of Queen Katherine continued even after her death. Katherine Parr died at Sudeley Castle on 7 September 1548 at the age of thirty-seven after the birth of her only child. Following the first Protestant funeral service for a king or queen of England, Katherine was entombed in the floor of St Mary's Chapel at Sudeley. The chapel was destroyed during the Civil War in the seventeenth century and all record of Katherine's burial place was lost. In 1782, some women visiting the ruins of the chapel discovered her tomb. With the help of a farmer, they dug down and came across her lead coffin. An inscription was found stating, 'Here lyeth Quene Kateryn, Wife to Kyng Henry VIII.' They opened it to find the body still perfectly preserved, but on first exposure to the air the process of decomposition began almost immediately. The body was reinterred, but inebriated workmen buried it upside down. The coffin was opened on two other occasions but eventually covered with rubble and forgotten.

By 1817, when the chapel was being restored, a search was made for the queen's remains. Eventually, the coffin was found. It was badly damaged and contained only a skeleton. It was repaired and reburied in a vault within the chapel. In 1862, the restoration of the chapel was completed and a new tomb with a marble effigy became her final resting place.

In October 2018, my wife and I took a trip to England and spent one day at Sudeley Castle in Gloucestershire and paid our respects at the tomb of Queen Katherine. I gave three copies of my self-published adaptation of her *The Lamentation of a Sinner* to the folks in the bookstore/visitors' centre, which they were very happy to receive. In response, I received a very gracious letter of thanks from Lady Elizabeth Ashcombe, the owner of Sudeley.

I have dedicated this book to her because of her tireless efforts to sustain the memory of Queen Katherine Parr.

It is my hope that in reading this book you will be informed by the remarkable life of Katherine Parr; edified by her Christian witness; and instructed by her clear teaching. In his prefatory letter to *The Lamentation*, William Cecil writes regarding Queen Katherine,

> By birth made noble, by marriage most noble, by wisdom godly; by a mighty King, an excellent Queen; by a famous Henry, a renowned Katherine. A wife to him that was a King to realms: refusing the world wherein she was lost, to obtain heaven, wherein she may be saved; abhorring sin, which made her bound, to receive grace, whereby she may be free; despising flesh, the cause of corruption, to put on the Spirit, the cause of sanctification; forsaking ignorance, wherein she was blind, to come to knowledge, whereby she may see; removing superstition, wherewith she was smothered, to embrace true religion, wherewith she may revive.[22]

Dr Donald G. Matzat
Wentzville, Missouri

I

THE TUMULTUOUS TUDORS

Henry Tudor, Earl of Richmond and figurehead of the House of Lancaster, defeated King Richard III of the House of York at the Battle of Bosworth Field in 1485. According to Shakespeare, Richard cried, 'My kingdom for a horse' before being killed on the field of battle. The crown was removed from his head and placed on the head of Henry Tudor, who became Henry VII, the last king to gain the throne of England on the field of battle.[1] The houses of Lancaster and York were a part of the Plantagenet dynasty, a huge, powerful family not only in England but throughout Europe. A series of civil wars identified later as the War of the Roses had been fought for control of the throne of England between the supporters of the two branches, culminating in Bosworth. After his victory, as promised, Henry married Elizabeth of York, the daughter of King Edward IV and niece of Richard III, bringing the two houses together and ending the War of the Roses. This marked the beginning of the tumultuous Tudor dynasty, which lasted until 1603 with the death of Elizabeth I, granddaughter of Henry VII and Elizabeth of York. A new symbol, the Tudor Rose, combined the white and the red, symbolising unity between the two houses.

For those of you who know little about sixteenth-century English history, please understand: catching a glimpse of the beginnings of the Tudor dynasty will bring us to the infamous

Henry VIII, who, through some unique circumstances, initiated the Protestant Reformation in England. Henry is famous for his six wives, the last being our heroine: Katherine Parr, the subject of this work. Many large, detailed volumes have been written about Henry and his six wives, and it is not my intention to scrutinise what might be considered insignificant details. However, as we consider the life and faith of Queen Katherine Parr, wife number six, it is important to 'set the stage' and consider the plight of the five women who preceded her in marriage to King Henry. This will raise the question of why Katherine Parr, a beautiful, sensual, intelligent and financially independent woman, would even consider marrying this king, who was at that time an irascible, obtuse, violent, unpredictable and physically disgusting character – the question becomes all the more urgent when we learn that Katherine had another love interest.

The Tudor dynasty prevailed in a time marked by the call for reform within the Roman Catholic Church. Desiderius Erasmus (1466–1536) of Rotterdam, known as the 'Prince of the Humanists', called the Church back to piety, devotion and the study of Scripture. He wrote, 'Would that the farmer might sing snatches of Scripture at his plough and that the weaver might hum phrases of Scripture to the tune of his shuttle, that the traveller might lighten with stories from Scripture the weariness of his journey.' Erasmian reform was not directed at the theology and doctrine of the Church but at the dead formalism and ignorance of Scripture that was pervasive, not only among the laity but also the clergy. His proposed reforms were a reaction against medieval scholasticism in which the teachings of the Bible were mixed with the tenets of Greek philosophy, creating a separation between theology and personal piety. Erasmus promoted the 'philosophy of Christ', which could only take root within the human heart through the study of the original source of Christianity, the New Testament. Roland Bainton writes, 'The radicalism of Erasmus consisted in his spiritualising of religion to the degree that the external aids to worship were regarded as superfluous or even impediments:

prayers by rote, telling of beads, reverence for relics, adoration of images, including the crucifix, prayers for physical benefits to the saints and the blessed Virgin, dietary rules, the obligatory celibacy of the clergy – all these might go, but should not be rooted out by royal fiat. Conversion, not coercion, should be the method.'[2]

Erasmus is best known for his historic translation of the New Testament. For centuries, the West had only known the Vulgate version of the Bible, the translation into Latin by Saint Jerome at the beginning of the fifth century. Erasmus' edition of 1516 contained the original Greek text and a new Latin translation which corrected the errors of the Vulgate. Erasmus was sharply criticised by traditional theologians, who considered the Vulgate to be a sacred text. Erasmus wanted everyone (including women) to read the Bible.

In 1519, an obstinate German monk by the name of Martin Luther nailed his Ninety-Five Theses to a church door in Wittenberg, Germany, calling into question the abuses associated with the sale of indulgences – Papal grants remitting punishments in purgatory – and thus initiating the Protestant Reformation.

Erasmus and Luther were initially of the same mind. They both rejected medieval scholasticism, the sale of indulgences, the value of the disciplines of monastic life, the superstitions involving relics and pilgrimages, the exercise of papal authority and the dead formalism of the Church. However, they soon parted company. Erasmus believed Luther was going too far by attacking the doctrines of the Church, which, in his mind, retained validity because of their historicity. Because Erasmus refused to take sides, Luther labelled him a coward. The primary issue that separated the two men was free will. Luther taught that humans, incapacitated by sin, were unable to work out their own salvation and bring themselves to God. Erasmus, on the other hand, proposed that a reasoning human, informed by the teachings of the New Testament, could willingly, with a 'boost' from the grace of God, follow the example of Jesus. It is vitally important in assessing the religious life of Katherine

Parr that these two reforms – Erasmian reform and the Lutheran Reformation – are clearly distinguished. In the case of Queen Katherine, history and theology are inextricably joined.

While Erasmian reform gained wide popularity in sixteenth-century England, the conflict and turmoil created by the Lutheran Reformation on the Continent was mirrored by events in England during the reigns of Henry VIII and his children Edward VI, Mary I and Elizabeth I. In the middle of all this, exerting profound influence upon Henry and his children, stands Katherine Parr. Queen Katherine was probably one of the most influential queens in English history, yet she is largely forgotten.

Henry VII and Elizabeth of York had a happy marriage and produced four surviving children: Arthur, Margaret, Henry and Mary. Arthur, as the eldest son, was Prince of Wales and heir apparent to the throne of England. Before dealing with the historical interplay between Arthur and Henry, however, let's briefly discuss the significance of the two girls.

The older daughter, Margaret, was Queen of Scots from 1503 until 1513 by marriage to James IV of Scotland and then, after her husband died fighting the English, became regent[3] for their son James V of Scotland from 1513 until 1515. She was the grandmother of Mary, Queen of Scots, and great-grandmother of James VI and I, who ruled both Scotland and England after the death of Elizabeth I and for whom is named the King James Version of the Bible. Margaret's second husband was Archibald Douglas, 6th Earl of Angus, but the marriage was unpleasant and she sought a divorce. By this time, her younger brother was on the English throne as Henry VIII. Being at that time a good, conservative Catholic, he opposed the divorce – an ironic detail considering his later attempts to dissolve his own marriage. Margaret and Angus eventually reconciled.

Mary was the fourth child of Henry and Elizabeth of York and was considered one of the most beautiful princesses in Europe. As children, Mary and her brother Henry shared a close friendship. In 1507, during the reign of her father Henry VII, eleven-year-old Mary was betrothed to Charles I of Spain, who later became the ruler of the Holy Roman Empire and before whom Martin Luther, in 1521, would make his 'Here I stand!' defence. In 1513, during the reign of Mary's brother Henry VIII, Cardinal Thomas Wolsey, Henry's Lord Chancellor, cancelled the betrothal and made a peace treaty with France. As part of this, the eighteen-year-old Mary married the fifty-two-year-old King Louis XII and became Queen of France in October 1514. Rumour had it that Mary wasn't very happy with the arrangement because she was in love with Henry's best friend, Charles Brandon, the Duke of Suffolk.

On her journey to France, Mary was accompanied by four English maids of honour, one of whom was Anne Boleyn. However, her marriage to King Louis XII was short-lived; Louis died just two months later. Some suggested he was worn out by exhaustion in his bedchamber, while others claim he died of gout. Whatever the case, Henry sent Charles Brandon to France to bring Mary home, even though he knew there was a romantic interest between the two. He made Brandon promise not to propose to Mary since he had other plans for his beautiful sister. But Mary had other ideas. In March 1515, before leaving France, the two were secretly married – an act that was technically treasonous. Henry was furious. He spared Brandon's life on account of their long friendship, but imposed a huge financial penalty. Charles' and Mary's eldest daughter, Francis, would marry Henry Grey, Marquis of Dorset, in 1533. Another daughter, Lady Jane Grey, was under the tutelage of Katherine Parr and was the 'mourner' at Queen Katherine's funeral. Lady Jane Grey was later crowned queen for nine days and is one of the most tragic figures in English history.

Mary died in 1533 at the age of thirty-seven, and a few months later the forty-nine-year-old Brandon married his fourteen-year-old ward Catherine Willoughby. After his death in 1545, Catherine Willoughby Brandon, Duchess of Suffolk, a staunch, brash outspoken defender of the Lutheran Reformation, became close friends with our heroine, Katherine Parr, influencing her religious beliefs and partially financing the publication of her seminal work, *The Lamentation of a Sinner*.

We now need to return to the past to see how Henry, the younger son of Henry VII and Elizabeth of York, became the infamous King Henry VIII.

Arthur, Prince of Wales, the firstborn son of Henry VII and Elizabeth of York, embodied the unification of the two warring houses of Lancaster and York and his birth signalled the official end to the War of the Roses. He was the heir apparent to the throne, finding his ancestry in both houses. Named after the legendary King Arthur, he was the great hope of the newly established House of Tudor.

The fledgling Tudor dynasty needed both military and financial support. To form an alliance with Spain against France, Henry VII proposed Arthur's marriage to Catherine of Aragon, daughter of the Catholic Monarchs, Ferdinand II of Aragon and Isabella I of Castile and (the same Queen Isabella who financed the Christopher Columbus's 1492 expedition). The Treaty of Medina del Campo (27 March 1489) stipulated that Arthur and Catherine wed as soon as they reached canonical age, which was sixteen for boys and fourteen for girls. However, once Catherine reached canonical age the families grew impatient, so a papal dispensation was sought to allow the underage Arthur to marry Catherine. It was duly issued in February 1497, and the couple were officially betrothed. Catherine's dowry was set at a princely 200,000 crowns, but there was one issue that King Ferdinand insisted had to be resolved before the marriage could take place.

Edward Plantagenet, 17th Earl of Warwick, was the son of George Plantagenet, 1st Duke of Clarence, and a nephew of Edward IV, and therefore a claimant to the English throne. If the Yorkist line were the true line, as most people thought, and if the succession belonged to males, as was again the common assumption, then Warwick's claim was stronger than Henry's.[4] After King Richard's death in 1485, Warwick, only ten years old, was imprisoned in the Tower of London by Henry VII. King Ferdinand, concerned for the security of his daughter's future royal status, demanded Warwick's execution before the marriage went ahead. On 28 November 1499, Warwick was beheaded for treason on Tower Hill. Catherine is said to have felt very guilty about Warwick's death, and believed her trials in later life were punishment for it. David Starkey comments, 'She, too, was to discover that her marriage to Arthur had been made in blood – Warwick's royal blood.'[5]

In 1501, fifteen-year-old Arthur and sixteen-year-old Catherine, with great pomp and ceremony, were married at St Paul's Cathedral in London. Following the ceremony, Arthur and Catherine left for Baynard's Castle, directly to the south of St Paul's, where a bedding ceremony was orchestrated by Arthur's grandmother Lady Margaret Beaufort. The bed was sprinkled with holy water, after which Catherine was undressed, veiled and reverently laid in bed, while Arthur, in a shirt and gown, was escorted into the bedchamber. The bed was blessed by the Bishop of London, who prayed for the marriage to be fruitful. After this – the only recorded public bedding of a royal couple in fifteenth-century Britain – the couple were left alone. Thus began one of the most controversial wedding nights in history.[6] The question of whether the marriage was actually consummated would have profound future implications.

The young couple established their household at Ludlow Castle in Wales, where young Arthur took on administrative responsibilities. In March 1502, the two fell ill. Catherine recovered, but Arthur died on 2 April 1502 at Ludlow, six months short of his sixteenth birthday. It was thought that the illness was the mysterious 'sweating sickness' that would plague England in a series of epidemics.[7] The news of Arthur's death reached Henry VII's court late on 4 April. The king was roused from sleep by his confessor, who told him that his dearest son has departed to God. Henry burst into tears. Grief-stricken and emotional, he had his wife brought into his chambers, so that they might receive the tragic news together.

On 8 April, a general procession took place for the salvation of Arthur's soul. A dirge was sung in St Paul's Cathedral and in every parish church in London. On 23 April, Arthur's body, which had been embalmed, sprinkled with holy water and sheltered with a canopy, was carried out of Ludlow Castle and into the parish church of Ludlow. On 25 April, his body was taken to be entombed at Worcester Cathedral. As was customary, Catherine did not attend the funeral.

After the period of intense mourning was over, Henry VII faced the challenge of avoiding the obligation of returning Catherine's 200,000-ducat dowry by keeping her in the country. After the death of Arthur, Catherine remained in England. She went through some difficult times, especially at the death of her mother, Queen Isabella, in 1504. In 1507 she held the position of ambassador of the Crown of Aragon to England. She was the first female ambassador in European history. Henry VII, meanwhile, renewed his efforts to seal a marital alliance between England and Spain by suggesting that Catherine marry his second son, ten-year-old Henry, who was now the Prince of Wales and heir apparent to the throne. A dispensation from Pope Julius II permitting the marriage was received. Canon law, based on Leviticus 18:16, forbade a man to marry his brother's widow. Catherine testified that her marriage to Arthur was never consummated and was therefore not valid, even though there was evidence to counter her claim. The issue remains debatable. What really happened in the marriage bed of Arthur and Catherine, God only knows.

On 27 June 1505, the eve of Prince Henry's fourteenth birthday, he announced that he would not marry Catherine. He said, 'I protest vehemently against it and am [utterly] opposed to it.'[8] A pubescent fourteen-year-old boy might not have relished the idea of marrying a twenty-year-old woman. However, Alison Weir indicates that in the late summer and autumn of 1506 'a bond of affection began to develop between them, and the gap between their ages to seem narrower.'[9]

King Henry VII died in April 1509, and his seventeen-year-old son duly became King Henry VIII. The new king quickly reversed his earlier decision, declaring that he would indeed marry Catherine, claiming that it had been his father's dying wish. Whether or not this was true, Henry only knows. According to David Starkey, 'The truth seems to be that Henry VIII married Catherine because he wanted to. He wanted her father, Ferdinand of Spain, as an ally in the war which he intended to wage against France. He wanted to be married to show that, despite his youth, he was fully adult and able to wield sovereignty without limitation. And finally, despite the fact that Catherine was twenty-four-and-a-half years old to his eighteen, and that she was four feet something to his six feet two inches, she was still young enough and attractive enough to be wanted for herself.'[10]

A low-key affair, Henry's wedding to Catherine was held at the friar's church in Greenwich on 11 June 1509. On 23 June 1509, Henry led Catherine from the Tower of London to Westminster Abbey for their coronation, which took place the following day. Finally, after seven years of waiting, Catherine of Aragon was now the Queen of England, the first wife of Henry VIII.

2

THE KING'S GREAT MATTER

Henry and Catherine's honeymoon lasted far longer than the customary 'first month after marriage, when there is nothing but tenderness and pleasure'. Instead, many months passed while the king, queen and court devoted themselves to rounds of entertainment. 'Our time is ever passed in continual feasts,' Catherine informed her father.[1] By most accounts, theirs was generally a happy marriage, despite Henry's numerous affairs. Since Catherine was frequently pregnant, passion was obviously involved. Starkey commented that Catherine made Henry's shirts and that, to his dying day, he never lost his taste for the black-thread embroidery round the collar and cuffs that was known as Spanish work.[2] The royal couple apparently loved each other and worked well together as king and queen.

In 1513, Henry went to France on a military campaign and in his absence appointed Catherine regent in England with the titles Governor of the Realm and Captain General. (Thirty years later, Queen Kathrine Parr would also be appointed regent in England as Henry went off to another war against France; they were the only two queen consorts[3] to be afforded that honour.) In the absence of Henry, the Scots decided to invade from the north. Catherine had to muster the troops, and despite being heavily pregnant at the time, she rode north in full armour to give an impassioned speech to the army. While Henry won his battle in France, his queen successfully defended the homeland against a Scottish invasion.

Henry and Catherine were devout Roman Catholics. Agnes Strickland, quoting from Sebastiano Giustiniani, an Italian who lived in England, describes Henry as being very devout. On the days when he went hunting he heard Mass three times, but on other days it was as often as five times. He had vesper service every day in the queen's chamber. Catherine, on the other hand, was very pious and self-denying, almost a nun in her performance of religious duties. She would rise at different times of the night for prayers. She fasted on Fridays, Saturdays and all the saints' days, confessed every week, and received the Eucharist every Sunday. For two hours after dinner, one of her attendants read books on religion to her.[4]

While Henry and Catherine shared the same faith, as a boy Henry's tutor was William Blount, 4th Baron Mountjoy, a friend and disciple of the humanist Erasmus. Henry was trained in the manner and style of Erasmus, making him the first Renaissance king of England. This would become evident later, when Henry became the 'pope' of England. On Henry's accession in 1509, Mountjoy had become a trusted servant of the king. By 1512, he had become Queen Catherine's Lord Chamberlain. As we will see later, the king's 'Great Matter' would place Mountjoy in a terrible position.

On the horizon there loomed a threat to the royal couple's staunch Roman Catholic beliefs in the form of the Lutheran Reformation. Even the minds of some of Henry's English subjects were being poisoned by these new ideas. The king was initially a staunch supporter of the papacy and an opponent of the Reformation; indeed, he was engaged in a virulent exchange with Martin Luther in 1521. In 1520, Luther had written *The Babylonian Captivity of the Church*, in which he critically examined the Seven Sacraments of Rome in the light of Scripture. Although published in Latin, a translation of this work had quickly been published in German by Thomas Murner, an opponent of Luther. Murner had hoped that people would withdraw their support from Luther if they were aware of his radical views, but the opposite happened. The translation helped to spread Luther's views across Germany.

The virulence of Luther's language, however, did cause some offence, as did its harsh condemnation of the papacy. Henry fired off a stinging response entitled *Defence of the Seven Sacraments*, in which he referred to Luther as 'the little monk who spews up against the pope'. Henry commented to his friend Thomas More, a noted humanist scholar, 'We will set forth the pope's authority to the uttermost.' He would come to regret these words.[5] Whether or not Henry wrote this treatise is in fact debatable. It has been suggested that it is actually the work of Cardinal Thomas Wolsey, Henry's Lord Chancellor, or Thomas More. More did admit that he was the editor, 'a sorter out and placer of the principal matters therein contained'.[6] Regardless, Henry was afforded the honorary title 'Defender of the Faith' from Pope Leo X, a title that the Church of England would apply to every subsequent monarch. The pope was so ecstatic over the work that he even awarded an indulgence to anyone who read it.

Martin Luther angrily responded in 1522 with *Against Henry, the King of England*, in which he said that Henry's work was overflowing with lies and that Henry was the 'king of liars'. Luther also declared that Henry's ranting made him come across like 'a livid whore on the street'. According to Alison Weir, Luther accused Henry of 'raving like a strumpet in a tantrum' and spoke of 'stuffing such impudent falsehoods down his throat'.[7] It was this work that prompted the humanist Erasmus, who had originally supported Luther, to publicly take issue with both Luther's theology and his tone.[8] Erasmus believed that debates within the Church should be conducted in a brotherly, non-combative manner.

Luther's reaction had perhaps been typical of his personality, but it was also unfortunate. Later, in 1526, King Christian II of Denmark told Luther that Henry was changing and moving closer to the Reformation. It was suggested that an apology from Luther might help swing Henry to the Protestant side, so he wrote a humble apology to King Henry:

Grace and peace in Christ, our Lord and Saviour. Amen. Indeed, most serene and illustrious King, I ought greatly to fear to address your Majesty in a letter, as l am fully aware that your Majesty is deeply offended at my pamphlet which I published foolishly and precipitately... What impels me to write, abject as I am, is that your Majesty has begun to favour the evangelical cause, and to feel disgust at the abandoned men who oppose us. This news was a true gospel, tidings of great joy, to my heart. I cast myself with the utmost possible humility at your Majesty's feet, and pray and beseech you, by the love and cross and glory of Christ, to deign to leave off your anger, and forgive me for what I have done to injure your Majesty, as Christ commands us in His prayer to forgive each other. If your serene Majesty wishes me to recant publicly and write in honour of your Majesty, will you graciously signify your wish to me, and I shall not delay, but shall do so most willingly. Although I am a man of naught compared to your Majesty, yet we may hope that great good may come to the evangelical cause and to God's glory if opportunity is given me of writing the King of England on this subject.[9]

Luther was given bad information. At this early stage, Henry had no intention of moving toward the Reformation. He took advantage of the opportunity to embarrass Luther by translating his apology into English and making it known. Henry was as vicious in his response as imaginable, accusing Luther of deflowering a nun and of leading scores of thousands to their deaths in the Peasants' War.[10,11]

In 1527, in a letter to his friend Wenceslas Linck discussing the matter, Luther referred to Henry as a Satan worshipper. He wrote, 'Persuaded by the king of Denmark, I wrote a humble and suppliant letter to the king of England [Henry VIII]; I had high hopes and wrote with a guileless and candid heart. He has answered me with such hostility that he sounds ... as if he rejoiced in the opportunity for revenge. These tyrants have weak, unmanly, and thoroughly sordid characters that make them unworthy of serving any but the rabble ... I disdain them and their god Satan.'[12] In hindsight, Henry would probably have been wise to accept Luther's apology and encourage him 'to write in honour' of him. It might have changed Luther's mind when his opinion was sought regarding that which came to be known as the 'King's Great Matter'.

Catherine was pregnant on seven occasions, but only one child, daughter Mary, survived. On 1 January 1511 she did give birth to a son, Henry, Duke of Cornwall. There was great rejoicing, but the child died after fifty-two days. As a result, Henry grew convinced that his marriage to Catherine was cursed because it was contrary to God's law. Leviticus 18:16 stated, 'Thou shalt not uncover the nakedness of thy brother's wife: it is thy brother's nakedness,' and Leviticus 20:21, 'If a man shall take his brother's wife, it is an unclean thing ... they shall be childless.' But there is another side to the story. Pope Julius had sanctioned the marriage based on Deuteronomy 25:5, which states that if one brother dies without a son, his widow must not marry outside the family. Her husband's brother shall take her and marry her and fulfil the duty of a brother-in-law to her. This is called Levirate marriage. While the Leviticus verse applies if the brother is still living, the Deuteronomy verse applies if the brother died without a male heir. So, Pope Julius was right, according to Old Testament law, to grant the dispensation.

Ignoring the verse in Deuteronomy, Henry claimed that Pope Julius was wrong in granting the dispensation and that his conscience was sorely burdened to the extent that his soul was suffering. Catherine strongly insisted that her marriage to Henry's brother Arthur was never consummated, but there was contrary evidence. On the morning after 'the bedding ceremony', Arthur announced to his friends that he was thirsty because 'he had spent the night in Spain'. There was also the alleged existence of bloody sheets. Of course, Henry would have known whether Catherine was a virgin (which many believe she was). Thus began the 'King's Great Matter', his desire to have his marriage to Catherine declared null and void.

Henry was properly concerned that he did not have a male heir. According to Alison Weir, 'His concern for the succession and the future of his kingdom was sincere and genuine.'[13]

Without a legitimate male, there could again be a battle for the throne as in the earlier 'War of the Roses'. Henry did have a son: Henry Fitzroy, the child of his mistress Elizabeth 'Bessie' Blount. This proved to Henry that their failure to produce a male heir wasn't his fault. In 1525, the six-year-old Fitzroy was elevated to become Duke of Richmond and Somerset. Sir William Parr, Katherine's uncle, was appointed his chamberlain. There was some indication that King Henry wanted his bastard son included in the succession, but Henry Fitzroy died in 1536, aged seventeen, before it could be formalised.

Henry was unwilling to accept Princess Mary as his only heir to the throne. He believed that women were inferior and therefore unfit to rule, and he was not prepared to seek a solution to his dynastic weakness by wedding Mary to any of his rivals, real or potential, in the hope that she would provide grandsons. He wanted a male heir of his own body, not hers.[14] Of course, Catherine did not agree. She was convinced that Mary was able to rule, as her own mother, Isabella of Castile, had done in Spain.

There was no hope for Henry to have a male heir if he remained married to Catherine of Aragon, who was now beyond childbearing years. Her once slim appearance had drastically changed, causing King Francis I of France to describe her as being 'deformed'. British historian David Starkey wrote that her 'once trim figure broadened, and layers of fat swelled her face and body. By the time she reached the menopause, which seems to have come to her very early at about thirty-five, she was nearly as wide as she was tall.' What made it worse, of course, was that she had married a husband who was younger and better-looking than she, and who had kept his youth and looks longer.[15]

Waiting in the wings was the beautiful and infamous Anne Boleyn. Anne was the daughter of Thomas Boleyn, 1st Earl of Wiltshire, and his wife, Lady Elizabeth Howard. She had moved to France as one of the maids of honour for Henry's sister Mary, who was to marry King Louis XII. Two months later, after the death of Louis, Mary was called home, but Anne remained in France as a lady-in-waiting to Queen Claude of France. Anne returned to England in early 1522 and became one of Queen Catherine's ladies-in-waiting.[16]

Henry began to pursue Anne in 1526. He fell madly in love and became obsessed with her. He sent her gifts and wrote her love letters, which, interestingly enough, are in the Vatican Library – probably sent to Rome by those loyal to Catherine as evidence of the king's infidelity. Henry offered Anne the opportunity to become his 'official mistress', but she declined, stating that she would only share his bed if she became his wife. Anne's sister Mary had once become Henry's mistress only to be discarded, and Anne was not interested in the same fate. Henry was growing frustrated. Cardinal Campeggio, who would be sent to England to adjudicate in the Great Matter, later wrote to his master Pope Clement, 'He sees nothing, he thinks of nothing but Anne. He cannot do without her for an hour, and it moves me to see how the King's life, the stability and downfall of the whole country, may hang on this.'[17]

So, considering all the motives, what was the primary reason for Henry to seek the annulment? Peter Marshall suggests that the king's actions only make sense in the light of his protestations of being truly, utterly convinced that his marriage was unlawful, an abomination in the eyes of the Lord. Why else would the Lord punish him by withholding the son his rank and piety deserved?[18] Was it really a matter of his conscience, though, or was it simply down to his passion for Anne Boleyn? Or was it all about the lack of a male heir? I have a hard time believing that his conscience was really bothering him. Why did it take over twenty years before his conscience kicked in? Considering his antics, I doubt whether Henry VIII had a very sensitive conscience. Agnes Strickland writes, 'His first step was to complain to his confessor that his conscience troubled him for having married his brother's widow, but it seems strange that that inward monitor had been silent for so many years.'[19]

There is no doubt that Henry was obsessed with Lady Anne, but according to historian Alison Weir she was 'merely a catalyst, and the indications are that Henry would have pursued an annulment at some stage anyway, for overriding all other considerations was his desperate need for a male heir'.[20] The idea that his primary motive was unrequited passion for Anne Boleyn, while rich material for a romantic storyline, is unrealistic, especially when you consider that their eventual marriage lasted only three years since Anne did not produce a male heir. Anne was accused of adultery and beheaded. How could Henry have executed the love of his life?

In May 1527, Anne appeared with Henry for the first time at a public gathering. Henry was impatient. By showing her off, he made clear that his troubled conscience was intimately linked to her. By November the following year, the king had invited his chief subjects to Bridewell Palace and laid his cards on the table. Standing before the throne, he did his best to justify his need for an annulment of his marriage. He reminded his audience how peace had prevailed during his reign and confessed to them his fear of dying without a male heir to succeed him, when, 'for want of a legitimate King, England should again be plunged into the horrors of civil war'.[21] He assured them that this was his only motive for annulment, and perhaps they believed him.

In 1527, Henry had sent his Secretary of State, William Knight, to Rome to present two documents to Pope Clement VII. The first dealt with the annulment of the marriage to Catherine, and the second with his subsequent marriage to Anne. Unfortunately for him, the mutinous troops of Holy Roman Emperor Charles V had sacked Rome and taken Clement into captivity. Clement was terrified of Charles, who also happened to be the nephew of Catherine of Aragon. Knight met with Clement and concluded that Clement was 'utterly untoward ... in the King's Great Affair'.[22] Henry therefore placed the entire matter in the hands of his Lord Chancellor, Cardinal Thomas Wolsey, demanding that the cardinal get the annulment or suffer the consequences.

Wolsey appealed to Pope Clement, and the aforementioned Lorenzo Campeggio was sent to England under the guise of having the authority, together with Cardinal Wolsey, to determine the case. Campeggio was in a tough spot since Charles V was pressuring Clement to reject Henry's petition to divorce his aunt. A very slow-moving Campeggio arrived in London in October

1528 and sat with Wolsey through many days of testimony. Both Henry and Catherine testified. The primary issue was whether the dispensation from Julius II for Henry to marry Catherine was proper since witnesses affirmed that her marriage to Arthur had been consummated, which Catherine vehemently denied. Finally, Campeggio gave his decision, and it was no decision. He deflected the final decision to the Roman Curia, the administrative assembly of the papacy, which would not be in session for nearly another year.

Henry was furious, and Cardinal Wolsey, his dear friend and trusted chancellor for many years, became the object of his wrath. Wolsey was stripped of both his position and his wealth. It was later discovered that he was plotting against the future Queen Anne, and while on his way to face the charges in London he died, at Leicester, on 29 November 1530. In Wolsey's stead Henry appointed the noted conservative Renaissance humanist Thomas More, who was not a cleric but a lawyer. While Henry was moving closer to Reformist views, especially pertaining to his role as king, Thomas More busied himself burning Reformist advocates at the stake.

The English king was on a collision course with the Roman Church and the supremacy of the pope in religious matters. Being a Renaissance king and a humanist, Henry was undoubtedly familiar with Erasmus' attitude toward the papacy. In 1519, in his *Ratio Theologiae*, Erasmus stated, 'Some assert that the universal body of the Church has been contracted into a single Roman pontiff, who cannot err on faith and morals, thus ascribing to the pope more than he claims for himself, though they do not hesitate to dispute his judgment if he interferes with their purses or their prospects. Is not this to open the door to tyranny in case such power were wielded by an impious and pestilent man?'[23] Erasmus often lampooned the clericalism, monasticism, superstitions and abuses of the Church, but remained a faithful Roman Catholic. Luther spoke of Erasmus being as slippery as an eel; only Christ can grab him.[24] Yet, Erasmus' assessment of the papacy must have bolstered Henry's resolve.

As Henry mulled over this matter, angrily assessing the stubbornness of the papacy to grant his request, he probably began to question the necessity of England submitting to a pope who seemingly had little concern for the future stability of England. Henry was the king; why couldn't he also be the king over the Church? The English Church might be better off with him as its head than it would owing allegiance to a weak and vacillating pope. This notion held great appeal for the king, and once it had taken root in his mind, a break with Rome was inevitable.[25]

In his 1973 biography of Katherine Parr, Anthony Martienssen claims that sometime in 1529 Henry was given a copy of Niccolò Machiavelli's book *The Prince* by his advisor Thomas Cromwell, who claimed that is was the greatest book he had ever read on the art of practical government. Martienssen goes on the suggest that it was the political philosophy of Machiavelli that largely informed Henry's decision to assume control of the Church of England.[26] This is highly unlikely given the fact that Cromwell was not Henry's Lord Chancellor – and therefore entitled to offer such forthright advice – until 1534 and that *The Prince*, though written in 1513, was not printed until 1532. While there is no evidence to suggest that Henry's decision was informed by Machiavelli, it is probably true that his later response to events such as the Pilgrimage of Grace (of which more later) was patterned after Machiavelli's postulate that it was better for a king to be feared than to be loved.

There were two events that both informed and solidified Henry's position against papal supremacy. In 1528, William Tyndale, an English scholar who was also responsible for producing the first English Bible taken directly from the Hebrew and Greek, published *The Obedience of the Christian Man*. In this work, Tyndale argued from Scripture that the king of a country and not the pope was the supreme head of that country's Church.

The story goes that Anne Boleyn owned a copy of the book, but Wolsey had confiscated it. Anne begged Henry on bended knee to have Wolsey return the book to her, which he did. She then gave it to Henry to read. The king was thrilled with the book.[27] Another version of the tale has it that Anne's maid had a copy of the book which she gave to Anne, who gave it to the king, who allegedly exclaimed, 'This book is for me and all kings to read.'[28] Whichever scenario is true, we can assume that Henry read the book. It should be noted, however, that the supremacy of the king was in fact a minor point in Tyndale's work; he was more focussed on the supremacy of Scripture in all matters and the need for the Bible to be in the language of the people, so it could be read and studied.

Thomas Cranmer, a generally unknown Cambridge prelate, was responsible for the fatal blow to papal jurisdiction in England. In the summer of 1529, Cranmer suggested to the king's advisors that his Great Matter was not a religious matter but one of ethics and morality, and that the scholars of the great universities of Europe were the only ones capable of giving an impartial verdict on the legitimacy of the king's marriage. Henry loved the idea. The humanist ideal gave greater credence to the scholarship of the universities than the decrees of a singular pontiff. Cranmer prepared a 'brief' outlining the king's case, and Henry's court contacted the major universities of Europe for opinions. With very few exceptions the universities approved the planned annulment of the marriage. Of the sixteen European universities canvassed, only four supported the queen.[29] According to Alison Weir, the whole process was not above board: 'Henry's agents had canvassed most of the European universities on the issue of the validity of the king's marriage, and where it was felt necessary, bribes were issued to the learned divines in order to obtain the opinions the king hoped to hear.'[30]

It is interesting to note that Henry's agents also sought the opinion of Jewish rabbis, and the king had also purchased a copy of the newly published Bomberg Talmud to investigate its position on his marriage. Henry's agents reported mixed opinion among the rabbis. Some said that Levirate marriage was no longer practised, and that the Leviticus verse applied. Others had a contrary opinion. Some dismissed the issue by stating that both Old Testament references applied only to Jews.[31]

The opinion of the leader of the Reformation, Martin Luther, was also sought. Robert Barnes, one of the leading advocates of the Reformation in England, was a part of the group of scholars who met at the White Horse Tavern in Cambridge to discuss the teachings of Luther. Somehow, he became involved in the Great Matter and came to Wittenberg in 1531 seeking Martin Luther's opinion. Luther, who had been embarrassed by Henry's response to his letter of apology, must have relished the opportunity to retaliate. In a letter to Barnes, Luther stated his opinion. Barnes returned to England and delivered the letter to the king. Luther's opinion was contrary to Henry's plans and did not endear Barnes to the king:

> Under no circumstances will he be free to divorce the Queen to whom he is married, the wife of his deceased brother and thus make the mother as well as the daughter[32] into incestuous women. Even if the King might have sinned by marrying the wife of his deceased brother, and even if the dispensation granted by the Roman pope might not have been valid (I do not debate this now), nevertheless it would be a heavier and more dreadful sin [for the King] to divorce the woman he had married; and this especially for the reason that then the King, as well as the Queen and the Young Queen, could be forever charged with, and considered as, being incestuous people ... Regarding the other reason – whether you are fabricating it, or whether it is true – that the King is searching for a son, an heir to the kingdom, but that the Queen gives birth only to girls, who doesn't see that this is an even less valid argument? Who will assure the King either that this present Queen will not give birth to a boy (if age does not hinder it), or that the other Queen, the one whom he is to marry, will give birth to boys?[33]

Luther went on to say that if the issue was Old Testament law, Henry was right in marrying Catherine according to Deuteronomy 25:5. While Luther makes valid points, he does not give enough credence to Henry's desire for a male heir. He even refers to the notion as a possible fabrication. Henry's concern was legitimate.

Regardless of Luther's opinion, as far as Henry was concerned, the theological and moral judgments of the divorce had now been declared. He wrote to Clement that 'we do separate from our cause the authority of the see apostolic'.[34] However, Henry and Anne had to jump through one more hoop before being married. Armed with the positive responses from the universities and the principled reasoning of William Tyndale, Henry was certain that his Great Matter was soon to conclude, but he feared one thing: international response, perhaps in the way of armed conflict initiated by the Catholic countries of France or Spain.

In the winter of 1532, Anne and Henry journeyed across the Channel to Calais to meet with King Francis I of France to hopefully enlist his support for their intended marriage. Francis duly obliged. While in Calais, Anne had openly lived with Henry as his consort. She had behaved and been treated as his queen, and she had been given Francis's blessing.[35] It has been assumed that Henry and Anne began conjugal relations while in France, for Anne was soon to become pregnant.

Shortly after returning to England, Henry and Anne married in a secret ceremony on 14 November 1532. Since Henry's marriage to Catherine had not yet been annulled, Henry was now a bigamist. With Anne pregnant, the November marriage was legitimised somewhat in a private ceremony held in the chapel at Whitehall Palace on 25 January 1533.

The task of informing Catherine of Henry's marriage to Anne fell to Lord Mountjoy, who was the head of the queen's household. He led the group entrusted with the task of urging Catherine to accept the king's new marriage and acknowledge herself dowager princess – which the indomitable Catherine of course resolutely refused. This task was too much for Mountjoy, who begged Thomas Cromwell to release him from the responsibility since he had long been a friend and supporter of Catherine. Henry's first wife never accepted Anne as queen, referring to her as the 'king's concubine'. She retired to Kimbolton House, where she would die in January 1536. She was buried at Peterborough Abbey. Until death, she referred to herself as the Queen of England. Anne reacted to Catherine's death with great rejoicing.

Events now moved quickly. Upon the death of William Warham, Archbishop of Canterbury, Henry, with the permission of Rome, elevated Thomas Cranmer to the newly vacated post. In a special court convened at Dunstable Priory on 23 May 1533, Cranmer declared the marriage of Henry and Catherine to be null and void. Five days later, he declared the marriage of Henry and Anne to be good and valid. The Great Matter had been settled.

On 1 June 1533, Anne was crowned Queen of England in a magnificent ceremony at Westminster Abbey. The Imperial ambassador, Eustace Chapuys, thought the coronation was 'a cold, meagre and uncomfortable thing', and the London crowds evidently agreed with him, for again they watched in silence, few bothering to cheer.[36] Carolly Erickson writes, 'Through it all Queen Anne rode unabashed, regal, triumphant. She paid little heed to the jeers and mockery around her, and none at all to the appraising stares directed at her person. She carried her head proudly, not only to keep in place the jewelled circlet she wore but from habit, for she had a long and graceful neck and knew how to show it to advantage. She was at her best that day, her colour high from excitement and her cheeks rosy in the cool spring air.'[37]

Elizabeth Barton, the so-called 'nun of Kent', was a popular visionary and prophetess of the time. Some of her predictions had been accurate. On two occasions she met with King Henry to bolster his stance against the heresies of the Protestant Reformation, but when Henry married Anne and declared himself the head of the Church of England, Barton turned against him. Around 1532 she began prophesying that Henry would quickly perish if he remarried; she even claimed to have seen the place in hell to which he would be consigned. Since it was high treason to speak of the death of the king, on 20 April 1534, at twenty-eight years old, Elizabeth Barton was hanged at Tyburn for treason along with five of her chief supporters.

In March 1534, Pope Clement finally ruled on the matter. His verdict was that the king's marriage to Catherine was lawful and legitimate, and he threatened Henry with excommunication if he didn't return to his lawful wife. Henry ignored the threat, and in September both Henry and Cranmer were excommunicated; Henry also lost his title of *Defender of the Faith*.

On 3 November 1534, the first Act of Supremacy was passed. By this Act, Henry was declared the supreme head of the Church of England and together with all subsequent monarchs was granted the title *Defender of the Faith* – what Clement revoked, Parliament granted. This officially marked the beginning of the English Reformation. Parliament acted with succession in mind, recognising that future stability depended on the existence of a male heir to the throne. Next came the passage of the Treasons Act, under which anyone who rejected the Act of Supremacy could be found guilty of treason. Thomas More, Henry's friend and former chancellor, denied the king's authority; he was convicted of treason and beheaded. Protestant sympathiser Thomas Cromwell, a lawyer who had been secretary to Cardinal Wolsey, became the king's secretary and chief minister. Henry VIII was now effectively king and pope in his own realm, with complete jurisdiction over his subjects' material and spiritual welfare.[38] The year 1537 saw the Irish Supremacy Act passed by the Irish Parliament, establishing Henry VIII as the supreme head of the Church of Ireland.

Henry and Anne settled into married life at Greenwich Palace, awaiting the birth of their first child and hoping that it would be a boy. Henry had fulfilled all his promises to Anne. He had married her and saw to it that she was crowned with as much pomp as if she were a reigning monarch. It was now up to Anne to deliver her part of the bargain by presenting the forty-two-year-old Henry with the son he needed more desperately than ever, not only to ensure the succession but also to justify the risks he had taken to marry Anne. The birth of a male heir would bring many waverers and dissidents over to his side.[39]

3

'DIVORCED, BEHEADED, DIED...'

On 15 September 1533, Queen Anne gave birth to a girl who was named Elizabeth after her grandmothers Elizabeth of York and Elizabeth Howard. While Henry and Anne welcomed the birth, it was a source of great disappointment. Henry consoled Anne with the words, 'You and I are both young and by God's grace, boys will follow.' All prophetic markers led them to believe that it would be a boy. Letters announcing the birth of a prince had already been prepared; now, with an 's' added, they were dispatched abroad.[1] Henry cancelled a joust that he had planned in honour of his new son.

If Henry and Anne had only known that this little baby was destined to become England's greatest queen and to rule for nearly forty-five years, their attitude would have been different. More than this, it was Katherine Parr who was largely responsible for forming the life of this little girl and turning her into the woman she became. In 1534, the First Act of Succession made Princess Elizabeth the heir to the throne and declared Princess Mary, daughter of the king by Catherine of Aragon, illegitimate.

Anne became pregnant on two other occasions, both times suffering miscarriages. In January 1536, on the day of Catherine's funeral, she miscarried a male child of almost four months. Much of the existing gossip abounding in King Henry's court comes from the correspondence of Eustace Chapuys, the Imperial ambassador of Emperor Charles V. Chapuys had been loyal to Queen Catherine and an enemy of Anne Boleyn, whom he referred to as the 'king's concubine'.[2] Regarding the miscarriage, he reported that the foetus 'seemed to be a male child which she had not borne three and a half months'. Chapuys further reported that Henry scarcely said anything to Anne, except that he saw clearly that God did not wish to give him male children.[3]

Five days before, on 24 January 1536, Henry had been unhorsed in a jousting tournament and knocked unconscious for two hours. His leg was injured – an open sore would remain throughout his life. Some point to this injury as the cause of the king's alleged personality change, turning him into an oft angry and erratic tyrant. Anne blamed her miscarriage on her fear relating to this event and the fact that she knew Henry was already plotting his next marriage, to Jane Seymour, one of Anne's ladies-in-waiting. Agnes Strickland writes, 'Henry had grown tired of her and was carrying on a flirtation with the beautiful Jane Seymour, one of her attendants.'[4]

Henry was now faced with the task of getting rid of wife number two, and his secretary and chief minister Thomas Cromwell knew it. He set about gathering all sorts of damaging information about Anne, accusing her of treason, adultery, and incest with her brother George. The most damning evidence was a conversation reported between Anne and Henry Norris, the king's most trusted aide,[5] in which Anne teased Norris that he would want her as his wife should the king perish.[6] To discuss the death of the king in this way was regarded as high treason. Anne was put on trial and convicted on all counts. On 19 May 1536, Anne was beheaded. Graciously, Henry had imported a skilled swordsman from France to make sure of a clean cut. In his *Acts and Monuments,* John Foxe records her final words before her execution:

The words of this worthy and Christian lady at her death were these: 'Good Christian people! I am come hither to die, for according to the law, and by the law, I am judged to death; and therefore, I will speak nothing against it. I am come hither to accuse no man, nor to speak anything of that whereof I am accused and condemned to die; but I pray God save the king, and send him long to reign over you, for a gentler or a more merciful prince was there never; and to me he was ever a good, a gentle, and a sovereign lord. And if any person will meddle of my cause, I require them to judge the best. And thus, I take my leave of the world, and of you all, and I heartily desire you all to pray for me. O Lord have mercy on me! To God I commend my soul.'[7]

Because of her depiction in Foxe's *Acts and Monuments*, Anne was later acknowledged as a martyr and heroine of the English Reformation. Foxe wrote, 'It may be suspected some secret practising of the papists here not to be lacking, considering what a mighty stop she was to their purposes and proceedings, and on the contrary side, what a strong bulwark she was for the maintenance of Christ's gospel, and sincere religion, which they then in no case could abide.'[8]

This issue has been widely debated. John Foxe was known to exaggerate, and his depiction of Anne Boleyn might have been intended to bolster the image of her daughter, Queen Elizabeth, who was on the throne when he was writing. Anne did receive the Sacrament while in prison, and questioned whether she would go to heaven because of her many good works, contrary to the primary Reformation principle of justification by faith. While Anne Boleyn rejected papal supremacy and acknowledged Henry as head of the Church, her personal piety remained Erasmian Roman Catholic. According to Susan James, 'In 1536 as queen, Anne refused to support the publication of a work which approved of justification by faith and communion in both kinds.' Justification by faith was a central and pivotal tenet of Protestant belief, and Anne's reluctance to support such a tenet shows a reluctance to enter into the full spirit of the Reformation.[9] This was also true of Henry until the day he died. His funeral was a traditional Catholic Mass with prayers for the dead in purgatory. The only legitimate Protestant queen was Katherine Parr, who embraced the Lutheran teaching of justification by faith and was nearly arrested for doing so.

Within a fortnight of Anne's execution, Henry married the aforementioned Jane Seymour in a wedding at Whitehall Palace. Starkey sums up Jane's appeal to Henry:

> Jane was everything that Anne was not. She was calm, quiet, soft-spoken (when she spoke at all) and profoundly submissive, at least to Henry. In short, after Anne's flagrant defiance of convention, Jane was the sixteenth century's ideal woman (or at least the sixteenth century *male*'s ideal woman).[10]

The next month, Parliament passed the Second Act of Succession, 1536 which removed Elizabeth from the succession, consigning her to illegitimacy along with her sister Mary. They were both banished from court.

In October 1536, a popular rebellion known as the Pilgrimage of Grace arose in the north under the leadership of lawyer Robert Aske. This uprising was a protest against Henry's break with Rome and the subsequent dissolution of the monasteries, which was instigated by Cromwell to eliminate relics and superstitions and for financial reasons. 'The monasteries' central role in popular piety as places of pilgrimage to miracle-working images or relics. These images and relics offered comfort to the people, as well as providing nice little earners for the monks.'[11] The rebellion failed, and the leaders were executed. Robert Aske was hung in chains at York. During the rebellion, Katherine Parr, who at the time was married to Lord Latimer, was held hostage at Snape Castle in Yorkshire together with her stepchildren and threatened with death if her husband did not return and join the rebellion.

In early 1537, Queen Jane became pregnant. She went into confinement in September and gave birth to a healthy, highly coveted male heir, the future King Edward, on 12 October 1537 at Hampton Court Palace. The issue of succession was settled. However, soon after the birth Jane became seriously ill, probably suffering puerperal fever, a bacterial infection that was a common hazard for mothers during childbirth in those days.[12] Two weeks after Prince Edward's birth, on 24 October, Jane passed away. She was buried on 12 November 1537 in St George's Chapel at Windsor Castle. She was the only one of Henry's wives to receive a queen's funeral, and was probably Henry's favourite given that she provided him with a male heir. When Henry eventually died, he was buried beside her in the grave he had made for her.

Following the death of Jane Seymour, Henry seemed in no hurry to find a fourth wife: 'For Henry, as we have seen, being in love, or at least being able to imagine himself in love, was a prerequisite for marriage,' David Starkey explains. 'But he tended to fall in love with a woman only when he was falling out of love with another one. It was thus that Anne had succeeded Catherine and thus in turn, as her own star waned, that Anne had been displaced by Jane. But Jane died while Henry was still in love with her – or, at least, not much out of it. Moreover, the fact that she died giving him a son meant that he came to love her more dead than alive.' So, the question was asked, would the king marry again?[13]

In the years following Henry's injury in 1536, drastic changes took place in the personality and appearance of the proud king. Alison Weir writes,

For an active man, it was a cruel blow, and the effect upon Henry's already uncertain temper was disastrous. As his frustration at his enforced inactivity grew, along with the pain he suffered, he would become increasingly subject to savage and unreasonable rages. He was nearly forty-five now, growing bald, and running to fat; as he grew older, he would become more and more addicted to the pleasures of the table, and more and more gross. He would also, with each passing year, become more egotistical, more sanctimonious, and surer of his own divinity, while still seeing himself as a paragon of courtly and athletic knighthood. The discrepancy between image and reality was one he could not bring himself to face.[14]

Even though Henry had renounced the authority of the Pope, making himself the Supreme Head of the Church of England, his basic theology remained Roman Catholic. Being a man of intelligence and following the lead of Erasmus, his primary opposition to Roman Catholicism focused upon questionable relics and foolish superstitions. In 1538, Cromwell, with Henry's blessing, directed the clergy to provide English translations of the Bible in some convenient place within their churches where the parishioners may read them. The result was the Great Bible, the first authorised English translation, based primarily upon Tyndale's earlier translation. While some saw this as a sign that Henry was warming to the Reformation, it was in fact down to the influence of Erasmus, who believed the Bible should be in the hands of the people. For a while, until he realised its implications, Henry supported the translation of the Bible into English and the observation of a more straightforward form of religious service.[15]

Thomas Cromwell now undertook the task of seeking to more closely align England with the Lutheran Reformation in Germany. This was a two-pronged effort. On the one hand, an alliance was sought between England and the German Schmalkaldic League,[16] which would be advantageous for both England and the German Lutherans since Emperor Charles V provided a threat to both parties. At the same time, Thomas Cromwell was hoping that Lutheran Germany would provide the next wife for Henry VIII. Cromwell's efforts would end very badly.

In seeking to establish an alliance with German Lutherans, the English engaged in much diplomacy, communication and discussion. In 1536, seeking to define the doctrine of this new Church of England, Parliament passed the Ten Articles. The first article stated that Scripture and the Creeds defined the essence of the Christian faith. While much Catholic doctrine was retained – prayers to the saints, purgatory and prayers for the dead, for instance – the superstitions connected with idols and ceremonies were rejected. The Real Presence of the Body and Blood of Christ in the Sacrament of the Altar was affirmed, but there was no mention of transubstantiation, that the substance of the bread and wine changed into the Body and Blood of Christ. Justification by faith was rejected and the necessity for good works for salvation affirmed. No threat was appended to the Ten Articles identifying those who denied them as guilty of heresy, which would have been punishable by death. These articles were the basis for discussion between Henry and the Lutherans, and it seemed that some headway was being made.

On 1 October 1538, a legation of the Schmalkaldic League left London for Germany carrying a letter from King Henry to John Frederick, Elector of Saxony, head of the Schmalkaldic League of Germany and close friend and patron of Martin Luther. Henry praised the members of the legation for their piety and learnedness and expressed his hope that Philip Melanchthon, Luther's 'right-hand man' in the Reformation and author of the *Apology of the Augsburg Confession*, and other learned men would soon come to England in order to conclude the matter – that is, an alliance between Henry and the league.[17]

Henry appreciated the writing of Philip Melanchthon, the right-hand man of Luther and professor at the University of Wittenberg. Melanchthon was highly regarded throughout Europe as a humanist scholar. Henry disagreed with Luther's understanding of justification by faith because he felt Luther derogated good works. Not understanding the points of theology, he felt that Melanchthon gave good works a greater dignity even though Melanchthon always viewed good works as a consequence of justification, not a cause – they were necessary but not for salvation. At the suggestion of Robert Barnes, Melanchthon dedicated his 1535 edition of his seminal work *Loci Communes* (Common Places in Theology) to King Henry. Henry esteemed this honour highly, and sent him 200 gold florins, with a very gracious letter, in which he calls Melanchthon his 'dearest friend' and signs himself 'Your friend Henry, King'.[18] This stipend was more than Melanchthon would earn in one year as a professor. As a result, Henry invited Melanchthon on two occasions to visit England and to assist in the formation of the English Church, but Elector John Frederick did not give him leave to take the trip. He probably did not trust Henry – and with good reason. Perhaps he also did not appreciate Melanchthon's seemingly conciliatory posture.

In the early summer of 1539, all hopes for unity between the Lutherans and King Henry VIII were dashed when Parliament passed Henry's Act for the Abolishing of Diversity in Opinion, otherwise known as the Act of Six Articles. The principal article reaffirmed transubstantiation, the position that the bread and wine in the Lord's Supper is 'in substance' the Body and Blood of Christ. The remaining five articles ruled that Communion be rejected 'in both kinds', that the marriage of priests was unlawful, that monastic vows should be kept, that Masses for the dead were allowable and that confession to a priest was both necessary and desirable. English Protestants referred to the 'Six Articles' as the 'bloody whip with six strings'. It seems apparent that, following the lead of Erasmus, Henry was willing to move against the dead formalism, monastic abuses, relics and superstitions of Catholicism but not touch its basic theology. Both Thomas Cromwell and Archbishop Cranmer were taken aback. Cranmer was forced to send his wife back to Germany. To disagree with the Six Articles was considered heresy and punishable by death.

Cranmer's approach to marriage was unique. In 1532, on a trip to Nuremberg in Germany, he met the Lutheran reformer Andreas Osiander, who happened to be married with a family. Over dinner, Osiander introduced Cranmer to his niece Margarete, and soon after Cranmer did the unthinkable for a priest in service to King Henry: he ignored his vow of celibacy and married this Lutheran woman. Sometime in the 1530s, she travelled to England. During his time as Archbishop of Canterbury, his marriage remained a secret, and his wife well hidden. With the passage of the Six Articles through Parliament, which included strict observance of clerical celibacy, it became too dangerous for Margarete and their daughter Margaret to remain in England. Cranmer arranged for their exile in Germany. Cranmer was separated from his family for the remaining eight years of King Henry VIII's reign. While he could have easily followed the practices of some of his fellow clerics and procured a mistress, he had chosen marriage. Perhaps from his perspective, fornicating with a mistress was a far more serious sin before God than breaking a vow made to the Church. It is hard to believe that Henry was not aware of Cranmer's marriage and simply turned a blind eye as he felt indebted to him because of the archbishop's tireless efforts to solve the Great Matter.

As a result of the Six Articles, the Lutherans felt betrayed by Henry. Martin Bucer, one of the leaders of the Reformation, who had been exiled from Strasbourg and moved to England in 1539, blamed Elector John Frederick for Henry's Six Articles, claiming that the outcome would have been different if he had agreed to send Melanchthon to England. Bucer felt that Melanchthon was the only person who could have effectively debated the issues with Henry. 'The Elector, whose sagacity in this matter cannot be denied, understood very well that Henry was merely anxious to unite with the Evangelical party from impure motives, particularly his matrimonial matters.'[19]

In a letter to Elector John Frederick in October 1539, Martin Luther agreed with the decision of the elector and dismissed Bucer's claim: 'We are not obligated to try further to deal with the King; there is little hope for such an undertaking. Perhaps God does not wish his gospel to be touted by this King who has such a bad reputation.'[20] There is no telling how Frederick felt about Luther's comments regarding King Henry since he was about to become the king's brother-in-law.

After a few months spent mourning the loss of Queen Jane, Henry had set out to find wife number four. After seeking prospects in France and being rejected, he pursued Christina, Duchess of Milan, but she, knowing the king's history with his wives, candidly refused, declaring that if she had two heads 'one should be at his Grace's service.'[21] Thomas Cromwell all the while continued to recommend Anne of Cleves to Henry as a possible choice. Anne was the sister of Duke William of Cleves, but more importantly her older sister Sibylle was married to Elector John Frederick. Since amiable discussions were still taking place between Henry and the Lutherans, this was shrewd diplomacy from Cromwell. In the spring of 1538, negotiations began.

After seeing a miniature portrait of Anne painted by the court painter Hans Holbein, Henry agreed to the marriage.

On 4 September 1539, the marriage treaty was signed by the Duke of Cleves at Düsseldorf.

Anne began her long journey to England to marry the king, arriving in Rochester on 30 December to be housed in the Bishop's Palace in the city. Henry was anxious and couldn't wait to see his new bride, so he set out to Rochester to meet her in disguise and was incredibly disappointed and disgusted by her appearance. He brutally referred to her as a 'great Flanders mare'.[22]

Henry tried to get out of the marriage contract but to no avail. On 6 January 1540, Henry made Anne of Cleves his fourth wife. The morning after, Thomas Cromwell came to the King's Privy Chamber and asked how he liked the queen. Henry's made himself clear:

> Surely, my lord, I liked her before not well, but now I like her much worse! She is nothing fair and have very evil smells about her. I took her to be no maid by reason of the looseness of her breasts and other tokens, which, when I felt them, strake me so to the heart, that I had neither will nor courage to prove the rest. I can have none appetite for displeasant airs. I have left her as good a maid as I found her.[23]

In her book *Anna of Kleve*, Alison Weir states that she puzzled for months over what Henry meant by these remarks. Henry seemed to be indicating that Anne was not a virgin.[24] Yet in a previous book Alison Weir reported a conversation between Anne and her ladies-in-waiting regarding whether Anne was still a virgin. 'How can I be a maid and sleep every night with the king?'[25] Anne appeared incredibly naïve when it came to the marital relations between a husband and wife. She seems to have believed that if a gentleman so much as kissed her then she would be with child.[26] While she had claimed to be a virgin, from Henry's perspective she was 'no maid'.

Even though Henry was angry with Cromwell over the whole affair, on 17 April the king surprised everyone by creating Cromwell Earl of Essex. According to Alison Weir, 'this was another example of the King's subtle cruelty. By lulling Cromwell into a sense of false security, he hoped to exact a more satisfying revenge, which would be as unexpected as it was deadly.'[27]

On 24 June, Anne was commanded to leave the court and was informed that the king was reconsidering the marriage. Shortly afterwards, Anne was asked for her consent to an annulment, which she gave. The marriage was annulled on 9 July 1540 on the grounds of non-consummation. Anne decided to remain in England and was treated very well, receiving a generous settlement including Richmond Palace and Hever Castle – the latter of which had once belonged to Anne Boleyn. In fact, Henry and Anne became good friends, and she was referred to as 'the King's Beloved Sister'. When it came to matters of religion, Anne was ambivalent. While she was Lutheran in name, she would embrace Roman Catholicism in later years when it was politically expedient.

Unfortunately for Thomas Cromwell, he was not to enjoy the same fate as Anne of Cleves. Even though he had been honoured by the king a few months earlier, he became the scapegoat for the failed marriage. In short order he was accused of treason and beheaded on 28 July 1540. On the same day, Henry married wife number five, seventeen-year-old Catherine Howard.

Catherine Howard was one of the daughters of Lord Edmund Howard and Joyce Culpeper. Her paternal aunt Elizabeth Howard was the mother of Anne Boleyn. Therefore, Catherine Howard was the first cousin of Anne Boleyn, and the first cousin once removed of Elizabeth, Anne's daughter. Soon after the death of her mother (in about 1528), when Catherine was aged about five, she was sent with some of her siblings to live in the care of her father's stepmother, the Dowager Duchess of Norfolk, at Chesworth House in Horsham, Sussex. As a result of the dowager duchess's lack of discipline and her frequent absences at court, Catherine became influenced by some older girls there who allowed men into the sleeping areas at night for entertainment. Catherine was not as well educated as some of Henry's other wives; she has often been described as vivacious, giggly and brisk, but never as scholarly or devout.

Catherine Howard was, therefore, already a woman with a past when, in late 1539, she was appointed one of Anne of Cleves's maidens during the approach to Anne's ill-fated wedding. After that marriage was annulled, it did not take long for Henry to notice the exciting seventeen-year-old Catherine Howard, and they were soon married. 'It is easy to read Henry's motives,' writes David Starkey. 'Physically repelled by Anne of Cleves, and humiliated by his sexual failure with her, he sought and found consolation from Catherine. We can also guess that sex, which had been impossible with Anne, was easy with her. And it was easy because she made it easy. Henry, lost in pleasure, never seems to have asked himself how she obtained such skill. Instead, he attributed it all to love and his own recovered youth.'[28]

With the Six Articles firmly in place and Protestant reformer Thomas Cromwell out of the way, Henry's religious policies became far more conservative. Cromwell was succeeded by the conservative Thomas Wriothesley, Earl of Southampton and former secretary to the Privy Council. Stephen Gardiner, Bishop of Winchester, remained the king's secretary. The two men advised King Henry that diplomacy – specifically the prospect of an alliance with the Roman Catholic Emperor Charles V against France – required a halt to religious reform. Together, they set out to purge England of those holding Protestant views. In a letter to Elector John Frederick, Martin Luther had some interesting things to say about Stephen Gardiner:

One also has to consider the people who are now in power and favour around the king. They too have no consciences. The man from Winchester, while traveling around the country, is accompanied by two unchaste females dressed in men's clothing, yet he declares that the marriage of priests is contrary to God's law. He is so arrogant as to say in public that he intends to maintain against the whole world that the thesis, 'We are justified by faith,' is wrong. Among tyrants he is the greatest; prior to this year he pushed for the burning of two people solely on the ground of transubstantiation, and so the proverb is true: like master, like servant.[29]

Two days after the execution of Cromwell, Robert Barnes, who had delivered Luther's anti-annulment statement to Henry and who was also involved in pursuing the marriage of the king to Anne of Cleves, was burned at the stake with two other Protestant sympathisers. To level things up, as it were, three men loyal to the pope who denied the royal supremacy were hanged for treason.

The marriage between King Henry and Catherine Howard lasted a scant sixteen months. Henry was originally enamoured of her, and young Catherine was thrilled to be Queen of England, but Henry had very little to offer a teenage girl. Catherine was described as young, joyous and carefree. Henry was now nearing fifty and ageing rapidly. The abscess on his leg oozed pus continually and emitted a horrible odour. Also, the king had become exceedingly fat: a new suit of armour, made for him at this time, measured 54 inches around the waist.[30] It is no wonder that young Catherine sought her pleasures elsewhere. In addition to a previous affair with a Francis Dereham, she had also committed adultery with King Henry's groom, Thomas Culpeper. Her affairs soon came to light. In December 1541, Culpeper was beheaded while Dereham was hanged, drawn and quartered. Both their heads were put on spikes and displayed on London Bridge. Two months later, Catherine Howard was beheaded for treason.

Henry was sorely disappointed by the infidelities of his young queen. Ambassador Chapuys reported to Charles V, 'This King has wonderfully felt the case of the queen, his wife. He has certainly shown greater sorrow and regret at her loss than at the faults, loss or divorce of his preceding wives.' Perhaps, then, it was time for Henry to reconsider his relationship with his 'sister' Anne of Cleves. Chapuys further reported that 'the Lady Anne of Cleves has greatly rejoiced at [Catherine's fall], and that in order to be nearer the King she is coming to, if she is not already at, Richmond.'[31] A formal diplomatic attempt from Anne's brother to restore the marriage was unceremoniously rejected by King Henry, which Anne found very difficult to accept. For some reason, Henry simply found Anne of Cleves to be repulsive as a wife.

In dealing with the affairs of state, especially in matters of religion where he was essentially the 'pope' of England, Henry's behaviour was impulsive and erratic. While he desired the enforcement of his Six Articles and allowed the bishops freedom to deal with those who held opposing, Protestant views, he was not consistent. At times, loyalty and friendship motivated the king to turn a blind eye to the violation of the articles he had set in place. For Henry, personal affection counted for more than political (or theological) correctness.[32]

In 1542, Thomas Wriothesley and Bishop Stephen Gardiner plotted against Archbishop Cranmer, seeking to unseat him. They sought Henry's permission to arrest Cranmer and send him to the Tower, and the king obliged. However, unbeknown to them, Henry was being duplicitous. Cranmer, regardless of his Protestant leanings and the fact that he was married, had provided the final solution to Henry's Great Matter. The king would not soon forget that.

On the night before the Privy Council would meet to accuse and arrest Cranmer, Henry summoned the archbishop to his presence. He informed Cranmer that the next day he was to be arrested and sent to the Tower. When Cranmer protested, Henry replied brutally, 'Think you to have better luck that way than your master Christ had?' But Henry was not really going to let Cranmer's fate be decided by the man's fellow councillors. Instead, Henry gave Cranmer his ring to produce when the council tried to arrest him.

The summons came the next day and Cranmer was called before the Privy Council. When the charges were levelled against him, Cranmer brandished the king's ring. Some of the councillors immediately rushed to the king's apartment to abase themselves and seek the king's mercy, and thereafter, while Henry lived, Cranmer was untouchable.[33]

Then there is the interesting, if not comical, plight of Sir George Blagge. Blagge was a politician and soldier who served in Parliament from 1545 to 1547 and was a good friend of King Henry. For some reason, he had the endearing nickname of 'pig'. Blagge attracted attention to himself because he openly denied the Roman

Catholic doctrine of transubstantiation in contravention of the Six Articles. This was reported to Thomas Wriothesley, who had Blagge arrested. As soon as Henry heard of this arrest, he sent for Wriothesley and severely rebuked him, demanding Wriothesley draw up a pardon for his good friend at once. On his release Blagge hurried to thank his protector, the king, who cried out, 'Ah! my pig, are you here safe again?' 'Yes, sire,' came the reply, 'and if your majesty had not been better than your bishops your pig had been roasted ere this time.'[34]

Henry had become the new pope of England. At his pleasure, those who were loyal to Rome and denied Henry's role as the Supreme Head of the Church of England were either hanged or beheaded for treason. On the other hand, those with Protestant leanings who rejected the Six Articles were burned for heresy, unless the king chose to grant them a reprieve.

The stage was now set for the entrance of queen number six: Katherine Parr, a beautiful, wealthy woman, twice widowed. When Henry proposed, she reluctantly accepted despite the fact that she was in love with another man. Anne of Cleves, believing herself to be of greater beauty than Lady Parr, commented, 'A fine burden Madam Katherine has taken upon herself!'[35]

Yes, it was indeed a 'fine burden' that Katherine had taken upon herself by agreeing to become Henry's sixth wife, yet no woman was more suited to be by Henry's side during the final four years of his life.

4

BEFORE HENRY

There are people who appear on the stage of history and at first glance seem relatively insignificant. For some reason, their accomplishments, influences, writings and courage in the face of adversity are largely ignored. Henry's first three wives are historically significant. He was married to Catherine of Aragon for twenty-four years, and she gave birth to Mary, who became queen. While Anne Boleyn was queen for only three years, she was one of the instruments in Henry's break with Rome and gave birth to Elizabeth, who reigned as queen for forty years. Jane Seymour was queen for just one year but died as a result of giving birth to Edward, who would succeed Henry as king; she was also Henry's favourite and he chose to be buried by her side. After this come the last three. Catherine Howard contributed nothing to English history and lasted sixteen months before losing her head. Anne of Cleves really doesn't count since literally nothing happened between them and the marriage was annulled after seven months. Finally, there is Katherine Parr, who was married to Henry for the last four years of his life.

According to an early biography by Agnes Strickland, Katherine was primarily Henry's nursemaid and would sometimes 'remain on her knees for hours bathing and bandaging his ulcerated leg, for he would not permit anybody to touch it but her'.[1] Such a characterisation is largely debunked by Katherine's modern biographers. Susan James is correct in saying that Katherine Parr has been marginalised in much of the literature of the period due primarily to a lack of research into her life and activities.[2] It is also true that Katherine's reputation 'took a major hit' after the death of Henry and her marriage to Thomas Seymour, and so she was largely forgotten. But times have certainly changed. More has been written about Katherine Parr in the last twenty-five years than in the previous four centuries. Across this new literature, the consensus appears to be that Katherine was one of the more important queens in English history.

Katherine Parr was probably born in 1512, the oldest child of Sir Thomas Parr, Baron of Kendal, and Matilda or Maud (née Green), daughter of Sir Thomas Green of Northamptonshire. Her siblings were William, who became 1st Marquess of Northampton and would later encourage Queen Katherine to publish her *The Lamentation of a Sinner*, and Anne, who married Sir William Herbert and thus became Lady Herbert. The two sisters remained close, with Anne taking a place in Queen Katherine's inner circle.

Katherine's father, Sir Thomas Parr, was the son of Sir William Parr and Elizabeth FitzHugh. Through his mother he was a descendant of King Edward III of England.[3] Thomas' forebears were members of the northern Parr clan of Kendal, an influential presence in southern Westmorland. Since his mother and grandmother before him were royal ladies-in-waiting, Thomas enjoyed a privileged upbringing at the English court. According to biographer Susan James, the young Thomas most likely studied under Maurice Westbury of Oxford, learning (among other things) classical Greek and Latin as well as modern languages.[4] He had thus acquired all the polish and poise necessary to thrive at court.[5]

Thomas Parr had links with the religious community. He was related to Sir Thomas More, the noted humanist scholar, as More's first wife, Jane, was Parr's niece by marriage, thereby making More his in-law.[6] Parr appreciated More and respected his intellect. More would be executed in 1535 for refusing to acknowledge Henry VIII as supreme head of the Church. Parr also advocated the teachings of his cousin Sir Cuthbert Tunstall, a close friend of the family.

They shared a great-great-grandfather, Sir Thomas of Thurland Castle. Tunstall, who became Bishop of Durham, was a committed Roman Catholic and advocate of the internal reform initiated by Desiderius Erasmus. Unlike More, Tunstall accepted with some hesitation the supremacy of King Henry over the Church. In the question of Henry's divorce, Tunstall acted as one of Queen Catherine's counsellors. Tunstall was a victim of the ever-changing religious landscape of England. After Henry's death Tunstall was imprisoned throughout the reign of Edward VI, and his bishopric revoked. He was only set free and restored when Mary I took the throne. When Elizabeth ascended the throne, Tunstall refused to take the Oath of Supremacy. He was arrested, again deprived of his dioceses, and held in Lambeth Palace until his death.

The Parrs were seated in Kendal Castle in Cumbria, in the north-west of England. The castle was in a poor state by the time of Katherine's birth, and the Parrs made their townhouse in London's Blackfriars district their primary home. It is here that Katherine was born. Her mother, Maud, was a close friend and attendant of King Henry's first wife, Catherine of Aragon, and remained at court during her pregnancy, continuing her service to the queen. Maud was faithful to Queen Catherine and continued to serve her until her death. Indeed, Katherine was named after Queen Catherine, who was also her godmother. So, Henry's last wife was named after his first wife.[7] Her father, Sir Thomas, was a good friend of King Henry and this favour was shown in his appointments. Thomas was the High Sheriff of Northamptonshire and Lincolnshire, and Comptroller to the King. According to David Starkey, Katherine's father 'was well born, rich and well connected. He was blessed with children. And, above all, he enjoyed the royal favour.'[8]

Katherine's family was growing in wealth and favour when Sir Thomas suddenly died of the mysterious 'sweating sickness' in November 1517, leaving as head of the household Katherine's mother, who was pregnant at the time with their fourth child (which she miscarried). Cuthbert Tunstall was the executor of Thomas' will, which made provision for his wife and children.

Katherine and Anne were to receive dowries while the bulk of the estate was to be inherited by his only male child, William.

While it was expected that Maud should remarry to establish her household, as a spirited, independent woman, this was not in her plans. She set out to make her own way. Gaining prominence as one of Queen Catherine's attendants, she was given her own suite of rooms at court, meaning she was often away from home. While she was away, the children were cared for by the servants at Rye House in Hertfordshire, which became their permanent home not long before their father's death. It was leased from one of Sir Thomas Parr's many cousins and would remain their chief residence until Maud's own death fourteen years later. Undoubtedly, Katherine learned a great deal from the strength, independence and determination displayed by her mother.

Maud understood the importance of male protection and involvement in her children's lives. She was fortunate to be able to call upon her late husband's brother, Sir William Parr of Horton, and Cuthbert Tunstall for assistance. Together, they provided a further resource for the future of her family.[9] Katherine was fond of her uncle William, and as an eight- or nine-year-old child wrote a dedication to him in her father's Book of Hours,[10] which became his possession: 'Uncle, when you do on this look, I pray you remember who wrote this in your book. Your loving niece, Katherine Parr.'[11]

Maud oversaw the education of her children, which was undoubtedly influenced by her husband's relationship with Thomas More and Cuthbert Tunstall, both followers of Erasmus and committed Roman Catholics. There is evidence to suggest that Katherine received a good education. She was proficient in French and Italian and perhaps even knew some Greek and Latin. She was also taught mathematics, which she would put to good use in her later capacity as Lady Latimer and Queen of England. In addition, she was schooled in manners and courtly etiquette, developing an easy conversational style. She could sing well and play music. With all this in mind, she was aptly suited for life at King Henry's court.[12] Of all the wives of Henry VIII, she was the most intellectual.

It has been suggested that Katherine lived at court with her mother and was educated alongside Princess Mary, and that a wonderful friendship developed between the two children.[13] This is highly unlikely since Katherine was three years older than Mary, and Mary had her own household.

Katherine was known to have been highly skilled in needlework, but there is debate over whether she enjoyed it or in fact saw it as an activity beneath her potential status. Agnes Strickland in 1882 wrote, 'When a little girl she never could bear to sew, and often said to her mother, "My hands are ordained to touch crowns and sceptres, not spindles and needles."'[14] According to biographer Linda Porter, the story is almost certainly apocryphal.[15] It is unlikely that Maud would have put up with such conceit, and the statement is too prophetic to be true. Allegedly, young Katherine had come up with the idea due to the reading of some astrologer who saw her stars aligned for greatness. It's fiction, not fact. Strickland nonetheless acknowledges that Katherine's embroidery – specimens of which survive today – shows unusual skill and industry,[16] certainly not the work of one who despised the practice.

In 1523, when Katherine was eleven,[17] Maud set out to find her a husband, and she had one in mind. During a meeting with her late husband's cousin Lord Dacre, Maud suggested the marriage between Katherine and Lord Dacre's grandson Henry, the teenage heir of Lord Scrope of Bolton. Dacre liked the idea and felt that the young Katherine would be a good match for his grandson. Maud wrote a letter to Henry's father suggesting the match. To make a long story short, Lord Scrope stubbornly demanded more than the considerable dowry Maud offered, and she resisted. Scrope also demanded the dowry be paid to him and if the marriage was terminated by the death of either party, he would keep the money. So, the match failed. Probably just as well, since young Henry Scrope died one year later. If Katherine had married him, she would have been a widow before the age of thirteen.

In 1529, when she was seventeen, Katherine finally married Sir Edward Burgh (Borough), son of Sir Thomas Burgh and grandson of 2nd Baron Edward Burgh of Lincolnshire. There is much confusion over this marriage since there are two Edwards, the grandfather and the grandson. In her 1882 work Agnes Strickland wrote that 'Katharine was married twice before she became the wife of Henry VIII. Her first husband was Lord Edward Borough, a middle-aged widower with several children, who died a short time after the marriage.'[18] Alison Weir said that 'some confusion exists as to the identification of this gentleman, some sources naming him as Sir Edward de Burgh, who died before April 1533. He was, in fact, Sir Edward's grandfather, another Edward de Burgh, second Baron Borough of Gainsborough in the county of Lincolnshire.'[19]

The research of Susan James, Linda Porter and David Starkey confirms that Katherine married the grandson Edward, not the grandfather. In her will, dated May 1529, Maud Parr acknowledges that Katherine married Edward, the son of Sir Thomas Burgh, not his father. The old man was insane, and Maud Parr would never have married her seventeen-year-old daughter to a lunatic. The Burgh family seat was Gainsborough Old Hall, an attractive and prominent building that still stands today.[20] After the marriage contract was signed, Katherine began her long journey north.

Since Edward was in his twenties, he had not established his own household. Katherine therefore moved into the home of Edward's parents. Sir Thomas 'ruled the roost' with sharp talons, and Katherine had to establish a good relationship with her father-in-law to avoid a miserable life. Linda Porter writes, 'Her father-in-law was a man of his times and, as master of the household, he expected obedience.'[21] Sir Thomas Burgh held some Protestant views, although the full extent of his faith is unclear. He kept a Protestant chaplain in his household and had favoured the king in his Great Matter, and later the quasi-Protestant Anne Boleyn would appoint him as her Lord Chamberlain. Some biographers suggest that it was through the influence of Sir Thomas that Katherine rejected her Roman Catholic upbringing and embraced the Reformation. Elizabeth Norton writes, 'Maud Parr was entirely conservative in her religious faith, and Catherine was raised as a Catholic, as was everyone of her generation. At some point during her early life, Catherine turned towards the religious reform and, while there is no evidence of when this occurred, the likelihood is that it was due to the influence of Sir Thomas Burgh during Catherine's time at Gainsborough.'[22]

However, this is not feasible because, as we will see, Katherine's next husband was a fiercely committed Roman Catholic. In addition, her later writings in 1544 and 1545 still reflected traditionalist Roman Catholic piety. She embraced the Reformation when she came to understand justification by faith between 1545 and 1546. It would seem to me that Burgh's heavy-handed Protestant legalism would have had the opposite effect of confirming her Roman Catholic upbringing. Katherine only remained under the roof of Sir Thomas Burgh for two years, after which Edward set up his own household about 12 miles away.

In 1531, Maud Parr died. She was only thirty-nine and her children mourned her passing. In her will, executed by Cuthbert Tunstall, she left Katherine many fine pieces of jewellery including 'my bed of purple satin, panelled with cloth of gold' and 'my beads [rosary] of lignum [a kind of hardwood] always dressed with gold, which the ... Queen's Grace [Catherine of Aragon] gave me', as well as a third of her ample collection of jewels. These included, in addition to several hundred pearls, eighteen substantial pieces ranging from 'a ring with a table diamond, set with black enamel, meet for my little finger' to a 'tablet with pictures of the King and the Queen'.[23]

In the spring of 1533, at the age of twenty-one, Katherine became a widow. Edward died of some unknown illness. Katherine was now alone. Following his death, she may have moved in with Lady Strickland, who was the widow of Katherine's cousin Sir Walter Strickland, at the family residence of Sizergh Castle in Westmorland: 'There is a tradition in the family of the Stricklands of Sizergh Castle in Westmorland that Catherine spent the year of her widowhood – 1533 – with them, demonstrating her notable needlework on a piece of embroidery still at the castle. Although this tradition is unsubstantiated – apart from the needlework – it may well be true.'[24]

In the summer of 1534, Katherine married John Neville, 3rd Baron Latimer, a kinsman of Lady Strickland. Latimer had been married twice before and was twice Katherine's age. He had two children by his first wife, Dorothy: John, aged thirteen, a difficult, rebellious teenager; and Margaret, aged nine, to whom Katherine became a loving stepmother. Young John would become 4th Baron Latimer on the death of his father in 1543. After this he married Lucy, daughter of Henry Somerset, who was the maid of honour for Catherine Howard and became a part of Katherine Parr's inner circle of ladies. John Neville's life would take a turn for the worse after Queen Katherine's death in 1548; he was accused of rape, murder and assaulting a servant, and was sent to Fleet Prison. His sister, Margaret, was betrothed to her cousin Ralph Bigod but never married. She later became a lady-in-waiting for Queen Katherine but died tragically at the age of twenty-one in 1546.

Through her marriage to Lord Latimer, Katherine now gained a title. She was Lady Latimer, the wife of Lord Latimer. 'During her nine-year marriage Katherine developed an affection for her husband deep enough to cherish a remembrance of him, his New Testament with his name inscribed inside the cover, which she kept with her until her death.'[25] She moved into Snape Castle in North Yorkshire. Katherine now had a home of her own, a title, and an influential husband. Alison Weir writes that the new Lady Latimer settled comfortably into her first experience of mature married life. She ordered her household, cared for her stepchildren and accompanied her husband on his occasional trips to London. Lord Latimer had a house conveniently located in the capital for attending King Henry's court.[26]

Lord Latimer was a staunch supporter of the Catholic Church and, because of the religious consequences, had opposed the annulment of Henry's marriage to Catherine of Aragon and his subsequent marriage to Anne Boleyn. If Katherine had already embraced the Reformation, this marriage would not have been a good fit.

At the time that Katherine had married Lord Latimer, drastic changes were being legislated in London. Both the Act of Supremacy and the Treasons Act were passed. The First Act of Succession made Elizabeth, the daughter of Henry and Anne, first in the line of succession and declared Mary, the daughter of Catherine of Aragon, illegitimate. In addition, Thomas Cromwell was closing and plundering the monasteries and abbeys. This created great anger and bitterness among the committed Catholics of the north. It was this last that was to play an important role in Katherine's life, for after only three years of marriage the Lord and Lady Latimer were embroiled in the great northern uprising known as the Pilgrimage of Grace, a demonstration against Henry's policies.

The initial uprising took place in Lincolnshire but was rapidly put down and the leaders were executed. The rebels of the north regrouped at Yorkshire and became organised under the leadership of lawyer Robert Aske. Lord Latimer was one of the first noblemen to join the rebellion. He claimed that he had been captured and forced to participate, but there are many indications that he was a very willing participant. According to biographer Elizabeth Norton, 'Lord Latimer does appear, as did many other noblemen, to have quickly agreed to espouse their point of view and it is difficult to distinguish between duress and free will in the actions of the lords and gentlemen who were captured and forced to lead the rebels.'[27] David Starkey comments, 'The idea of "being compelled to lead" is a strange one. Were the gentle and noble Pilgrims really coerced? Or did they connive? The question has been much debated, by contemporaries and historians alike.'[28]

While the rebellion endured, Latimer actively participated and probably hoped that it would succeed in restoring the 'old religion'. Perhaps Katherine, after spending two years under the heavy-handed Protestant legalism of Thomas Burgh, shared his views.

The rebels demanded that the heretical works of Luther and other reformers be destroyed; that the authority of the Pope be restored; and that Henry's eldest daughter, Mary, the daughter of Catherine of Aragon, be declared legitimate. They also demanded that the suppressed abbeys and monasteries be restored and that a parliament be held at Nottingham or York to further address their concerns. Of course, there was no way Henry was about to acquiesce to their demands.

After a period of armed conflict, in negotiations through the Duke of Norfolk Henry granted a pardon to all involved in the uprising and promised that a parliament would be convened to discuss their demands – a promise he never intended to keep. When the decision was announced to the rebels, they disbanded.

Henry summoned the leaders, especially Robert Aske, to come to court at Christmas in 1536. Aske was confident of the graciousness of the king, but he was totally deceived if he thought that Henry meant to keep his promises. In 1537, Aske was executed and hung in chains at York. Lord Latimer, on the other hand, had far more personal experience with the King and was not convinced by his display of graciousness toward the rebels. After Christmas, he left Katherine at Snape and hurried south to explain to Henry his actions during the rebellion, leaving Katherine alone with the two children.

When the rebels in the area learned that Latimer was heading south to plead his case with the king, they decided he was a 'turncoat' and attacked Snape Castle. Katherine and her stepchildren were held hostage and the house was ransacked. There is no evidence that either Katherine or the children were harmed. Word was sent to Latimer, who was returning from London, that his family would be killed if he did not return immediately: 'Catherine and her household must have been in great trepidation as hostages of such unpredictable and desperate men. Fortunately, her ordeal did not last very long. When Lord Latimer returned, he managed to persuade those who had taken possession of his home to depart. It would be pleasant – and not unreasonable – to believe that Catherine's demeanour also helped to defuse the situation.'[29]

The king and Thomas Cromwell heard conflicting reports concerning Latimer. Was he a prisoner or a conspirator? If he was a conspirator, he could be found guilty of treason and forfeit his estates, leaving Katherine and her stepchildren penniless. Latimer was pressed to condemn the actions of Robert Aske, and he complied. Probably Katherine's brother William Parr and his uncle William Parr, 1st Baron Parr of Horton, who both fought against the rebellion, intervened to save Latimer's life.

As a side note, Katherine's younger brother William was a courtier and making a name for himself. He had married Anne Bourchier, 7th Baroness Bourchier, daughter of Henry Bourchier, 2nd Earl of Essex. In 1541, Anne created a scandal when she deserted William to elope with her lover, who happened to be the prior of St James's Church in Surrey. She was repudiated by Parliament in 1543, whereupon William received Anne's lands and titles and became the Earl of Essex. Under the reign of Mary, he was convicted of high treason and sentenced to death but was released. His titles were restored to him by Elizabeth I. He died in 1565 and was entombed in the chancel of St Mary's Church in Warwick. Queen Elizabeth paid for his funeral and burial. While William's tomb was known and readily identified, the tomb of his sister, Queen Katherine, was lost for over two hundred years.

Although no charges were levelled against Lord Latimer, his reputation, which reflected upon Katherine, was tarnished for the rest of his life. Over the next seven years, the family spent much of their time in the south. In 1542, during their time in London, Lord Latimer attended Parliament, and Katherine spent the time visiting with her brother William and her sister Anne at court. Through the influence of her mother, Maud, Anne had become one of Catherine of Aragon's ladies-in-waiting at the age of thirteen. After Maud's death, Anne became a ward of King Henry. She served all six of Henry's wives. In 1538, she married Sir William Herbert.

Katherine loved the atmosphere at court, so different from that of the rural estates she had known. She became acquainted with the latest trends, not only in matters of religion, which eventually became very important to her, but also in the more mundane matters such as fashion and jewellery.

By 1542, Lord Latimer's health had worsened. Katherine nursed him until his death the following year. In his will, Katherine was named as guardian of his daughter, Margaret, and was put in charge of her affairs until she came of age. When Margaret died at the age of twenty-one, she stated in her will, 'I am never able to render to her grace sufficient thanks for the godly education and tender love and bountiful goodness which I have ever more found in her highness.'[30] Later, this 'bountiful care and tender love' would be directed to Henry's daughter Elizabeth. Lord Latimer left Katherine various properties, and as a result she became a fairly wealthy woman.

Since her mother had been the dear friend of Catherine of Aragon, Katherine renewed her friendship with the former queen's daughter, Lady Mary. Since they were about the same age and their mothers were close friends, they must have had a previous relationship. It has even been suggested that they may have been educated together,[31] although this is unlikely. By February 1543, Katherine had established herself as part of Mary's household. It was here that she caught the eye of the king and was offered a proposal that, for some reason, she could not refuse.

5

WHY MARRY HENRY?

It took Henry some time to recover from the disappointment and embarrassment of being cuckolded by his teenage queen, Catherine Howard. Nevertheless, the king was soon on the prowl again, seeking a sixth wife. On 29 January 1542, the Imperial ambassador Eustace Chapuys reported that his majesty had given a great supper for sixty-one ladies – twenty-six at his own table and thirty-five at an adjacent one.[1] Yet he found no one to meet his expectations.

Strangely, in February 1543, King Henry began to show a great deal of attention to his once estranged daughter, Lady Mary. Chapuys further reported to Charles V that 'the king has shown the greatest possible affection and liberality to the Princess, and not a day passes but he goes to visit her in her chamber two or three times with the utmost cordiality.'[2] While Henry was indeed fond of Mary and had never shown her so much attention, he had ulterior motives involving her attendant Lady Latimer. He sent a gift of dresses for Mary but also for Lady Latimer. Even though she was still married to her ailing husband at this time, Katherine was beginning to get the hint that Henry had sized her up as his possible sixth wife.

What would prompt Henry to choose Katherine Parr as wife number six? According to Derek Wilson, 'Probably that calm acceptance of duty she was demonstrating. He had had his fill of meddlesome beauties and foreign princesses. Catherine was still young and attractive, and combined with these attributes had maturity and intelligence.' In addition, the king was also well disposed towards the Parr family. Anne had risen to become senior woman of the chamber to the last two queens and William was captain of the ceremonial guard of Gentleman Pensioners.[3] Both Catherine's siblings had become prominent and dependable members of the royal entourage.[4]

However, there was a problem. Katherine already had her heart set on another. Lord Admiral Thomas Seymour, brother of the late queen Jane Seymour and uncle to heir apparent Prince Edward, was the most eligible bachelor at court. He was quite a catch. He had a magnificent speaking and singing voice, wrote poetry, dressed with flair, and, like his brother Edward, could boast of actual exploits in battle.[5] Carolly Erickson writes that the admiral was, by general repute, a man of hearty sexual appetites who looked on women in frank appraisal and was more of an opportunist than a gentleman.[6] Despite the court rumours regarding his character, it's not surprising that he should have appealed to Katherine after her marriage to the aged Lord Latimer. Nor is it unreasonable to believe that Thomas was genuinely attracted to her. Katherine was a slim, elegant and accomplished woman with hair the colour of burnished gold, a warm personality and exemplary private life that perhaps masked a hidden sensuality that a man with his experience of the world might have detected even while she was still married.[7] Despite the turmoil surrounding Lord Latimer's illness and death, Katherine was in love – likely for the first time.

No details are reported concerning the romance between Katherine and Thomas Seymour prior to her marriage to King Henry; everything written about their relationship is mere conjecture. David Starkey writes, 'We do not know when they met, or when their evidently mutual attraction began. Probably it was before Latimer's death. If so, she handled her feelings with her usual wisdom and discretion.'[8]

After her marriages to Edward Burgh and Lord Latimer, who was twice her age, Katherine finally had the opportunity to follow her heart. And who could blame her? She was truly in love with Thomas Seymour, and the very thought of marrying King Henry must have been repulsive. After the betrayal of Catherine Howard, the king had plunged into old age. Alison Weir writes of how he had changed from the dashing prince of Christendom:

> The king was ... so fat that such a man had never been seen. Three of the biggest men that could be found could get inside his doublet. At fifty-two, he was already an old man, with an old man's set ways and uncertain temper. His bad leg sometimes rendered him immobile and needed constantly redressing; on occasions it stank ... All the same, he presented himself as a prospective bridegroom with all the assurance he had displayed to Anne Boleyn nearly twenty years before, and it was obvious that he would not brook any refusals.[9]

For Henry, the only real downside in choosing Katherine as his sixth wife was her apparent infertility – after two marriages, she had no children. At fifty-one, Henry still expected a sexual relationship with his wife, although he was apparently intermittently impotent.[10]

In seeking the hand of Lady Katherine, Henry also knew that he had a rival in Thomas Seymour. In the early spring, he resolved to remove him from the picture by appointing him ambassador to the Netherlands. News of this appointment must have been devastating for Katherine. Thomas had already become aware of the king's interest in Katherine and, not wanting to start a rivalry with the king, was beginning to back off. Perhaps in the back of his mind he might have figured that Katherine's marriage to the king was not a bad idea. She would probably outlive Henry, and being married to a former queen would be advantageous. As future events would demonstrate, Seymour was a schemer, seeking any means for his personal advancement – a trait Katherine was later to discover, and for which Thomas would eventually lose his head.

Even with Seymour out of the picture, Katherine was still resolved not to marry the king if she could find some way to avoid it. Of course, in the back of her mind was the plight of Henry's five previous wives. She knew that two of them had lost their heads for in some way displeasing him, and she also knew that, given Henry's present state of mind, she could become the third.

The exact date is not known, but probably in early May 1543 Henry made his intentions known and proposed: 'Lady Latimer, I wish you to be my wife.' He did not expect an immediate response and gave Katherine some time to think about it, although he surely did not entertain the possibility that she might refuse. But why would Katherine Parr – a beautiful, independent, financially secure woman in love with another man – marry the obtuse, violent, physically repulsive King Henry? In telling Katherine's story, this is a very important question.

Most of Katherine's biographers see a higher purpose and suggest that she had an ulterior motive in marrying King Henry: gaining the ear of the king to promote the Reformation. They assume that Katherine had embraced the Lutheran Reformation by the time of her marriage to Henry. David Starkey writes, 'Henceforward Catherine was a woman with a mission. She was marrying Henry at God's command and for His purpose. And that purpose was no less than to complete the conversion of England to Reform.'[11] Alison Weir suggests that the Pilgrimage of Grace led Katherine to embrace the Protestant cause: 'It may have been around this time that Katherine first became interested in Protestantism, a leaning she would be forced to conceal for many years; it was not until much later that she would be able to embrace openly the Lutheran faith.'[12] Elizabeth Norton adds, 'Catherine saw Henry's proposal as the will of God and, from that moment onwards, she prepared for her marriage with a new purpose, seeing it as an opportunity to do God's work and spread her reformist beliefs.'[13]

There is no doubt that when Katherine married Henry she held 'Reformist beliefs', but these were Erasmian ideas and most certainly not the radical notions of Martin Luther. The only evidence to suggest that Katherine was a proponent of the Lutheran Reformation at the time of her marriage to King Henry was a reference by John Foxe in his *Acts and Monuments* claiming that Katherine was seen by the reformers as the perfect instrument whereby they could influence the king. They put heart and soul into encouraging the marriage, grateful that the king's inclinations at last coincided with their hopes.[14] If such an appeal to the reformers is factual history, it may be explained by Katherine's advocacy of the teachings of Erasmus, who was often viewed as a precursor to the Reformation; indeed, it was said that Erasmus laid the egg that Luther hatched. Of course, Erasmus denied this claim, stating that what Luther hatched was a different bird. The reforms of Erasmus, which Katherine can be seen to have embraced, entailed restoring sincere piety to the Catholic faith and elevating the study of Scripture. In this sense, she was a 'reformer'. Her appeal for those who desired to see reform was her piety, not her theology. Their hope was that her piety would eventually lead her to the truth – which it did.

In assessing the religious landscape of sixteenth-century England, what is most frustrating is the failure of historians and biographers to define terms and to distinguish the reform touted by Erasmus and his humanist disciples, including both King Henry and Queen Katherine, from the radical views of Luther and the Protestant Reformation. There was a marked difference between Erasmus and Luther. Derek Wilson points out, 'Where Erasmus and Luther parted company was over some of the finer points of doctrine (such as free will) and the German's belligerent rejection of those who disagreed with him. The two men had drunk from different streams. Luther had imbibed the brackish waters of *anfechtung*, an intense and unremitting spiritual conflict. Erasmus had quaffed from the limpid spring of reason.'[15] Janel Mueller comments, 'Erasmus, despite his adherence to the Catholic faith and his dispute with Luther, by the mid-sixteenth century had come to be regarded as a proto- or quasi-reformer, incurring strong condemnation from certain Catholics and varying degrees of admiration from Protestants.'[16]

The Lutheran Reformation began in 1517 when Martin Luther nailed his Ninety-Five Theses to the church door in Wittenberg, calling into question the practice of selling indulgences. As the movement developed, various doctrines were presented and formulated that were contrary to the teachings of the Roman Catholic Church and which Luther was called upon to defend. The primary issue was the question of righteousness. Luther and his followers taught justification by faith, calling into question the entire Roman approach, including the monastic system, indulgences, prayers for the dead, purgatory, the various definitions of good works, the saints, and so on. While Erasmus' reforms were in opposition to ignorance and dead formalism, the Lutheran Reformation was about truth. The reformers declared, 'We are saved by grace alone, through faith alone, based on Scripture alone.' To promote the Reformation was to declare those truths that were contrary to the teaching of Rome. When Katherine married Henry, it is very evident that she had not embraced the truths that defined the Lutheran Reformation.

It is said that the English Reformation began when Henry rejected the authority of the pope, but nothing changed regarding the truths of the religion Henry embraced. While he did, following the views of Erasmus, move against meaningless rituals, superstitions and relics, and allowed the English Bible to be put into the hands of the people, he simply replaced the pope. According to the Act of Six Articles (1539), England theologically remained a Catholic country apart from the authority of Rome. Taking advantage of the king's hatred of heresy and desire for unity, the conservatives, led by Bishop Gardiner, set in motion a further expression of official doctrine which appeared in 1543 under the title *The Necessary Doctrine and Erudition for Any Christian Man*, commonly known as the King's Book. The doctrine of justification by faith was totally rejected. Cranmer tried to save the doctrine by arguing that, while true faith was accompanied by good works (in other words, faith was not *alone*), it was only faith that justified. However, Henry would not be persuaded, and the text was amended to read that faith justified 'neither only nor alone'.[17] The King's Book affirmed that each person had the free will to do the good works leading to their justification.

In 1529, Henry made a concerted effort to eliminate the threat of the Protestant Reformation by banning books that were went contrary 'to the faith Catholic' or against the 'decrees, laws and ordinance of Holy Church'. In 1530, further efforts were made to prevent the dissemination of 'blasphemous and pestiferous English books, printed in other regions and sent into this realm', decreeing that subjects were not to 'buy, receive, or have' any 'erroneous books' and ordering that no book in English 'concerning Holy Scripture' be printed 'until such time as the same book or books be examined and approved by the ordinary of the diocese where the said books shall be printed'.[18]

To further the Lutheran Reformation meant having access to banned books and speaking contrary to the Six Articles and the King's Book. While Katherine eventually did speak out, after her discovery of justification by faith in 1546 as evidenced in *The Lamentation of a Sinner*, she was nearly arrested for doing so and her privy chamber was examined for evidence of banned books. Regardless, these were most certainly not her beliefs when she married Henry. In other words, she didn't marry Henry to further the Lutheran Reformation since it is historically evident that at that time she had not embraced the truths that defined the Lutheran Reformation.

Katherine Parr was born and raised a pious Roman Catholic. Her mother, Maud, attended Catherine of Aragon until the day she died. One of the men who oversaw her education was Cuthbert Tunstall, a committed Roman Catholic and follower of the humanism of Erasmus. To suggest, as does Elizabeth Norton,[19] that Katherine rejected her Roman Catholic upbringing because she spent one year under the roof of the 'Reformist' tyrant Thomas Burgh is, to say the least, highly tenuous. It is more likely that the opposite took place.

Katherine's second husband, Lord Latimer, was a committed traditional Roman Catholic who had reluctantly accepted the Act of Supremacy. Latimer also opposed the destruction of the abbeys and monasteries and evidently was a part of the Pilgrimage of Grace. Did Katherine, as a subservient wife, share her husband's views? While she obviously accepted Henry as the head of the Church of England, there is nothing recorded regarding her views on the Pilgrimage of Grace. David Starkey suggests that Katherine did not embrace the Pilgrimage of Grace because she was already committed to reform.[20] If by 'reform' Starkey is referring to that promoted by Erasmus, I would agree, since Erasmus opposed the abuses of the monasteries. If he is referring to the Lutheran Reformation, I would strongly disagree. Katherine's biographers fail to recognise the influence of Erasmus upon her religious beliefs. The key concern should in fact be to pinpoint the moment in Katherine's life when she rejected Erasmus and embraced Luther.

The marriage of Katherine and Henry was strongly endorsed by both Lord Chancellor Thomas Wriothesley and King's Secretary Stephen Gardiner, two key conservatives who were committed to rooting out Protestant heresy. It was Gardiner, not Thomas Cranmer, who conducted the marriage ceremony of Henry and Katherine. Linda Porter writes, 'It seems safe to say that when she married Henry there was nothing about Katherine that set alarm bells ringing with him or with conservatives like Stephen Gardiner.'[21] When learning of the king's interest in Lady Latimer, Wriothesley and Gardiner must have gone to great lengths to determine the religious leanings of the new queen. As they happily assented to the union, they surely heard nothing in the court gossip to suggest that she was a crypto-Lutheran Protestant.

Katherine was one of Lady Mary's attendants. Lady Mary, the daughter of Henry and Catherine of Aragon, was a strong advocate of the 'old religion' as evidenced by her later reign as 'Bloody Mary' when over 280 advocates of the Reformation were executed. Maud Parr, Katherine's mother, had faithfully served Mary's mother Catherine of Aragon until Maud's death in 1531. After her marriage to Henry, Katherine and Mary had a connection and became very close friends and constant companions. Katherine acted as her older sister and confidante. Elizabeth Norton writes, 'What is also evident from the first year of Catherine's marriage is that she was often with her stepdaughter, Princess Mary, and the two women were exceptionally close.'[22] In a correspondence with the Emperor, Imperial ambassador Eustace Chapuys writes regarding the queen's friendship with Mary, 'With regard to the maintenance of friendship, she said she had done, and would do, nothing to prevent its growing still further: and she hoped that God would avert even the slightest dissension, as the friendship was so necessary.'[23]

If they had harboured differing religious views, as many suggest, this would have obviously created tension and hindered their relationship. After being coerced and threatened, Mary had reluctantly agreed to the Act of Supremacy, declaring the king to be the head of the Church of England. Katherine certainly knew this and must have been aware of Mary's true loyalty to Rome, but it didn't faze her. She probably sympathised with Mary's plight. I'm sure there were numerous times when Katherine and Mary, both pious Romans Catholics, would pray the rosary together, Katherine using her mother's beads that had been a gift from Mary's mother.

If Katherine had embraced the Reformation, it would have been highly unlikely that she would broker the king to place Mary back in the line of succession. The last thing any advocate of the Lutheran Reformation would want is Princess Mary on the throne of England – a notion later justified by events following the death of Edward.

If Katherine hoped to moderate Mary's loyalty to Rome, as has been further suggested,[24] she certainly wasn't successful. This is mere conjecture based on the faulty assumption that Katherine had embraced the Reformation by this time. There is no evidence to suggest that Katherine attempted to influence Mary's pro-Catholic stance. If Katherine had undertaken such a mission, it would not have escaped the notice of Eustace Chapuys, the Imperial ambassador, and been reported to Emperor Charles V. It seems that very little escaped the notice of Chapuys when it came to Lady Mary.

By appearance Katherine was indeed a pious person, and that piety was evident in the daily routine of her household. Probably in early 1544, Francis Goldsmith, who had a place in her household, wrote Katherine a letter thanking her for bringing Christ into the palace. He wrote, 'Your most rare goodness made days that were seldom such, truly Sundays now. Your most pious service and your carefulness of life have redounded from your most exalted station as things that we perceive never to have been done before in a royal house especially.'[25] Goldsmith goes on to credit 'our most serene and invincible Prince' (King Henry) for making such piety possible.

Katherine's biographers quote the Goldsmith letter to demonstrate that Katherine was importing her 'reformist beliefs' into the daily routine of her household.[26] Susan James surmises that the piety defined by Goldsmith 'is not rooted in the old religion but in the new'. She says that 'it is difficult to know what to make of this letter unless it is accepted as a statement of the new queen's commitment to the reformed faith,'[27] but this is not the case. Certainly, the Goldsmith letter does not reflect the so-called 'old religion' but rather the 'new learning', piety and commitment to the study of Scripture of the Erasmian reform. Katherine having appeared to be pious doesn't make her Protestant. Acknowledging sin and focusing upon the death of Christ on the cross is an integral part of Catholic piety as promoted by Erasmus. There is nothing in the Goldsmith letter to indicate that Katherine was importing the radical views of Luther, which King Henry opposed, into her daily devotions.

Through the influence of Cuthbert Tunstall, a friend of the humanist scholar Erasmus, Katherine became a student of the latter figure, who of course remained loyal to the Church in Rome and was committed to its reform from within. Erasmus was no friend of Luther or the Lutheran Reformation. He believed that Luther had gone too far. He staunchly rejected Luther's *On the Bondage of the Will*, in which he argued against Erasmus' idea that humans had free will to do good or evil, for obvious reasons. Erasmus believed that man was capable of doing the good works that would merit salvation – a view also held by Katherine. Luther's *On the Bondage of the Will* was an attack upon the entire Erasmian system. As a follower of Erasmus, Katherine promoted piety and encouraged the study of Scripture within her household and believed that the Bible should be in the hands of the common people. This motivated her to later undertake the task of overseeing the translation of Erasmus' *Paraphrases* into English 'to guide English Scripture readers into less contentious paths'. Erasmus *Paraphrases*, or rewritings of the Gospels, were composed between 1517 and 1524. Brandon Withrow is correct to be sceptical: 'But was Katherine a reformer of religion as well when she became queen? Early biographers and admirers often portray Katherine as an unabashedly Reformed queen when she entered the throne in 1543. This portrayal is largely derived from the high praise Katherine received from John Foxe in his popular *Acts and Monuments*. It is true that Katherine left the throne as a Protestant calling for Reformation, but initially she was, to be precise, more a follower of Erasmus.'[28] William Haugaard confirms: 'Katherine was attached to that form of sixteenth-century Christianity known as "Erasmianism".'[29]

The demonstration of Katherine's piety is evident in her devotional writings. No queen, including the alleged Protestant queen Anne Boleyn, had ever published personal devotional writings. Katherine's religious piety was exemplary as affirmed by Goldsmith, but what was the nature of that piety? To determine whether a person was a proponent of the Lutheran Reformation you must discover what that person believed and confessed. Being a proponent of the Reformation did not merely mean aligning yourself with a specific group but rather adopting a theology as presented in the Lutheran *Augsburg Confession* or perhaps John Calvin's *The Institutes of the Christian Religion*. Both were published at the time and were probably readily available in Protestant circles. In the first years of her marriage to Henry, had Katherine embraced the very simple and primary elements of Reformation teaching, specifically justification by faith? Did she have 'reformist beliefs'? This question is not difficult to answer. All you must do is examine the theology Katherine espoused in her devotional writings.

In 1544, Katherine anonymously published her first book, *Psalms or Prayers*, an English translation of the Latin Psalms published by noted humanist Bishop John Fisher around 1525. Fisher, together with Thomas More, was executed in 1535 for his refusal to acknowledge Henry as the Supreme Head of the Church of England. At first glance, it appears strange that Katherine would choose to undertake the laborious task of translating from Latin into English the works of a man who had been her husband's greatest adversary and was considered a traitor. Janel Mueller comments on this seeming inconsistency: 'Despite their total political discrediting, the intrinsic spiritual value of Fisher's and More's religious writing remained in high esteem among knowledgeable contemporaries.'[30]

In her work, Katherine speaks of doing penance. She writes, 'I have not done penance for my malice, but have increased in much vanity.'[31] And again, 'Forgive me all my sins, O Lord God almighty, for Thy own sake put out of Thy sight my heinous offenses, for according to Thy goodness, Thou hast promised forgiveness of sins ofttimes to them that do penance.'[32] Janel Mueller comments, 'Parr's rendering of the Latin *poenitentia* as "penance" (rather than repentance) aligns her with a traditionalist stance, since penance in the English context was always understood as entailing oral confession to a priest.'[33] The second of Martin Luther's Ninety-Five Theses declares, 'This word (repentance) cannot be understood as referring to the sacrament of penance, that is, confession and satisfaction, as administered by the clergy.'

On several occasions, Kathrine affirms Fisher's position that obedience to the commands of God and individual goodness leads to salvation. In both these examples, her translation is totally contrary to the basic teachings of the Reformation and are clearly aligned with King Henry's conservative Six Articles and the King's Book. Janel Mueller further writes, 'In Lutheran (and much other Reformation) theology it is axiomatic that sinful humankind cannot keep God's commandments and covenants. While good works are the necessary fruits of salvation, they cannot earn it. But Parr's rendering in *Psalms or Prayers* concur with Fisher's repeated affirmations of a role for human cooperation in the dynamic of salvation.'[34]

Her second book, published in June 1545 with the king's approval as *Prayers or Meditations*, was the first book published by a woman in England under her own name. The title page reads,

'Prayers or Meditations, wherein the mind is stirred, patiently to suffer all afflictions here, to set at naught the vain prosperity of this world, and always to long for the everlasting felicity.'[35] She based her meditations upon Thomas a' Kempis' fifteenth-century Catholic devotional book *Imitation of Christ*. C. Feno Hoffman points out that 'preceding the prayers is the sixty-page "meditation", which could hardly have a Protestant tone since it is borrowed from the *Imitation of Christ*,'[36] which most certainly did not present Reformation teaching.

While her meditation is replete with words of self-abasement, decrying her sinful condition, she has no answers for her quandary. She addresses Jesus Christ as 'my most loving spouse, who shall give me wings of perfect love, that I may fly up from these worldly miseries and rest in thee.'[37] She is seeking God. She makes statements such as 'Give me Lord, therefore, heavenly wisdom, that I may learn to seek and find thee'[38] and 'For as long as any transitory thing keepeth me back, or hath rule in me, I may not freely ascend to thee.'[39] While Katherine appeared to be a pious woman, her notion that she could seek after God, find him and ascend to him was Roman Catholic meditative theology. If Katherine was a proponent of the Reformation and embraced either Lutheran or Calvinist teaching, there is no way she would author and publish books that are replete with Roman Catholic theology. On the assumption then that the Catholicism inherited from her family upbringing and from her first two marriages had not been seriously challenged when she published *Prayers or Meditations*, there is, nevertheless, evidence that by the end of 1545 Catherine had given serious thought to the message of the reformers.[40]

The content of her 1545 *Prayers or Meditations* is totally different from that presented in her 1547 *The Lamentation of a Sinner*, the first published 'conversion narrative' in England. In *The Lamentation of a Sinner*, Katherine knows exactly what she believes. Her theology is defined and precise. Her eyes have been opened. She has discovered that the answer to her lament is faith in the person and work of Jesus Christ and the 'Book of the

Crucifix'. C. Fenno Hoffman states, 'In the second of her religious publications, however, *The Lamentacion (sic) of a Sinner*, first published November 5, 1547 (some nine months after Henry's death), Catherine unmistakably and in her own voice described – but without dating it – a radical change in her religious views. *Lamentacion (sic)*, indeed, may be read – perhaps should be read – as a repudiation of *Prayers or Meditacions (sic)*.'[41]

Randall Martin states that Katherine's *Lamentation of a Sinner* circulated in manuscript at court by November 1545.[42] Martin is undoubtedly basing his information on the undocumented, unreliable conjectures in the 1973 Anthony Martienssen biography of Queen Katherine. I find Martin's claim highly unlikely. If the *Lamentation* was a repudiation of her *Prayers or Meditations*, which appears to be the case, Katherine would not have had enough time to define and research her conversion experience and write about it.

Katherine had a conversion experience and embraced the teachings of the Lutheran Reformation, particularly the truth of justification by faith, between the time she published those two works. It probably took place sometime at the end of 1545 or the beginning of the tumultuous year of 1546. It was then that she began to discuss points of theology with her husband the king, since they had issues to debate. Before that time, their views on religion were aligned. To suggest that Katherine had embraced the Reformation prior to her marriage to Henry is to minimise the importance of her conversion from trusting in her own efforts to faith in Jesus Christ, which is the central truth of the Reformation. Derek Wilson observes, 'Though Catherine nowhere in her writings revealed the precise circumstances of her conversion, it is difficult to believe that it was not a dramatic, comparatively sudden occurrence, a moment of enlightenment, such as that which had befallen the monk, Martin Luther, as a result of studying the opening of St Paul's argument in his Letter to the Romans.'[43]

It is interesting but not surprising to note that Katherine's *Prayers or Meditations* became very popular among English readers of the sixteenth century and that numerous editions were published[44] while her *The Lamentation of a Sinner* seemingly lapsed into obscurity. For some reason, it is far more agreeable to human sensibilities, whether in the sixteenth century or the twenty-first century, to confess sins and cry out to God for mercy, facing an uncertain eternal destiny, than to acknowledge that mercy, forgiveness and eternal life have already been granted through Jesus Christ.

The doctrine of Henry's new Church of England, over which he was 'pope', according to Linda Porter, was 'a middle way neither Lutheran nor traditionally Catholic'. The king had fully endorsed the destruction of shrines, removal of images, cessation of pilgrimages and the assault on superstition that characterised the first phase of the Reformation in England. 'Yet Henry could not be reconciled to the teaching of Martin Luther … Justification by faith alone did not convince him, either. He believed there must be more to salvation and would not accept that good works and charity did not play their part in the redemption of the soul.'[45] I think it would be more accurate to say that the doctrine of Henry's new Church of England was an Erasmian brand of Roman Catholicism.

It is evident that for the first few years of their marriage, Henry and Katherine were of one mind when it came to issues of religion. Linda Porter is correct when she says that 'Katherine's personal beliefs in 1543 were still developing and there was nothing about this aspect of her life that troubled the king.'[46] While both Thomas Wriothesley and Stephen Gardiner, the two main 'heresy hunters' on the king's council, would later in 1546 seek to arrest her for heresy, at the time of the marriage they were both well pleased with Henry's choice of a sixth wife. Something had happened with Katherine to change their minds and seek her arrest.

So, back to the original question: if not to further the Reformation, why did beautiful, independently wealthy Katherine Parr, in love with another man, choose to marry Henry?

There are two items of correspondence written by Katherine Parr explaining the rationale behind her decision to marry King

Henry. The first is to her brother, Lord William Parr, and the other to Sir Thomas Seymour. While these letters are often quoted side by side, they represent two different time periods. The letter to her brother was written four months after her marriage to Henry, and the letter to Thomas Seymour was written after the death of Henry.

To her brother William she wrote:

> Right dear and beloved brother, we greet you well. Letting you wit that when it has pleased almighty God of his goodness to incline the king's majesty in such wise towards me, as it has pleased his highness to take me of all others, most unworthy, to his wife, which is, as reason it ought to be, the greatest joy and comfort that could happen to me in this world.
>
> To the intent, you being my natural brother, may rejoice with me in the goodness of God and of his majesty, as the person who by nature hath most cause of the same, I thought meet to give you this advertisement and to require you to let me sometime hear of your health as friendly as you might have done if God and his majesty had not called me to this honour: which I assure you, shall be much to my comfort.
>
> Katherine the Queen[47]

Katherine rejoices not that she chose Henry but that God had inclined the king's majesty to choose her above all others, even though she felt unworthy. She attributes the king's decision to choose her to God even though there is nothing to indicate that Henry was seeking the will of God in choosing his sixth wife. From Katherine's perspective, God was behind the scenes informing the king's decision. She assures her brother that the match 'shall be much to my comfort'. The word comfort in this sense does not imply offering strength and hope to one experiencing hardship, but rather 'ease and luxury'. William, as her natural brother, should also rejoice because he too will be the beneficiary of the same 'ease and luxury'.

It is clear from this letter that Katherine accepted the proposal of the king because of the great benefits she would reap. As we will later see, Katherine loved the temporal bounty that came with being queen. Linda Porter writes, 'She loved clothes and soon possessed a wardrobe stuffed with beautiful and expensive items: gowns, sleeves, kirtles, petticoats, partlets and placards in an array of colours, though the most common were crimson, purple and black.'[48] Her family would also experience the benefits of her position. Derek Wilson comments, 'It was within Catherine's power to make the Parrs the second dynasty in the land. On St George's Day (23 April) brother William's name was added to the select list of Knights of the Garter. Days later, he was appointed Lord Warden and Keeper of the Western March, responsible for law and order on part of the border. Catherine's brother-in-law William Herbert was knighted and received lands in Wales.'[49]

In the weeks following Henry's death on 28 January 1547, while she was supposed to be mourning the loss of her husband, Katherine rekindled her romantic relationship with Thomas Seymour. In a letter written probably in mid-February 1547, she wishes to assure Thomas that her interest in him is not some sudden emotion and that he was always her first choice. These thoughts are added as a postscript to a letter in which Katherine complains that Thomas's brother Edward had not come to her as promised to discuss some legal matter. Janel Mueller suggests that 'the phrasing of her subscription in this letter raise the possibility that she and Seymour by this early date had already exchanged vows ... to a privately contracted marriage.'[50] Katherine briefly describes the process that caused her to marry the king:

I would not have you to think that this my honest goodwill toward you to proceed from any sudden motion or passion. For, truly as God is God, my mind was fully bent the other time I was at liberty, to marry you before any man I knew. Howbeit God withstood my will therein most vehemently for a time and through his grace and goodness, made that possible which seemed to me most impossible; that was, made me to renounce utterly mine own will, and to follow his will most willingly. It were too long to write all the

process of this matter. If I live, I shall declare it to you myself.
I can say nothing but, as my lady Suffolk saith, 'God is a
marvelous man.'

By her that is yours to serve and obey during her life,

Katherine the Queen KP[51]

The following month, in a letter dealing with other issues, Thomas
adds the final thought, 'I beseech your highness to put all fancies
out of your head, that might bring you in any one thought, that
I do think the goodness you have showed me is of any sudden
emotion.' Seymour signs the letter, 'From the body of him whose
heart ye have.'[52]

A great deal has been written about Katherine's postscript
describing her alleged battle with God over whether she should
accept Henry's proposal. David Starkey puts his spin on the words
of Katherine: 'In this dilemma, Catherine, like a true believer,
turned to God for guidance. An answer came. But it was not
the one she wanted. She prayed again. The answer remained
the same. Still she resisted; still God was implacable.'[53] He
states that Katherine was marrying Henry 'at God's command'.
Starkey paints a pious picture of Katherine wrestling with God as
Jacob did at Peniel (Genesis 32:22–31), and, of course, as usual,
God won. Elizabeth Norton adds that 'Catherine saw Henry's
proposal as the will of God.'[54] Susan James writes, 'Catherine's
God voicing His imperatives in the voice of the new religion
forced her to subordinate her personal desires to His. The force
applied to accept God's will in the matter of her marriage was not
only a metaphysical imperative but a human one, urged by the
reformers.'[55]

This begs the question: how did God communicate his will to
Katherine? How did the answer come? How did God 'command'
Katherine? A 'metaphysical imperative' implies a command that
was transcendent or supernatural. How was this supernatural
command communicated to Katherine? How did she 'know' it
was the will and command of God for her to marry Henry? Was
it an angelic visitation? A voice from heaven? A dream or vision?

Perhaps she discovered a tablet of stone with the words engraved by the finger of God. 'Thou shalt marry Henry!' One cannot speak of the divine intervention in the affairs of men without defining the divine methodology.

I dealt with this issue some years ago in a book titled *The Lord Told Me, I Think*.[56] While in the parish ministry, I had encountered people who would claim that God told them something or that God was leading them to accomplish something. The theological fact is that it is not possible to claim that something is the will or command of God unless you can cite chapter and verse from the Word of God, the Bible. Therein God reveals His will and purpose. All other claims to divine guidance are mere opinions unless there is objective verification. The Virgin Mary knew it was the will of God for her to marry Joseph because of an angelic visitation, and there is no historical record of such an angelic visitation to Katherine Parr. Katherine could not have made the decision to marry Henry because she objectively 'knew' it was the will of God. It is epistemologically impossible. Nor would Katherine have made such a monumental decision to marry Henry based on her subjective impression that she 'thought' it was the will of God. Her decision was based on objective factors, not on her subjective whims and opinions. If one wishes to be cynical, one could say that Katherine, in explaining her decision to marry Henry to her present lover, used the 'God made me do it' excuse. Rather than acknowledging the selfish 'comfort' motive as she did to her brother, she chooses to blame God.

There is a far more reasonable explanation: Katherine is simply stating that when the time came to choose her next husband after the death of Lord Latimer, Thomas was her first choice. She had always loved him, but marrying him at that time was not possible since Thomas had backed off and Henry was sending him to the Netherlands. With the possibility of marrying Thomas removed, she was wrestling with the likely consequences of being married to King Henry: the personal luxuries and family advancements associated with queenship measured against the revolting prospect of crawling under the royal sheets with the disgusting personage of King Henry VIII. I don't believe Katherine would pray about this issue. It's not the kind of 'either/or' one would present to God for guidance. Finally, after struggling with the issue, she resolved to sacrifice her private dignity for the sake of the benefits of being Queen of England. There is no evidence to suggest that Katherine's decision was influenced by her 'reformist friends'. It is mere conjecture.

Katherine is writing in retrospect. A great deal had happened since her marriage to King Henry. Her life had changed. She had been converted from the 'papal riffraff' of Roman Catholicism and Erasmian piety to the Gospel truth of justification by faith. She had embraced the Reformation and had the opportunity to witness to the king and to others around her. She had composed her seminal work *The Lamentation of a Sinner*, which she hoped to have published.

She had exerted profound positive influence upon Henry's children, especially Elizabeth. As she looked back over her decision to marry Henry, which at the time was prompted by worldly concerns, she saw the hand of God at work in the total process in the same way she saw the hand of God at work inclining Henry to choose her. This was 'the hidden God' behind the scenes, accomplishing his will and purposes. This is the only possible explanation for her comments unless an angel visited Katherine revealing to her the will of God. Derek Wilson says that we can believe her when she says that it was obedience to God that made her accept Henry's proposal. This is true, but only in retrospect.

This is not strange. When I chose to marry a beautiful young lady, I can honestly say there was nothing spiritual about my decision nor did I seek the will of God. But as I look back over the blessings of the past fifty-six years, I can without any reservation declare, *God made me do it*. I heartily agree with Lady Suffolk – God is a marvellous man.

Katherine initially married King Henry to enjoy the 'comfort' of being the Queen of England and promote the advancement of her family. She probably surmised, knowing the health of the king, that it was not going to be a lengthy marriage. She was willing to make that sacrifice in order to reap the benefits. In answering the question of Katherine's motivation in marrying Henry, her letter to her brother William four months after her marriage to Henry should carry far more weight than her postscript written to her lover following the death of Henry.

6

HENRY AND KATE

Katherine accepted the king's proposal in June, and they were married on 12 July 1543 at Hampton Court Palace. The time of day is not recorded, nor is there any description of Katherine's dress. Agnes Strickland wrote, 'She exchanged her widow's weeds for bridal robes.'[1] William Herbert and Edward Seymour were among the gentlemen of the king's party, while Katherine was supported by her sister Anne, Jane Dudley and Catherine Brandon, Duchess of Suffolk, who would become one of Katherine's closest friends. Henry's two daughters, Mary and Elizabeth, were honoured guests at the wedding and witnessed Henry and Katherine's exchange of vows. On the day of her marriage, Katherine gave presents of bracelets set with rubies to both Mary and Elizabeth, along with a liberal sum of money.

It is worth noting that the officiant who joined the two in marriage was not the Archbishop of Canterbury, Thomas Cranmer, which would have been expected, but rather Stephen Gardiner, Bishop of Winchester. This must have been Henry's choice, and it perhaps suggests that Cranmer, a Protestant who had argued a few months earlier for the inclusion of justification by faith in the King's Book, had temporarily fallen out of favour with the king. At the same time, a wide-ranging heresy hunt was taking place in Cranmer's own diocese of Canterbury.[2] Gardiner was determined to burn Cranmer for Protestant heresy – and with good reasons – yet it would not happen. Even though Henry disagreed with Cranmer's position on justification by faith, he was loyal to Cranmer, who had been instrumental in finding a solution for Henry's Great Matter.

The marriage was met with acclaim. The Conservative Lord Chancellor Thomas Wriothesley, who would later become an enemy of the queen and seek her arrest for heresy, wrote joyously to the Duke of Suffolk:

> I doubt not of your grace knowing ... that the king's majesty was married on Thursday last to my lady Latimer, a woman, in my judgement, of virtue, wisdom and gentleness most meet for his highness; and sure I am his majesty had never a wife more agreeable to his heart than she is. Our Lord send them long life and much joy together.[3]

Somehow, the Roman Catholic Imperial ambassador Eustace Chapuys was kept out of the loop and was unaware that the marriage had taken place. He soon became an admirer of Katherine, however, noting her graciousness and kindness, particularly to Lady Mary, the princess he had worked so hard to support for a decade. He commented to the Emperor Charles V that Katherine was 'praised for her virtue'; he added that she was 'of small stature, graceful, and of cheerful countenance'.[4]

There was one person who was not thrilled by the king's choice of Katherine, and that was Anne of Cleves. She had, so Eustace Chapuys claimed to have heard, 'taken great grief and despair at the king's espousal of this last wife, who is not nearly so beautiful as she, besides that there is no hope of issue, seeing that she had none with her two former husbands'.[5] 'She would rather,' Chapuys had heard, 'be stripped to her petticoat and return to her mother than remain longer in England.'[6] Since Anne was three years younger than Katherine, she probably thought of herself as a better candidate for child-bearing even though at the time of her marriage to Henry she seemed to be ignorant of the process whereby the blessed event occurs.

One of Katherine's first tasks as queen was to appoint her household. Catherine Howard's household had been disbanded in November 1541 and for two years the queen's apartments stood vacant. Katherine surrounded herself with friends and family. Sir William Parr, her uncle, became her chamberlain, the chief officer in her household. Her sister, Anne Herbert, was her most prominent attendant. With years of service to Henry's earlier wives under her belt, she was well qualified. Her young stepdaughter, Margaret Neville, the daughter of Lord Latimer, together with her cousin Lady Maud Lane, the daughter of Sir William Parr of Horton, and Lady Elizabeth Tyrwhitt were ladies-in-waiting. These ladies would later form Queen Katherine's 'Bible book club'. Catherine Brandon, Duchess of Suffolk, became a friend, but though she was present at the marriage ceremony her influence seems not to have been significant until 1545. Katherine was closest to her sister Anne and stepdaughter Margaret.

According to Alison Weir, 'Once the Queen's household had been organised, the King took his bride to Windsor, where he celebrated his marriage by having three Protestant heretics, Robert Testwood, Anthony Pearson and Henry Filmer, burned to death.'[7] John Marbeck, the noted musicologist, was also arrested but released. The arrest and interrogation was carried out by Dr John London, one of Bishop Gardiner's agents. We don't know how Katherine responded to this event. Amazingly, Agnes Strickland writes that Katherine 'knew well enough that the murder of these humble reformers was a blow aimed at herself, and that Gardiner was playing a bold game against all those professing her religion'.[8] It is unlikely that Gardiner, having endorsed Henry's choice of a new wife and conducted the wedding ceremony two weeks earlier, had now somehow discovered that Katherine had embraced the Reformation and had turned against her. Elizabeth Norton adds, 'The persecution of the four Windsor men was to prove only the first attack on Catherine's co-religionists during her time as queen.'[9] It seems that once historians accept the erroneous notion that Katherine married Henry for the purpose of advancing the Reformation, future events are often viewed through that lens.

Shortly thereafter, the newlyweds had to flee London because of an outbreak of plague. This meant that they were almost continuously together for the first six months of their marriage, as

Henry always stayed well away from any possible sites of infection. Katherine got to know the manors and hunting lodges that Henry possessed. Henry rarely hunted on horseback anymore, so he had new standings built in the woods from which he could shoot game. His wife, a keen huntswoman and archer of some prowess, could enjoy the pastime at his side.[10] They spent an extended honeymoon getting to know each other.

One of Katherine's reasons for marrying Henry was the potential advancement of her family, and she was not disappointed. On 23 December 1543 at Hampton Court Palace, Catherine's brother, William, was granted the title of the Earl of Essex and her uncle was elevated to Lord Parr of Horton. Katherine undoubtedly felt vindicated in her decision to marry Henry.

As their relationship developed, Henry came to truly love his new wife, and Katherine was perhaps growing in affection for her new husband, regardless of his condition and appearance. Four months after the marriage, she wrote to her brother expressing joy that Henry had chosen her to be his wife. There must have been a meeting of the minds. Henry was a highly intelligent man, in possession of an exceptionally large library and able to converse on numerous subjects, and Katherine was the most intellectual of all his wives and a great conversationalist. They were both tutored by disciples of Erasmus and shared humanist views. Finally, Henry had someone with whom he could carry on an intelligent conversation, unlike his previous wife, the flighty seventeen-year-old Catherine Howard. They were becoming soulmates, and, as we will see later, Henry trusted her judgments. While there must have been *some* physical element to their relationship, it seems that it was no longer the primary consideration. It was a new experience for Henry to love a woman because of her mind and personality and not merely for her body. And Henry really did love Katherine, referring to her as his 'beloved Kate'. Linda Porter writes, 'The depth of his love for Katherine Parr has often been overlooked. He showered her with jewels and dower manors, showed marked favouritism to her family and was delighted to show her off whenever he could. Her company seems to have been a real source of pleasure to him, perhaps because of her personality but also because they shared many interests.'[11]

What about Katherine? Porter further writes, 'No one has ever seriously considered that she might have loved him, too; her feelings are most often characterised as a ruthless suppression of love for Thomas Seymour, finding its outlet in religious study and writing, coupled with a not all together attractive opportunism in taking the benefits of queenship. But Katherine was a complex woman emotionally, and if she was not in love with Henry when they married, she came to have real affection for him, through getting to know him, and through her attentions to his children.'[12]

The question of whether Katherine actually loved Henry is open to debate. The issue is not only Katherine's complex personality but also the complex nature of this thing we call love. Katherine was 'in love' with the handsome, dashing Thomas Seymour. This was a 'romantic love', or what the Greeks would define as *eros*. Derek Wilson makes the compelling observation that in struggling with the issue of whether to marry Henry, Katherine may have come to see her love for Seymour as being the lust of the flesh.[13] This may be true.

I do not think it is possible, because of his appearance, for any woman to fall romantically in love with King Henry, but Katherine loved him despite his appearance because of everything that he had done for her and for her family. She had received gifts and favours from the king beyond her wildest expectations. Henry was proud of her and spoke kindly to his 'beloved Kate', and for that she loved him. The proper Greek term might not be *eros* but rather *philia*, defining a warm friendship and affection. This love is, as we will see, discernible in some of her correspondence with the king.

Katherine has been inaccurately described as Henry's nurse and the woman who soothed his ills during his old age. In 1853, Agnes Strickland wrote, 'Henry had become so unwieldy from disease that he could not move without assistance, and his wife showed herself the most patient and tender of nurses. Sometimes she would remain on her knees for hours bathing and bandaging his ulcerated leg, for he would not permit anybody to touch it but her.'[14] This is highly unlikely. Linda Porter writes, 'Gender historians have examined her period as queen with renewed vigour, finding an altogether different woman from the cosy image of the nurse who tended Henry's damaged legs.'[15] In marrying Katherine, Henry was most certainly not looking for a nurse. He had a host of attendants and doctors to care for his ailing leg. Defining Katherine as merely Henry's 'nursemaid' is an insult to her talents and intelligence.

Katherine readily embraced all the luxurious 'perks' of her position. She was determined to show the glory of England's queen to the world, which was conveyed in her sumptuous dress. The textiles she chose throughout her reign were an opulent mix of costly fabrics. She loved clothes and soon possessed a wardrobe stuffed with beautiful and expensive items in an array of colours, all in the latest fashion. In her first year as queen, 117 pairs of shoes were delivered.[16] Her jewellery was designed by the renowned jewellers of the day. As well as ensuring that she looked like a queen, Katherine made certain that those around her wore clothes to reflect their positions in her household. Her favourite colour was crimson, and she saw to it that her associates and footmen received new uniforms in her favourite colour.

But her luxury went beyond dress and clothing. Even in personal matters, which had nothing to do with showing to the world the glory of England's queen, her vanity was outrageous. The queen's lavatory was one of the most opulent in the whole of Tudor England. It had a crimson velvet canopy, cushions covered in cloth of gold and a seat of crimson velvet for the royal posterior. A removable commode was covered with red silk and ribbons, attached with gilt nails. In addition, Susan James writes, 'In a time when few people paid much attention to personal hygiene, Catherine indulged in milk baths taken in a leaden bathtub. Orders were sent out for expensive oils, almond, olive and clove, for perfumes and unguents, rose water and breath lozenges.'[17] Her spaniel, Rig, must have looked splendid in his 'collar of crimson velvet embroidered with damask gold' and its rings of silver gilt for attaching his lead.[18] Whatever Katherine wanted, Katherine got.

Katherine had five portraits commissioned and in each painting she was sumptuously dressed.[19] Linda Porter comments, 'There were more portraits of Henry VIII's sixth wife than any other sixteenth-century queen of England, except for Elizabeth.'[20] Of course, Elizabeth reigned for forty-five years, not four. A portrait of the royal family, painted by an unknown artist, included King Henry, the queen and all three of Henry's children. Katherine once sat for the queen's portrait but when the painting was unveiled, much to her dismay, the body was hers but the face was that of Jane Seymour. Susan James suggests, 'One reason, apart from this passion for art, which may have impelled Catherine to order so many portraits of herself as queen was the no doubt profoundly irritating custom of the king to have new portraits of the royal family include not his present wife but his former one.'[21] Perhaps Henry felt there were enough portraits of Queen Katherine on display in the various castles.

There was a pleasure-loving side to Katherine. Her household ate and drank heartily, danced and sang. She kept hounds and hawks for her hunting and various small birds and parrots to amuse her. She loved music and kept a troupe of minstrels to play for her. She had an interest in drama and her own company of players performed before both her and the court. Like the king, Katherine also employed fools to amuse her, with records noting that in 1546 she had a male fool called Thomas Browne and an unnamed female fool.[22] Katherine was an energetic, indulgent, determined woman who set about establishing an image and role for herself as the Queen of England. Everything was going according to plan. It may be true that any physical relationship with the obese, disgusting king was distasteful to her, yet it was well worth the sacrifice.

Alongside Katherine's love for the pleasures of the world there was also her piety and spirituality, as evidenced by the Goldsmith letter, her translation of the psalms of John Fisher from Latin to English and her study of Thomas a' Kempis's *Imitation of Christ* resulting in her first two books. How does one reconcile these two aspects of her life? Katherine, a student of Scripture, must have known that the Bible said, 'Love not the world nor the things of the world. If anyone loves the world, the love for the Father is not in them.'[23] She probably compartmentalised her life, believing that her piety and lifestyle were not related. In so doing, she was merely following the lead of her husband who could appear pious and religious while not batting an eyelid when having someone tortured and executed. Henry, as he saw himself, was God's representative on earth, and Katherine was his beloved wife. Perhaps Katherine's displays of piety were simply part of an attempt to create an image.

Amid this seeming incongruity, there was an event looming on the horizon that would change her attitude, jeopardise her relationship with the king, threaten her life and turn her entire world upside-down. As a result, she wrote in *The Lamentation of a Sinner* that 'Christ was meek and humble in heart; and I most proud and vainglorious. Christ despised the world with all its vanities; I made it my God. Christ came to serve his brethren; and I desired to rule over them. Christ despised worldly honour; and I much delighted to attain it. Christ loved the base and simple things of this world; and I esteemed the most fair and pleasant things. Christ loved poverty; and I wealth.'[24] If there was any doubt as to why she married Henry, her words put them to rest. She loved material wealth, coveted worldly honour, and desired to rule as queen. She was an opportunist who became a reformist.

Henry was not disturbed by his wife's opulent lifestyle but took pleasure in seeing Katherine play her role with style and enthusiasm. She made him proud. Here was an intelligent woman with whom he could readily discuss affairs of state; indeed, Henry recognised Katherine's value and she was permitted to play a prominent role in foreign diplomacy.[25] He trusted her enough to even place her in charge of his entire realm.

In 1542, the Emperor Charles V and Francis I, King of France, had gone to war, and Charles was eager to secure an alliance with Henry. In a departure from his previous marriages, Henry permitted Katherine to play a role in the negotiations with the emperor. Charles himself believed that Katherine was influential and wrote to his ambassador, Eustace Chapuys, in March 1544 that 'to conclude, you are doing the right thing in keeping on good terms with the queen; do not fail, whenever the opportunity offers, to address her.'[26] These remarks were probably prompted by the impression he received of Katherine from his ambassador after the visit of Don Manriquez de Lara, Duke of Najera, to the English court the month before. This was Katherine's first foray into the world of foreign diplomacy, and she handled it with grace and flair befitting the Queen of England. After an audience with the king, the duke was ushered into the queen's chambers where he met and greeted Queen Katherine and Lady Mary. Katherine entertained the duke with an evening of music and dancing. The duke's secretary, Pedro da Gante, was very impressed with the queen: 'The Queen has a lively and pleasing appearance and is praised as a virtuous woman. She was dressed in a robe of cloth of gold, and a petticoat of brocade with sleeves lined with crimson satin, and trimmed with three-piled crimson velvet: her train was more than two yards long. Suspended from her neck were two crosses, and a jewel of very rich diamonds, and in her head-dress were many and beautiful ones. Her girdle was of gold, with very large pendants.'[27]

In July 1544, Henry, in league with Charles V, went to war against France. Having only married Katherine a year earlier, he left her in charge of the realm as queen regent. Thirty years before, when Henry went to war with France, his first wife Catherine of Aragon had also been named queen regent. These two queens were the only consorts in English history to be afforded such trust and honour.

On 7 July 1544, Henry declared, 'First, touching the Queen's highness and my Lord Prince, the King's majesty has resolved that the Queen's highness shall be Regent in his grace's absence.'[28] Assisting the queen in the performance of her duties would be Thomas Cranmer, Thomas Wriothesley, Stephen Gardiner, Edward Seymour, and the secretary William Petre. Katherine requested that her uncle and chamberlain Sir William Parr be added to the group, and the king consented. Her brother William was serving with the king in France at the time. Katherine, who had not yet celebrated the first anniversary of her marriage to Henry, was now the ruler over England. While she had an austere group of advisors, she was not merely a figurehead. According to Elizabeth Norton, 'It is clear however that Catherine retained the final say in matters.'[29] Susan James confirms that Katherine's intention to rule, and not merely to preside, was made quite clear from the outset.[30]

Katherine's first year as queen had given her time to get to know this small group of men appointed to assist her. From all indications, she worked well with them. If Gardiner and Wriothesley, the two 'heresy hunters', had disdain for the possibly Protestant Katherine, there could have been dissension in the ranks. Yet, Linda Porter writes, 'no evidence of dissension survives.'[31] Katherine's advisors submitted themselves to her regency. Undoubtedly, like the king, they trusted her judgment. Despite the fact that, as Linda Porter states, 'there were very few men in the sixteenth century who welcomed government by a female,'[32] Katherine's judgment and demeanour was evidently so sound that her authority was accepted and respected. Out of curiosity, I wonder how Katherine's domineering Protestant father-in-law Sir Thomas Burgh would have responded upon hearing that the little girl who had suffered under his austere patriarchal authority was now ruler of England.

Of course, those who claimed that Katherine had embraced the Reformation prior to marrying Henry found her working together with Cranmer as another hook on which to hang their unfounded conjectures. It is true that Henry had requested Cranmer to daily meet with Katherine. Elizabeth Norton writes, 'Catherine's religious beliefs were already well developed by the time that she became queen but, in Cranmer's company, she was exposed to new ideas and Henry's absence gave her a welcome opportunity to extend her religious beliefs.'[33] Elizabeth Norton ignores the equally significant fact that both Gardiner and Wriothesley were also a part of the group. It is perhaps just as reasonable to suggest that their influence moved Katherine in the opposite direction.

Before leaving for France, Henry in all probability would have made out a will. If so it no longer exists, but Elizabeth Norton suggests that 'in light of Catherine's appointment in 1544 as both regent and governor of Prince Edward, it almost certainly included a provision for Catherine to fulfil the role of regent, a role commonly given to the mother of a child king, although rarely accorded to a stepmother.'[34] After Henry's eventual death, Katherine was sorely disappointed that this position was not granted her.

Katherine ruled well and made some important decisions. She issued five proclamations dealing with a variety of issues ranging from the status of French citizens living in England to the price of armour, the arrest and trial of deserters and the movements of anyone exposed to the plague. It was also her role to maintain peace and stability at home while the king was in France, to aid the war effort with supplies of money and materiel and to communicate the king's successes when they came. She was also responsible for the welfare of young Edward, the heir to the throne – a vital consideration should the king suddenly die. As regent, she possessed considerable powers.

There were obvious concerns in London regarding the aged king going off to war in France. Eustace Chapuys reported that 'they are afraid of his suddenly failing in health, and also that, if they have to take care of his person, all military operations will necessarily be delayed and the march of their army slackened through it; besides which the king's chronic disease and great obesity require particular care lest his life should be endangered.'[35] But evidently this was not the case. Alison Weir writes that the campaign had worked wonders for his health. In fact, Henry was in his element, enjoying himself as much as he had on his earlier campaign in France more than thirty years before. It was a relief to find that, despite encroaching age and infirmity, he could still mount a horse and bully the French.[36] It appears that Katherine did not try to dissuade Henry from his purpose. She already knew her husband well enough to appreciate how important this was to him, and possibly also to her.

Five of the letters Katherine wrote to Henry at this time survive, and in them she filled him in on how things were going on the home front. This letter dated 31 July 1544 is particularly revealing because Katherine compares her love for Henry with her love for God:

> Although the discourse of time and account of days is neither long nor many, of your majesty's absence, yet the want of your presence, so much beloved and desired by me, makes me that I cannot quietly pleasure in anything until I hear from your majesty ... The time, therefore, seems to me very long with a great desire to know how your highness hath done since departing hence ... whereas I know your majesty's absence

is never without great respect of things most convenient and necessary, yet love and affection compels me to desire your presence ... Love makes me in all things to set apart my own commodity and pleasure and to embrace most joyfully his will and pleasure whom I love. God, the knower of secrets, can judge these words not to be only written with ink, but most truly impressed in the heart ... I make like account with your majesty as I do with God for his benefits and gifts heaped upon me daily, acknowledging myself always a great debtor unto Him in that I do omit my duty toward Him, not being able to recompense the least of His benefits: in which state I am certain and sure to die, but yet I hope in His gracious acceptance of my good will. And even such confidence I have in your majesty's gentleness, knowing myself never to have done my duty as were requisite and meet to such a noble prince, at whose hands I have received so much love and goodness that with words I cannot express it. Lest I should be too tedious unto your majesty, I finish this, my scribbled letter, committing you into the governance of the Lord, with long life and prosperous felicity here, and after this to enjoy the kingdom of His elect. By your majesty's most humble, obedient loving wife and servant, Kateryn the Queen, K. P.[37]

Katherine loves both God and Henry for the same reason. She loves God 'for his benefits and gifts heaped upon me daily', and she loves Henry because she 'received so much love and goodness that with words I cannot express it'. In both cases, Katherine's love was obviously not a romantic inclination but a response to benefits received. Her love for Henry was as real as her love for God.

By her own words, it is evident that in July 1544 Katherine had not yet embraced the fundamental truths of the Reformation. She acknowledges that she will never be able to recompense God for His goodness toward her but hopes that God will graciously accept her because of her good will. She is trusting in her own goodness. Katherine's theology is that of the King's Book and the theology of Erasmus, affirming that each person had free will to do the good works that would lead to their justification. Later, Katherine would acknowledge that God had already chosen and accepted her, not because of her good will but because of the merits of Christ, His blood and His righteousness.

Taking an opposite perspective, David Starkey interprets Katherine's words as a dangerous promotion of the doctrine of justification by faith:

> This was daring indeed. Not because of the extravagance of the comparison between Henry and the Almighty, which so grates on the modern sensibility. But rather because of the theology. For Catherine, the theologically literate Henry would have realised immediately, was explaining her relationship with him in terms of the doctrine of Justification by Faith. Man (and Woman too) the doctrine held, was wholly sinful. This meant that Humankind could never fulfil the commandments which God had laid down as necessary for salvation. By God's justice therefore all were condemned. The only hope was in God's charity: 'in his gracious acceptance of [human] good will', as Catherine put it. And this good will was shown, not by actions or 'works', but only by faith. The doctrine of Justification by Faith was the cornerstone of Lutheranism and ordinarily it was anathema to Henry. But when Catherine used it as an analogy to explain her own absolute, submissive love for him, even he found it acceptable.[38]

Even if one takes the leap to define Katherine's expression 'my good will' as meaning 'faith', Starkey is turning faith into a good work which merits the acceptance of God. In her own words, Katherine refutes Starkey's interpretation: 'Yet, we may not impute to the worthiness of faith or good works our justification; but ascribe and give the worthiness of it totally to the merits of Christ's passion; and declare and attribute the knowledge and perception of those merits to faith alone.'[39] One can neither present nor define the doctrine of justification by faith without reference to the blood and righteousness of Jesus Christ, for therein lies our justification.

It is not my intention to be unduly critical of David Starkey, who is perhaps the foremost expert in Tudor history, nor any of Katherine's other biographers. I am merely underlining the point that they erroneously claim that Katherine had embraced the Reformation prior to marrying Henry because they do not understand the fundamental truths of the Reformation – or perhaps they are confusing the reforms touted by Erasmus with the Lutheran Reformation. Following the lead of Erasmus, Katherine at this time in her life had no intention of adjusting the theology espoused by her husband the king. In her letter to Henry, seeking the acceptance of God because of her good will, Katherine is espousing traditional Catholic piety. William P. Haugaard writes, 'Katherine was attached to that form of sixteenth-century Christianity known as "Erasmianism".'[40]

Henry responded on 8 September 1544, informing the queen of the successful progress of the battle and ending his letter, 'No more to you at this time, sweetheart, both for lack of time and great occupation of business, saving we pray you to give, in our name, our hearty blessing to all our children, and recommendations to our cousin Margaret and the rest of the ladies and gentlemen, and to our Council also. Written with the hand of your loving husband. Henry R.'[41] He soon returned home claiming to have gained a great victory – which, as later events revealed, was not really the case. Charles had betrayed Henry, signing a peace treaty with France and leaving Henry and his forces high and dry. It appeared that Charles had never forgiven Henry for the way he had treated his aunt, Catherine of Aragon.

Katherine had established herself as an effective, dutiful and impressive queen. She was held in high esteem, having demonstrated her good sense and the strength and dignity she brought to the role of queen. But what was even more impressive was how she engendered a family life for Henry's children. King Henry was never the ideal father. Because of who their mothers happened to be, Mary and Elizabeth were at times outside of Henry's good graces; but now, with Katherine in the royal household, all this would change. Not only did Katherine affect the present, but by her relationship with Henry's children she also had an impact on the future of England – for better *or for worse*.

7

ONE HAPPY FAMILY

After accepting Henry's proposal, Katherine might have reviewed in her mind the family situation that she was about to take on. Although she had no children of her own, while married to Lord Latimer Katherine had been stepmother to Margaret and John, his children with Dorothy de Vere, who had died in 1503.

Margaret, born in 1525, was a nine-year-old girl at the time her father married Katherine. The pair had a great mother–daughter relationship, and Katherine chose Margaret to be one of her ladies-in-waiting upon her marriage to the king. Margaret died at the age of twenty-one, and in her will stated that she was unable to render Katherine sufficient thanks for the godly education, tender love and bountiful goodness which she had always found in her highness.

John was a different story. Born in 1520, he was a rebellious teenager when Katherine entered his life. Linda Porter writes, 'When first confronted with Latimer's son and heir, she was not quite twenty-two. She might have been forgiven for wondering whether the confidence of this sulking, lying, over-sensitive boy could ever be won.'[1] After the death of his father, John became the fourth Baron Latimer. Katherine continued to show kindness toward him and made his wife Lucy Somerset one of her ladies-in-waiting. After Katherine's death in 1548, John's life took a turn for the worse. He was accused of murder and rape and was sent to prison. Since this violence occurred only after his stepmother's death, Susan James surmises that perhaps Katherine had some control over the wayward John.[2]

While Katherine did have 'stepmother experience', nothing could prepare her for the dysfunctional family of Henry VIII: three offspring from three different mothers, each with a different story to tell. This presented a challenge to which the new queen was quick to turn her talents as a diplomat. Her approach varied with each child and it is the measure of her real affection for them and her understanding of their characters that with each child she had considerable success.[3] The oldest, Mary, went through the trauma of her parents' divorce. The middle child, Elizabeth, was not yet three years old when her mother was executed, and little Edward lost his mother when he was born. For the next five years Katherine Parr was something akin to a mother to Elizabeth and Edward, and a sisterly advisor to Mary. Her role was that of overseer more than anything else, for the children had their own households and followed an itinerant pattern that saw them move from one country house to another.[4]

With the Latimers, there was a stable family setting at Snape Castle. Henry's children, on the other hand, had minimal contact with their father, and the two girls variously fell in and out of favour with him. This was not really a family, but Katherine was determined to make it one. History may not have viewed Henry as an attentive parent, but he cannot be judged by the standards of our time. The royal children were brought up in accordance with accepted practice, where a separate household for the Prince of Wales and smaller establishments for princesses, often living together, were the norm.[5]

At the time of Katherine's marriage to Henry, Mary was twenty-seven years old, so four years Katherine's junior. She had enjoyed a happy childhood and was loved by both her parents. Henry probably spent more time with Mary than with either of his other children. She was very talented, intelligent and musical. By the standards of her day, she had been well educated, and was often used as a diplomatic pawn, engaged at different times to Dauphin Francis, Emperor Charles V and James V of Scotland, but nothing resulted. Unlike Elizabeth and Edward, Mary did enjoy some experience of family life, having the benefit in her childhood years of both a mother and a father.

Mary's world would be turned upside-down when her father began the five-year process of seeking the annulment of his marriage to her mother. She was eleven years old at the time. One cannot imagine what Mary felt seeing the anger and belligerence of her father and the deep sorrow of her mother. Finally, in 1533, Henry and Anne Boleyn were married, and Anne was coronated as the new Queen of England. The birth of Elizabeth in September 1533 meant that Henry was forced to deal with the status of his first daughter. Mary was declared illegitimate, told that she must expect her household to be reduced, and deprived of the title of princess.

Just before Christmas 1533, Mary was packed off to join the household of baby Elizabeth and to serve her half-sister as a maid of honour. Mary's own household shrunk to half a dozen loyal servants. Henry reduced her allowance so that she was forced to mend her own clothing, and demanded the return of her beloved jewels and the plate that had graced her table as a princess. As a result of the stress, Mary's health suffered. Bouts of illness would plague her for the rest of her life. Her encounters with Anne Boleyn, who came to see her daughter on several occasions, never ended well. Anne's attempts at reconciliation were flatly rejected, and she angrily departed. Mary consistently refused to acknowledge Anne as queen, and was forbidden to visit her mother, who died at Kimbolton House in 1536.

After a three-year battle with her father, Mary reluctantly signed the Act of Supremacy during Henry's marriage to Jane Seymour and was restored to the king's favour. She was provided with her own household, and returned to court. In 1541, Margaret Pole, Countess of Salisbury and Mary's beloved governess, was beheaded for allegedly being a part of conspiracy headed by her son Cardinal Reginald Pole. A year later, Henry brought Mary back to court permanently. He needed a woman to serve as hostess for his diplomatic gatherings, and Mary gracefully accomplished this role. No expense was spared in providing apartments for her both at Hampton Court and Whitehall. Mary had two possible suitors at the time, one of whom was the Lutheran Duke Philip of Bavaria, but nothing came to fruition.

Elizabeth, for her part, was declared illegitimate. She was ten when Katherine became queen. While Katherine had become the big sister to Mary, and they developed a very close relationship, she would become a mother to Elizabeth, who had lacked a mother's love and guidance for most of her young life. She was four months short of her third birthday when her mother, Anne Boleyn, was beheaded. Her new stepmother must have been a very welcome presence in her life.

Young Elizabeth was a very interesting girl. She was incredibly intelligent and by the time she met Katherine already spoke three languages. For some reason, probably out of guilt, Henry never felt comfortable in the company of Anne Boleyn's precocious daughter. Now, under Katherine's influence, he softened. Katherine was both intrigued and impressed by Elizabeth and undertook the task of supervising her education. Elizabeth's brilliant talents were brought out and encouraged by her gifted stepmother. If Katherine had a legacy, it was Elizabeth herself.

One of the first acts Katharine performed was to restore the king's daughter Elizabeth to her proper position at court. So, with Henry's approval, Katherine wrote to Elizabeth, inviting her to come to court. Elizabeth promptly responded and expressed her appreciation for Katherine's kindness, which she was sure she did not deserve. She promised that she would conduct herself in such a way that Katherine would never have cause to complain, and that she would be diligent in showing obedience and respect: 'I await with much impatience the orders of the King my father for the accomplishment of the happiness for which I sigh, and I remain with much submission, Your Majesty's very dear Elizabeth.'

While Henry was in France, Mary and Edward were with Katherine at Hampton Court Palace. For some reason, Elizabeth remained in London. She wrote a letter to the queen in Italian. After bemoaning her absence, she writes,

I am bound to serve you but also to revere you with daughterly love, since I understand that that your most illustrious highness has not forgotten me every time that you have written to the king's majesty... However, heretofore I have not dared to write to him, for which at present I must humbly entreat your most excellent highness that in writing to his majesty you will deign to recommend me to him, entreating ever his sweet benediction and likewise entreating Lord God to send him best success in gaining victory over his enemies so that your highness, and I together with you, may rejoice the sooner at his happy return. I entreat nothing else from God but that He may preserve your most illustrious highness, to whose grace, humbly kissing your hands, I offer and commend myself. From St James on the thirty-first of July, Your most obedient daughter and most faithful servant, Elizabeth.[6]

As a result, Elizabeth was summoned back to court, and she witnessed Katherine's conduct of business as queen regent. Katherine, this 'mere woman', easily and gracefully imposed her authority in a masculine world – something that Elizabeth would later be called upon to do. With all three children by her side, Katherine could report to King Henry in France: 'My Lord Prince and the rest of your majesty's children are all, thanks be to God, in very good health.'[7]

At the end of 1544, Elizabeth sent a remarkable New Year's gift to Queen Katherine: an English translation of Marguerite of Navarre's *The Mirror of the Sinful Soul*.[8] In her prefacing letter Elizabeth writes, 'I have ... translated this little book out of French rhyme into English prose, joining the sentences together as well as the capacity of my simple wit and small learning could extend themselves.' Describing the nature of the 'little book', Elizabeth writes how the author 'does perceive how, of herself and of her own strength she could do nothing that good is or prevaileth for her salvation, unless it be through the grace of God ... Trusting also that through his incomprehensible love, grace, and mercy she, being called from sin to repentance, doth faithfully hope to be saved.' After expressing her hope that Katherine might edit and thus improve the work, Elizabeth says, 'But I hope that after to have been in your grace's hands, there shall be nothing in it worthy of reprehension, and that in the meanwhile no other but your highness only shall read it, lest my faults be known to many.'[9]

It is not possible to determine the impact of this little work upon Queen Katherine. Many of the thoughts of self-abasement indicated in both *Prayers or Meditations* and *The Lamentation of a Sinner* might well have first struck Katherine as a result of reading it. As a New Year's gift in 1546, Elizabeth would present another of her translations to Katherine, but this time it would be far more radical than the thoughts of the Roman Catholic Marguerite of Navarre.

Little Prince Edward was six and the heir apparent when Katherine came into the picture. He is generally described as a sad and lonely little boy, seldom moved to laughter and unable to show affection. He had never known the love of a mother, and his father seldom visited him. Katherine quickly befriended him, becoming the only mother that he was ever to know. Edward would later describe her as his 'dearest mother', whom 'I do love and admire with my whole heart'. Alison Weir writes, 'It was left to Katherine Parr to alleviate the little boy's loneliness; it was slow progress, but she eventually won his affection, although it was too late to repair all the damage that had been caused by his early upbringing.'[10]

As he grew a little older, Edward began writing Katherine devoted letters, referring to her as his 'Most honourable and entirely beloved mother'. Of all his letters, only those to Katherine and to his half-sisters show any tenderness. His surviving letters from the tender age of nine or ten, written in English, Latin and French, demonstrate the depth of his education. Probably in late 1545, Edward wrote to Katherine in French:

I thank you very noble and excellent Queen for your letters that you sent me lately; not only for the beauty of your letters but also for the inventiveness of the same letters. For when

I saw your lovely writing and the excellence of your device that greatly surpass my own invention, I did not dare to write to you. But when I thought that your nature is so good that everything proceeding from a good spirit and will would be acceptable, I have written this letter to you from my house of Hampton Court. Edward[11]

In a Latin letter dated 13 May 1546, Edward expressed concern about the behaviour of his sister Mary. The young boy wrote, 'Preserve, therefore I pray you, my dear sister Mary from all the wiles and enchantments of the evil one; and beseech her to attend no longer to foreign dances and merriments that do not become a most Christian princess.'[12] One wonders if Katherine showed this letter to Mary and how she responded to being admonished by her ten-year-old half-brother.

When Katherine commended his education, Edward commended hers in turn. Thanking her for her last letter to him, he comments, 'I see that you have really applied diligence to Roman script, such that my tutor could not be persuaded but that your secretary had written them until he saw your name written equally well. I too was amazed. I also hear that your highness progresses in Latin language and in good literature, wherefore I am not a little affected with joy.'[13]

Edward ensured that he always remained in contact with Katherine. Only twelve days after the previous letter, he wrote again in Latin, 'Perhaps, you will wonder at my writing to you so often, that within so short a time, most noble queen and dearest mother. But for the same reason you can wonder at me thus doing my duty towards you. However, I now do this more willingly, because I have got a suitable messenger, my servant; and therefore, I could not write letters to you, to witness my fondness for you. May you fair very well, most noble Queen.'[14]

Katherine's kindness toward young Edward must have profoundly influenced his life. In August 1546 he wrote, 'I have very great thanks for you, most noble Queen and most illustrious mother, because you treated me so kindly when I was with you at

Westminster. Such benign treatment suffuses the coldness in me so that I love you more, although I cannot love you better.'[15]

Even though the first Christmas in 1543 at Hampton Court Palace was overshadowed by the threat of war with Scotland, it still must have been a joyous occasion for the entire family to be together at court.

In February 1544, Parliament passed the Third Act of Succession. This overrode the Act of 1534, which had vested the succession of the English crown in Henry's children with Anne Boleyn and therefore disinherited Mary, and the Act of 1536, which had handed the succession to Henry's children with Jane Seymour and therefore disinherited Elizabeth as well. This third Act established the new line of succession as follows: Edward; any children he was to have; any son Henry VIII might have with Katherine Parr; that potential son's possible children; children Henry VIII might have from marriages after Queen Katherine, if any; Mary; Mary's children, if any; and finally, Elizabeth followed by any children she might have. Credit for Mary and Elizabeth's restoration to the line of succession is often given to Queen Katherine. According to historian David Starkey, 'There is every reason to believe that Catherine had encouraged Henry in this decision, which, for better and for worse, shaped the future of England for the rest of the sixteenth century and beyond.' The third Act was a landmark in English history. It was the first time that the right of females to succeed to the throne was spelled out in statute law.

Queen Katherine, displaying love and wisdom, succeeded in bringing together the dysfunctional family of King Henry. She became a dear friend to the emotionally wounded Princess Mary and a loving mother to both Elizabeth and Edward. This largely forgotten queen would greatly affect the future of England.

Catherine 'Kat' Ashley was appointed as Elizabeth's governess in 1537, and she remained Elizabeth's friend until her death in 1565. Ashley would become a very controversial figure in later events involving Elizabeth and Thomas Seymour. She taught Elizabeth to speak four languages: French, Flemish, Italian and Spanish. When William Grindal, a student of the noted scholar

Roger Ascham, became her tutor in 1544, Elizabeth could write English, Latin and Italian. Under Grindal, she also progressed in French and Greek. After the death of King Henry, Katherine continued to oversee Elizabeth's education. Grindal died in 1548, and Katherine wanted Francis Goldsmith, who had long been her faithful supporter, to replace him, but Elizabeth had other ideas. Her choice was Roger Ascham. She had lost the young man Ascham had trained, and now she wanted the older scholar himself. A considerable battle of wills ensued, but Elizabeth got her way.[16] By the time her formal education ended in 1550, Elizabeth was one of the best-educated women of her generation.

Edward's two main teachers were Richard Cox and John Cheke. Cox, the Dean of Westminster, allegedly had Protestant leanings even though he did subscribe to the king's Six Articles. Cheke was an English classical scholar and one of the foremost teachers of his age. Later, under Mary's reign, in the face of threats to his life Cheke would recant his views and become a Roman Catholic, which included submission to the papacy. Because of his tutors, it is said that Edward was the first English king to receive a 'Protestant education'. Of course, Katherine Parr with her alleged 'reformist views' is credited with providing that education.

Here again we are confronted with the confusion of terms. What does it mean that Edward received a 'Protestant education?' Were Cheke and Cox Protestant because they were Lutherans or Calvinists, or were they Erasmian 'reformed' Catholics? Was Edward's education a 'reformed Catholic' Erasmian education or a Lutheran education? In 1529, Martin Luther published his *Small Catechism* for the training of children. In it he reviews the Ten Commandments, the Apostles' Creed, the Lord's Prayer, the Sacrament of Holy Baptism, the Office of the Keys and Confession and the Sacrament of the Eucharist. As an aid for instructors, Luther in 1529 also published his *Large Catechism*. It is outside the realm of possibility that Edward was taught his religion using these 'Lutheran Protestant' texts.

The 'Protestantism' that Edward was taught was not that of Luther but of Erasmus. Linda Porter writes regarding John Cheke,

'He was soon to develop a major influence over Edward, whose studies flourished under his direction. The child loved the world that his new tutor opened up for him and responded eagerly to a curriculum that in 1544 included memorising passages from Erasmus and the Bible and at the beginning of 1545 moved on to Latin composition.'[17] Erasmus rejected the traditional dogmatism of scholasticism, calling for a return to the original documents of Scripture. He believed that the goal of Christian piety was to draw close to God through a disciplined study of the Bible and a sincere devotion to Christ and his teachings. The Church, he believed, would be reformed internally and society remade by people of goodwill who followed the teachings of Christ and his apostles. The focus of Erasmus' educational program was learned piety or the 'philosophy of Christ'. He was critical of the ignorance, superstition, corruption and dead formalism present in many of the institutions of the Church. He wanted a return to simple Christianity which entailed knowing the Bible, loving Jesus, and living a good life. Theologically, Erasmus remained a Roman Catholic and later developed an utter disdain for the theology and tone of Martin Luther. I do not believe there is any doubt that Erasmian philosophy defined Edward's 'Protestant education'. It is inconceivable that Cheke and Cox would teach Edward the truth of justification by faith, the defining doctrine of the Lutheran Reformation, which King Henry had flatly rejected.

As Francis Goldsmith has remarked, Katherine turned every day into a Sunday. She held daily Bible studies, devotional readings and prayers for her ladies and any other visitors who might attend. Regarding the piety of Katherine and her ladies, Anthony Martienssen writes, 'The women sought to establish the New Faith as the principal faith of the kingdom. It needs to be repeated, perhaps, that this faith was not the Lutheran Protestant doctrine or the Calvinist creed of predetermination, but the humanist and Erasmian doctrine of simplicity, charity and gentleness.'[18] While this assessment is accurate for the early stages of Katherine's queenship, it did not take long for Martin Luther to enter the discussion.

8

FROM OPPORTUNIST TO REFORMER

Katherine married Henry VIII in order to reap the benefits of being the Queen of England. She was an opportunist, and this was an incredible opportunity to secure a life of luxury and to see to the advancement of her family. Indeed, Katherine attests to this herself – not merely in her letters to her brother or her evidently opulent lifestyle, but even in her own confession in *The Lamentation of a Sinner*.

Katherine was a 'reformist', following the lead of the humanist scholar Desiderius Erasmus. She brought the pious study of Scripture into her daily gatherings and sought to follow Christ, demonstrating a kind and loving demeanour, as outlined by Erasmus. Her theology, as reflected in her first two books – *Psalms or Prayers* and *Prayers or Meditations* – was traditionally Catholic in substance and consistent with the religious views of her husband, the king. Along with Erasmus, she did not challenge the teaching of Catholicism – teachings Henry continued to embrace – but emphasised a deepened piety and knowledge of Scripture. But Katherine's religious views were about to drastically change.

In her *Lamentation of a Sinner*, Katherine affirms that her eyes were opened to the truth of the Gospel, particularly justification by faith. This was a scandalous work in which she jettisoned Erasmus in favour of Luther and wrote in opposition to the firm position of her husband, the king. This was the first published 'conversion narrative' in England. Katherine went from being an opportunist to a reformer. John Foxe's claim in his *Acts and Monuments* that Katherine was seen by the reformers to be the perfect instrument whereby they could influence the king had been realised.[1]

Katherine provides no details regarding the circumstances that caused such a radical departure from Erasmus and set herself in opposition to the king and his heresy hunters. Derek Wilson's assessment makes sense: 'Though Catherine nowhere in her writings revealed the precise circumstances of her conversion, it is difficult to believe that it was not a dramatic, comparatively sudden occurrence, a moment of enlightenment, such as that which had befallen the monk, Martin Luther, as a result of studying the opening of St Paul's argument in his Letter to the Romans.'[2]

Luther's conversion narrative, identified as his Tower Experience, was the result of an intense struggle (*anfechtung*) over the issue of righteousness. Luther identified this experience as having greater significance for the Reformation than the posting of the 95 Theses. Katherine's experience was very similar. Susan James writes, 'The public voice and the private conscience have finally become one despite a cultural bias against the appropriateness of the female voice in published works. Mild-mannered Erasmeanism (*sic*) has given way to a proselytising Lutheranism central to the queen's deepest convictions.'[3]

Even though *The Lamentation of a Sinner* is a proselytising work, Katherine's tone is very different to Luther's. Her approach mirrors the gentler admonitions of Erasmus rather that the bombastic retorts of the German reformer, which likely has more to do with culture than with comparative zeal. Susan James acknowledges that an undercoat of humanism could still be glimpsed beneath the high gloss of Lutheran evangelicalism.[4]

When did Katherine have this radical conversion experience, and under what circumstances? Her *Prayers or Meditations*, presenting the work of the Roman Catholic Thomas a' Kempis, was written in the beginning of 1545 and appeared in print on 8 June 1545. We can assume that her eyes were opened to the truth of justification by faith sometime thereafter. In attempting to answer this question, I am alone. None of her biographers pursue the issue, and they largely ignore the obvious fact that she had a conversion experience. In that pursuit, it is possible to string together several events and perhaps arrive at an approximate answer. My best guess is January or February 1546.

Probably sometime in early 1545, Katherine undertook her most energetic project: translating Erasmus' *Paraphrases of the New Testament* into English. The *Paraphrases* were rewritings of the Gospels in Latin composed between 1517 and 1523 by the humanist scholar Desiderius Erasmus. Katherine focused her attention upon the Gospels and the Book of Acts. Her purpose was to 'guide English readers into less contentious paths'. The general editor of the work was Nicholas Udall, a controversial figure who had taught Latin at Eton College. The work was perhaps a general response to Henry's 1543 Act for the Advancement of True Religion, which restricted the reading of the Bible to clerics, noblemen, the gentry and richer merchants. Women of the gentry and nobility were only allowed to read the Bible in private.

Katherine herself probably translated Matthew and Acts. Luke was translated by Udall, and Mark by Thomas Caius of Oxford. Katherine had convinced Princess Mary to work on the Gospel of John, and while she did most of the work, chronic illness prevented her from finishing it. It was eventually completed by Mary's chaplain, Francis Mallet. Katherine encouraged Mary to affix her name to the work since she had done most of it, but left it to her discretion. The work was completed during Edward's reign in 1548 and dedicated to Queen Katherine. Edward ordered that a copy of the work should be placed in every church. Despite the animosity of religious conservatives, the first volume of the *Paraphrases* had a circulation of some 20,000 volumes between 1548 and 1551.[5]

Between Henry VIII's death in January 1547 and the end of that year, the conservative Stephen Gardiner wrote at least twenty-five indignant letters, mostly addressed to Edward Seymour, the protector of King Edward VI, arguing that the reforms initiated by Seymour were both theologically wrong and unconstitutional. As a result, he was incarcerated for a time in Fleet Prison. One of his letters was a scathing denunciation of the translation of the *Paraphrases*, especially Katherine's translation of Matthew. He referred to her abilities in dealing with the Latin as the work of a 'literate concubine'.[6]

Perhaps Katherine's completion of her work on the *Paraphrases* was her first step on the road to her conversion. She was confronted with the life of Christ: his humility, his kindness, his rejection of the things of the world. She indicates in *The Lamentation of a Sinner* that her awareness of sin came about as she compared her life with that of Christ. While conversion experiences are usually moments of epiphany, there are often many events and encounters leading to that pivotal moment.

Sometime during the year of 1545, Margaret Neville, the daughter of Lord Latimer and beloved stepdaughter of Queen Katherine, died at the age of twenty-one. We do not know the exact date of her death, but she had made out her will at the end of March. She wrote, 'That He (God) through the mercies of my saviour and only mediator Jesus Christ will now perform his promise unto me that death may have no power over me but that through his grace I may boldly say, "O death where is thy victory? O hell where is thy sting?", being above all other things most certain that trust in him shall not be confounded.' She bequeathed all her earthly belongings to my 'dear sovereign mistress, the lady Katheryne Parr, Queen of England, France and Ireland'.[7] Katherine must have been deeply saddened by her stepdaughter's death and moved by her confession of a sure and certain faith. We can assume that Thomas Cranmer, the Archbishop of Canterbury, who was an outspoken proponent of justification by faith yet protected by King Henry, ministered to Katherine during her time of grief. It might have been at this time that Katherine came to consider the notion of not merely attempting to imitate Christ but rather to receive Him as her righteousness.

In August 1545, Henry's good friend Charles Brandon, 1st Duke of Suffolk, died. Probably as a result, his wife, Catherine Brandon, returned to court and struck up a very close friendship with Queen Katherine. At one time it was rumoured at court that the king was considering her for his seventh wife, but this has no basis in fact. She was an outspoken supporter of the Lutheran Reformation, and her pet spaniel was named Gardiner. The duchess is credited with influencing Katherine's religious views, yet the nature of the influence is not defined. Perhaps she encouraged Katherine to study Scripture or to recognise that her forgiveness is based on the work of Christ alone. It may very well be true that, as a result of reading *The Lamentation of a Sinner*, Catherine Brandon herself discovered the truth of justification by faith and for that reason strongly encouraged Katherine to publish the work, as recorded on the title page. She also partially funded the publication.

There is one largely unnoticed event involving the precocious Princess Elizabeth that could very well have been a major contributing factor. As a New Year's gift in 1546, Elizabeth presented Katherine with an English translation of the first chapter of John Calvin's seminal work *The Institutes of the Christian Religion*, which had been published in Geneva in 1541. In the eyes of the conservatives, Calvin was considered more radical than Luther. You must admire young Elizabeth's originality and boldness.[8] Wriothesley and Gardiner, the two heresy hunters, must have been shocked that the daughter of the king not only possessed a copy of this radical work but translated the first chapter and presented it to the queen. In her prefatory letter, Elizabeth writes, 'But seeing the source from which this book came forth, the majesty of the matter surpasses all human eloquence, being privileged and having such force within it that a single sentence has power to ravish, inspire and give knowledge to the most stupid being alive in what way God wishes to be known seen and heard.'[9]

Obviously, out of love and respect for the work of young Elizabeth, Queen Katherine read this document. There is no evidence to suggest that reading this first chapter had any effect upon Katherine's beliefs except for the content of the chapter itself. If she had any hope of attaining a righteousness and holiness pleasing to God by her own efforts, as she described in her *Prayers or Meditations*, those hopes would be dashed by the words of this Swiss reformer. In that first chapter, Calvin wrote, 'But should we once begin to raise our thoughts to God, and reflect what kind of Being he is, and how absolute the perfection of that righteousness and wisdom and virtue to which, as a standard we are to be conformed, what formerly delighted us by its false show of righteousness, will become polluted with the greatest iniquity.'[10] Elizabeth was probably right in saying that a single sentence 'has power to ravish, inspire and give knowledge'.

In her previous writings, Katherine had never considered that the standard for righteousness to which she was to conform was the absolute holiness of God himself, which was of course impossible to reach. In her previous two works she held out the hope that by the grace of God she might become holy and by her own efforts ascend to him. Calvin's words must have been a lightning bolt. In her *Lamentation of a Sinner* she later confessed, 'And I, most presumptuously thinking nothing of Christ crucified, went about to establish my own righteousness.'[11] Perhaps at this point her eyes were opened to see that her only hope was to be found in the righteousness of *another*, the very righteousness of Christ to be apprehended by faith alone.

Putting these events together, I believe Katherine's eyes were opened to the truth of justification by faith sometime in early 1546. This newfound faith, whereby she had apprehended the promises of God, changed everything for Katherine. Her 'religious' views were no longer aligned with the popular piety of Erasmus, nor with the views of her husband the king. Henry clearly rejected Luther's understanding of justification by faith and held out the belief that good works were necessary for salvation. Katherine, with Luther, believed that good works were the result of being justified but contributed nothing to her salvation, which was found in Christ alone. Katherine had made a life-changing discovery and as a new convert her emotions were aroused. She would have been concerned about the spiritual well-being of her husband, who was still trusting in his good works for salvation. Realising that Henry did not have long to live, Katherine must have openly shared and discussed her newfound discovery with Henry.

While there is no evidence revealing the content of the discussions and debates between Henry and Katherine, the primary issue between them would have been the relationship between faith and works, especially the nature of faith, a subject that was covered comprehensively in *The Lamentation*. It is a shame that their theological discussions were not recorded. Whatever the content of their conversations on faith, Katherine seeming attempt to teach the king would not bode well.

Meanwhile, King Henry was growing tired of all the religious conflicts taking place in his realm. Henry started the reform in England by overthrowing papal authority and having himself declared the Supreme Head of the Church of England. By his various Acts and declarations, he had attempted to unify the doctrine of his new Church, but to no avail. Conflicts and controversies persisted, and Henry was growing frustrated. Often, he found himself with a burning taper in one hand and an axe in the other. With an even hand, Henry sent Catholics to the block for the repudiation of the royal supremacy and Protestants to the stake for the rejection of transubstantiation.

On Christmas Eve 1545, the rapidly ageing king made his final speech to Parliament. Unbeknownst to him, he was about to enter the final year of his life. This speech was one of Henry's finest presentations to his subjects. After commending Parliament for supporting his war effort in France, he continued, 'Although I with you, and you with me, be in this perfect love and concord, this friendly amity cannot continue, except you ... study and take pains to amend one thing, which is surely amiss, and far out of order ... which is that charity and concord is not among you, but discord and dissension beareth rule, in every place.' He placed the blame squarely on the shoulders of the preachers: 'Behold, what love and charity is amongst you, when the one calleth the other heretic and anabaptist, and he calleth him again, papist, hypocrite, and pharisee? Be these tokens of charity amongst you? Are these the signs of fraternal love between you?'

The king did not mince words: 'Amend these crimes, I exhort you, and set forth God's word, both by true preaching and example-giving, or else I, whom God hath appointed his vicar, and high minister here, will see these divisions extinct and these enormities corrected.' There was one issue that the king found particularly troublesome: 'And though you be permitted to read Holy Scripture, and to have the word of God in your mother tongue, you must understand ... only to inform your own conscience, and to instruct your children and family, and not to dispute, and make scripture a railing and a taunting stock against priests and preachers, as many light persons do. I am very sorry to know and hear how irreverently that most precious jewel, the word of God, is disputed, rhymed, sung and jangled in every alehouse and tavern.'[12] Despite his plea, however, disputes would continue – even within his own household.

On 24 November 1545, Parliament granted Henry VIII sovereign power over colleges, chantries[13] and hospitals, 'to alter and transpose and order them to the glory of God, and the profit of the commonwealth'.[14] The issue of shutting down the chantries, which existed to pray for the souls in purgatory, was most contentious but did eventually pass, because Henry needed the money. The seeming rejection of purgatory was theologically significant. Purgatory provided the final stage for the sinner to become righteous and enter heaven. It is no wonder that the conservative element in Parliament fought to retain the chantries. Rejecting purgatory implied a move toward the evangelical position that the shed blood of Christ was enough to forgive sins and provide righteousness.

The Act also threatened the endowments of the colleges of Oxford and Cambridge with confiscation as well. Cambridge's leaders knew where to turn and promptly appealed to Katherine in a flamboyant Latin letter written by Sir Thomas Smith. Katherine responded in February 1546, first admonishing Smith for 'showing off' by writing in Latin when he could well have written 'in our vulgar tongue', and then criticising the university for promoting profane learning like the Greeks at Athens years before. She encouraged them to focus upon 'Christ's reverent and most sacred doctrine, that it may not be laid against you as evidence at the tribunal seat of God, how ye were ashamed of Christ's doctrine. For this Latin lesson I am taught to say of St Paul "*Non me pudet evangelii* (I am not ashamed of the Gospel)".'[15] Katherine was becoming bold in her witness to Christ and his Gospel. Such a bold confession of the Gospel was sorely lacking in her own *Prayers or Meditations*. She was not the same person.

Opposition to her newfound faith was brewing. Probably sometime in 1544 Katherine and her ladies gathered for Bible study, discussion and prayer in her privy chamber. Katherine's lawyer, Francis Goldsmith, wrote her a letter in that same year describing the daily activities: 'Your most rare goodness has made days that were seldom such, truly Sundays now.'[16] This group included her sister, Anne Herbert, her cousin Lady Maud Lane, Lady Elizabeth Tyrwhitt and eventually Catherine Brandon. There is no doubt that Katherine was motivated to initiate this gathering due to her commitment to Erasmian reform, but discussions of Luther must have taken centre stage after her conversion. It also appeared that such a gathering was contrary to Henry's 1543 Act for the Advancement of True Religion, which decreed that women of nobility could only read the Bible in private. In other words, these ladies were charting a dangerous course.

Thomas Wriothesley and Bishop Stephen Gardiner had undoubtedly heard about what was going on in the queen's privy chamber, and they set out to charge the queen and her ladies with heresy. Their first move was to gain incriminating evidence from the confession of a certain Anne Askew. What made Anne Askew's professed heretical views of such importance to Bishop Gardiner was her rumoured close connection with Katherine's ladies at court. According to Anne's nephew, writing after her death, she was captured when a letter she was trying to send was intercepted. The letter was part of an organised letter-writing campaign on Anne's part to communicate with Queen Katharine herself. In prison, Anne had received money both from Katherine's sister Anne and from Lady Denny – both members of the queen's inner circle – as well as visits from Nicholas Throckmorton, a cousin of the queen.[17]

Anne Askew was a devout Protestant from Lincolnshire. Her husband, Thomas Kyme, was a committed Roman Catholic and had her thrown out of the house. Anne moved to London, where she met the radical Anabaptist Joan Bocher. Together they smuggled Tyndale's New Testament into England, and into the royal court under their skirts. While in London, Askew became a 'gospeller' or preacher. In March 1545, Kyme had Askew arrested and brought back to Lincolnshire, where he demanded that she remain, but she escaped and returned to London to continue preaching. She flatly rejected the doctrine of transubstantiation and openly ridiculed it.

One of the controverted issues in the research into the life of Katherine Parr is her relationship, if any, with Anne Askew. It is a fact that they grew up near each other and could have met during this time. Without the use of any references, Anthony Martienssen in his 1973 biography of Katherine Parr creates a scenario based on conjecture whereby Anne, identified as a former friend of Katherine's, visits with her and her ladies, giving a 'ministry report'.[18] Derek Wilson, in his book *The Queen and the Heretic*, a comparative study of Anne Askew and Katherine Parr, writes, 'Anne seems to have become something of a celebrity in the world of London's religious radicals and her views were more extreme than Catherine's. It would have been unwise to be seen as openly offering patronage. This does not mean that the two ladies in our story never met; merely that we have no evidence for such meeting.'[19] It is highly unlikely that Katherine would relate to or even approve of Anne Askew's 'gospelling.' In her *Lamentation of a Sinner*, Katherine speaks of certain 'gospellers' being contentious disputers of the Word of God. She writes, 'They are an offense and slander to the Word of God.'[20] Perhaps she had Anne Askew in mind.

Askew was associated with the more radical Anabaptist movement. Her primary issue was with the doctrine of transubstantiation. She believed the bread and wine in the Eucharist merely symbolised the body and blood of Christ rather than being changed into the same by the action of the priest. While Katherine does not deal with this issue directly in her *Lamentation of a Sinner*, her Lutheran position would embrace the Real Presence. Luther rejected transubstantiation but taught that the bread remains bread and the wine remains wine, but 'in, with, and under' the bread and wine is the real presence of the body and blood of Christ received in the eating and drinking. In addition, Katherine respected the sanctity of marriage and believed that the wife should submit to her husband. Obviously, by her actions, Anne did not accept this position.

In May 1546, Anne Askew was arrested and tortured on the rack in the Tower of London, becoming the only woman ever recorded to have suffered that fate. She was ordered to name likeminded women, especially those within the queen's household, but she would not. When the lieutenant of the Tower, Sir Anthony Knyvett, refused to continue the torture, Lord Chancellor Thomas Wriothesley himself and Sir Richard Rich continue to turn the rack to such a degree that both her arms and legs became disjointed, but Askew, despite the horrible torture, refused to comply and to renounce her beliefs. On 16 July 1546, Anne was carried on a chair to the place of execution and burned at the stake. While there was no evidence to suggest that Katherine Parr had anything to do with Anne Askew, she certainly did not condone her torture and execution.

On 8 July, five days before the torture of Askew, a proclamation for the discovery of heretical books was made, requiring that 'from henceforth no man, woman, or other person, of what estate, condition, or degree he or they may be, shall, after the last day of August next ensuing, receive, have, take, or keep in his or their possession the text of the New Testament of Tyndale's or Coverdale's'.[21] Katherine and her ladies did have in their possession a copy of Tyndale's New Testament.

Having failed to implicate the queen by torturing Anne Askew, Stephen Gardiner persisted, and his quest took a fortuitous turn. One day, in the king's chambers, he overheard a conversation between Henry and Katherine in which Katherine was arguing a specific point of religion. After Henry bid his wife goodnight and Katherine left, the king complained to Gardiner. 'A good hearing it is,' he fumed, 'when women become such clerks, and much to my comfort to come in mine old age to be taught by my wife!'[22] Gardiner replied, 'His Majesty should easily perceive how perilous a matter it is to cherish a serpent within his own bosom.' Gardiner suggested that the queen and her ladies should be arrested and examined. Henry agreed and signed an arrest warrant, but it appears that, as was the case in the attempt to arrest Thomas Cranmer, the king was being duplicitous. The king leaked his intention to his physician, Dr Wendy, probably with the hope that Katherine would be informed of the threat against her. Wendy shared the king's intentions with one of Katherine's attendants, who informed the queen. Upon hearing the news, Katherine became hysterical. Henry, hearing the screams of his wife, was wheeled into her room. Katherine lamented that she had displeased the king and that he 'had utterly forsaken her'. Henry reassured his wife of his favour, but Katherine was taking no chances.

The next day she instructed her ladies to get rid of all the incriminating evidence in her privy chamber, especially all the banned books, including Tyndale's New Testament. By the summer of 1546, following Katherine's discovery of justification by faith, the discussion in Katherine's privy chamber took an abrupt turn because Katherine herself had changed her view. No longer were the writings of Erasmus the basis for discussion. He had been replaced by Luther. If young Elizabeth had a copy of Calvin's *Institutes*, Katherine was probably in possession of some of Luther's writings, possibly even a copy of *The Augsburg Confession* and perhaps even Melanchthon's *Apology* of 1537. A lot of Katherine's theological definitions in *The Lamentation* seem to be taken directly from the Lutheran confessional writings. We do know she had a copy of the first chapter of Calvin's *Institutes of the Christian Religion*. So, in that privy chamber, there had to be a veritable wealth of condemning evidence. There might even have been an early draft of *The Lamentation* hidden away.

When Gardiner had her apartment searched, he found nothing incriminating.

That evening, Katherine approached the king in order to plead her case. 'I am but a woman,' she said, 'With all the imperfections natural to the weakness of my sex, therefore in all matters of doubt and difficulty I must refer myself to his majesty's better judgment; for God hath appointed you supreme head of us all, and of you, next unto God, will I ever learn.' But Henry would not hear it. 'Not so, by St Mary!' he cried. 'You are become a doctor, Kate, to instruct us, as often times we have seen, and not to be instructed or directed by us.' Katherine claimed that the king had misread her intentions. 'Indeed,' she replied, 'if your majesty has so conceived my meaning has been mistaken, for I have always held it preposterous for a woman to instruct her lord; and if I have ever presumed to differ with your highness on religion it was partly to gain information for my own comfort regarding certain nice points on which I stood in doubt, and sometimes because I perceived that in talking you were better able to pass away the pain and weariness of your present infirmity, which encouraged me to this boldness, in the hope of profiting by your majesty's learned discourse.' 'Is it even so, sweetheart?' Henry replied. 'And tended your arguments to no worse end? Then perfect friends we are now again, as ever at any time before.' And they kissed and made up.

Nobody told Lord Chancellor Wriothesley that the king had undergone a change of heart, so when he turned up the next morning with an armed guard of forty men to arrest the queen he found her in the gardens down by the river, joyful in her husband's company. As he approached, he was sent away with Henry's reprimands ringing in his ears. 'Knave, arrant knave', the king cried, 'beast and fool'. Katherine attempted to dissuade the king's anger. 'With as sweet words as she could utter, she endeavoured to qualify the king's displeasure, with request unto his majesty in behalf of the lord chancellor, with whom he seemed to be offended.' Touched by her seeming concern for a man who was her enemy, Henry responded, 'Ah! poor soul, thou little knowest how evil he

Catherine of Aragon
(1485–1536) Daughter of
King Ferdinand and Queen
Isabella of Spain. Originally
married to Arthur, eldest son
of Henry VII and Elizabeth of
York. Upon death of Arthur,
married the second son
Henry who became Henry
VIII. Was Queen of England
1509–1533.
(Metropolitan Museum
of Art)

Henry VIII (1491–
1547) Second son
of Henry VII and
Elizabeth of York.
Ruled
England 1509-
1547.
(Rijksmuseum)

Erasmus of Rotterdam (1466–1536) Known as 'Prince of the Humanists'. Called the
Church away from superstition and dead formalism to the simple 'philosophy of Jesus'.
Translated from the early manuscripts the New Testament into Greek, calling into ques-
tion the accuracy of St Jerome's revered Latin Vulgate. (Rijksmuseum)

Martin Luther (1483–1546) Instigated the Protestant Reformation by nailing his
95 Theses to the church door at Wittenberg, Germany, on 31 October 1517.
(Metropolitan Museum of Art)

Phil: Melanchton.

Philipp Melanchthon (1497–1560) Co-worker of Martin Luther. Wrote the *Apology to the Augsburg Confession.* Dedicated the second edition of his seminal work *Loci Communes* to Henry VIII for which he received a sizable stipend.

Tho: Moor L'Chancelour.

Thomas More (1478–1535) Lord Chancellor to King Henry VIII 1529–1532. Beheaded for refusal to accept the Act of Supremacy, declaring King Henry as head of the Church of England. Pope Pius XI canonized More in 1935 as a martyr. In 2000, Pope John Paul II declared him the patron saint 'of Statesmen and Politicians.'

John Fisher (1469–1535) Bishop of Rochester. Beheaded for refusal to accept King Henry VIII as head of the Church of England. Canonized by Pope Pius XI in 1935. Katherine Parr's first book, *Psalms and Prayers*, published anonymously in 1544, included the English translation of the Psalms of John Fisher.

Jane Seymour (1508–1537) third and favourite wife of King Henry. Queen of England from 1536 to 1537. Died after giving birth to her son Edward who became King Edward VI. The only one of Henry's wives to receive a queen's funeral. Henry was buried beside her in St George's Chapel at Windsor Castle.

A young Katherine Parr.

The ruins of Snape Castle, home of Lord Latimer, where Katherine was held captive during the Pilgrimage of Grace in 1536.

Hampton Court Palace. Sixteenth-century section built by Cardinal Thomas Wolsey, Lord Chancellor, 1515–1529, but given to Henry after Wolsey's fall from grace. Edward VI was born at Hampton Court and Henry and Katherine were married there in 1543.

Sir William Parr (1513–1571) 1st Marquess of Northampton, 1st Earl of Essex. Brother of Katherine and 'beloved uncle' to Edward VI. Listed on title page of *The Lamentation of a Sinner* as one who encouraged its publication.

Charles Brandon (1484–1545) 1st Duke of Suffolk and close friend to King Henry. Incurred the wrath of the king by marrying his sister Mary, without Henry's permission, after the death of her husband Louis XII of France, a potentially treasonous act. After the death of Mary, Brandon married his fourteen-year-old ward Catherine Willoughby who would become a close friend to Katherine Parr. She is noted on the cover of *The Lamentation of a Sinner* as one who encouraged its publication. (Metropolitan Museum of Art)

King Edward VI (1537–1553)
Son of Henry VIII and Jane Seymour.
After the death of Henry in 1547,
Edward was crowned king at the age
of nine. Upon his death in 1553, a new
line of succession was established naming Lady Jane Grey, great-granddaugh-
ter of Henry VII through his daughter
Mary Tudor. (Rijksmuseum)

A young Princess Mary (1516–1558)
Daughter of King Henry and Catherine
of Aragon. Became Katherine's close
friend. Upon the death of Edward VI
and after Lady Jane Grey, who had
been queen for nine days, was deposed
by Parliament, Mary, who had gained
popular support, became Queen Regent
and reigned 1553–1558. She reversed
the Protestant Reformation returning Roman Catholicism. She had 280
Protestant dissenters burned at the stake
including Thomas Cranmer. As such,
she is remembered as 'bloody Mary'.
(Rijksmuseum)

Elizabeth as queen (1533–1603) Daughter
of Henry VIII and Anne Boleyn. After the
death of Mary, Elizabeth reigned as queen
1558–1693 ushering in the Elizabethan
Age in English history. She reversed the
policies of Mary. The Thirty-Nine Articles
incorporated into the Book of Common
Prayer (1571) define the theological
Protestant stance of the Anglican Church
to this day. Elizabeth, 'the virgin Queen',
died in 1603 without an heir bringing to
an end the Tudor Dynasty. (Rijksmuseum)

Katherine Parr's *Prayers or Meditations* (1545), the first book published in England by a woman under her own name. Relies heavily upon Thomas a' Kempis' *Imitation of Christ*.

Inside pages of Katherine's *Prayers or Meditations*.

A letter from Katherine to Thomas Seymour (*c.* February 1547) in which Katherine complains that Thomas' brother Edward, the Lord Protector of King Edward, had failed to keep his promise to visit her. In her 'famous' postscript, Katherine explains that by marrying Henry she was following the will of God.

One of the rooms in Katherine Parr's Sudeley Castle as she would have seen it.

The reading room at Sudeley Castle.

The ruined tithe barn at Sudeley Castle.

Above: Sudeley Castle's splendid exterior.

Left: A surviving lock of Katherine Parr's hair, on display at Sudeley Castle.

St Mary's Chapel at Sudeley Castle, where Katherine is entombed.

Katherine's tomb within St Mary's Chapel.

Above: The beautiful scenery at Sudeley Castle. Along with the gardens and castle, the chapel can be seen, where Katherine rests to this day amid the Cotswold Hills.

Left: Katherine's coat of arms depicted in stained glass at Wroxton Abbey in Oxfordshire.

deserveth this grace at thy hands. Of my word, sweetheart! he hath been towards thee an arrant knave and so let him go.' Katherine and her ladies were no longer suspects, and Bishop Gardiner, seen as a troublemaker by the king, was banished from court. With Gardiner out of the way, Wriothesley became humbler and more compliant. The balance of power changed, and Henry appeared to be moving in a different direction.

In August 1546, the French admiral Claude d'Annebaut arrived at Hampton Court to sign a treaty in which Henry agreed to return Boulogne to the French in eight years upon the payment of an indemnity of 2 million crowns. Following the banquet on the first night, Henry, d'Annebaut and Thomas Cranmer retired to one of the gardens. While leaning on the shoulders of Cranmer and d'Annebaut, the king amazed his archbishop by mentioning a shared intention between himself and the King of France to mutually abolish the sacrifice of the Mass from religious services and institute a simple communion service in its place.[23]

While debate has raged over the king's intention in this conversation, the notion of eliminating the sacrifice of the Mass, in which the broken body and shed blood in the Eucharist is a re-sacrifice of Christ for the sins of the world, implies a belief that the one sacrifice of Christ on the cross was sufficient. This statement, together with the elimination of the chantries, represents a significant shift in the king's apparent move in an evangelical direction.

There is no evidence to suggest that the discussions of religion between Henry and his wife ceased. As the year wore on and it became more and more evident that Henry was soon to die, perhaps he welcomed Katherine's instructions about the mercy and goodness of God found in Christ. It appears that Katherine had every intention of sharing her *Lamentation of a Sinner* with Henry, and there is no evidence to suggest that she didn't. If Henry had remained a staunch enemy of justification by faith, there is no way this would have happened. Regarding her husband she wrote:

But thank the Lord, who has now sent us such a godly and learned King, in these latter days, to reign over us: that, with the virtue and force of God's Word, he has taken away the veils and mists of errors, and brought us to the knowledge of the truth by the light of God's Word, which was so long hidden and kept suppressed, that the people were nearly famished and hungered for lack of spiritual food. Such was the charity of the spiritual clergy, and shepherds. But our Moses, and most godly, wise governor and King, has delivered us out of the captivity and bondage of Pharaoh. By Moses, I mean King Henry the eighth, my most sovereign, favourable lord and husband: who, through the excellent grace of God, is suitable to be an expressed picture of Moses' conquest over Pharaoh. And by Pharaoh, I mean the Bishop of Rome, who has been and is a greater persecutor of all true Christians than ever was Pharaoh of the children of Israel.[24]

As autumn turned to winter in 1546, Katherine did not leave Henry's side until early December, and then the parting was his choice, not hers. The king's awareness of his own mortality had grown. Katherine must have been aware of his failing health. In December, he bid farewell to his wife and children and closeted himself with a small circle of advisors at Whitehall. The queen and the court moved to the castle at Greenwich. Whether Katherine was permitted to see Henry again after they parted in the beginning of December is unclear. It has been assumed that she did not. Since Henry was not a man who liked emotional scenes, a deathbed parting between husband and wife seems extremely unlikely.

On Thursday, 27 January 1547, Sir Anthony Denny, a confidant of Henry, told the king that 'in man's judgement, you are not like to live.' According to Linda Porter, 'Faced with this reality, Henry's thoughts turned to his immortal soul. He believed, he said, "the mercy of Christ is able to pardon me all my sins, yes, though they were greater than they be." But he did not ask for his wife and chose not to see a priest and receive last rites, saying that if it were to be any, it should be Dr Cranmer. He would, however, sleep for a while before he made up his mind.'[25] By the time Cranmer arrived at Henry's bedside, the king was no longer able to speak.

The archbishop exhorted Henry to show some sign that he placed his faith in Christ. In response, Henry squeezed Cranmer's hand. In this simple gesture, after all the conflicts arising from his establishment of the Church of England and the tragedies arising out of his six marriages, the king indicated a simple trust in Christ.

Shortly after, in the late hours of 28 January 1547, King Henry VIII of England died.

We do not know what influence Queen Katherine might have had upon the king in the final months of his life. While there is no doubt that she had tremendous influence upon the future destiny of England by her love for Henry's children, the future king and queens of England, it is also very possible, if not probable, that she also had an influence in determining by her faith and witness the eternal destiny of her husband.

If we could end the story of Katherine Parr right here, everything would end well. But there is more to be written. The decisions and behaviour of the dowager queen over the next eighteen months would greatly tarnish her reputation.

9

THE DOWAGER QUEEN

This is an extremely difficult chapter for me to write. It is a tragic ending to a rather remarkable story. Unbeknownst to Katherine, after the death of Henry she only had eighteen months to live. While there were certainly times of joy and satisfaction, for the most part those remaining months would bring resentment, jealousy, anger, discouragement and disappointment. If one chooses not to take seriously the personal impact of Katherine's conversion and discovery of justification by faith, her behaviour after the death of Henry presents no problem. But if you do take her life-changing conversion seriously, you are left with a mystery. You want to ask, 'Why, Katherine, did you do the foolish things you did?' Katherine Parr, after her discovery of justification by faith, could have become one of the leading lights in the actual – not Erasmian – Protestant Reformation in England. If she had remained close with her dear friend Princess Mary, who can predict how that might have mellowed the future queen, who has forever been labelled 'Bloody Mary?' Yet Katherine, by her own behaviour, caused her life to become one of mockery and derision.

Perhaps it is possible to offer a level of understanding of the antics of the dowager queen during the final eighteen months of her life. As Queen of England, Katherine Parr adopted the motto 'To be useful in all I do'. She must have been sorely disappointed that King Henry's will had not afforded her any power or position. Since she had served admirably as queen regent while Henry was in France and had proven to be a loving stepmother to Edward, she might have expected to be declared queen regent and protector for Edward, the heir apparent, who was only nine years old when Henry died. Instead, Edward lost not only his father but his adoptive mother. His care was placed into the hands of the Privy Council, who declared Edward Seymour, 1st Duke of Somerset and older brother of Jane and Thomas Seymour, Lord Protector over his nephew King Edward until Edward reached his majority and could rule in his own right. As fate would have it, the young king would never make it. Edward Seymour, meanwhile, became the most powerful man in England. His wife, Lady Stanhope, sought to gain prominence in her position. Katherine was now on the outside looking in. She was more or less 'put out to pasture', and her influence diminished.

Henry's decision – if indeed it was his choice – to bypass Queen Katherine was perhaps understandable. Being a young woman, she would probably remarry, possibly introducing unwanted sources of influence over the young king. Henry did grant Katherine a very generous financial allowance, however. Additionally, he decreed that she should be afforded the respect of the Queen of England as if he were still alive.

Following the coronation of her beloved stepson Edward VI on 31 January 1547, Katherine retired from court and moved to Old Manor in Chelsea, a property that had formerly belonged to Thomas More but had been confiscated following his execution and become the property of the Crown. She was at this time granted the guardianship of Henry's daughter Elizabeth, who moved in with her.

While Katherine had held affection for Henry, and probably even loved him because of everything he had done for her, she obviously would have felt little if any physical attraction to him. Since her first marriage had been arranged and her second had been to a man twice her age, Katherine, with her status being diminished, now decided to follow her heart and seek her own pleasure through a marriage of her own choosing. She chose romance over influence – and who could blame her?

The object of her affection was her former lover Thomas Seymour. Susan James rather sarcastically comments, 'In the privacy of her oratory Catherine may have comforted herself with the knowledge that she had exchanged the lusts of earthly love for the divine salvation of the spirit, but with Henry dead, the entire situation now changed and the comforts of religion quickly proved less satisfactory than the comforts of Sir Thomas Seymour's arms.'[1] As early as mid-February 1547, less than a month after Henry's death, Katherine had reached out to Seymour, writing to him, 'I would not have you think that this my honest good will toward you to proceed of any sudden motion or passion ... my mind was fully bent the other time I was at liberty, to marry you before any man I knew.'[2]

Following Henry's death, Thomas Seymour, whom the Privy Council appointed 1st Baron Seymour of Sudeley, returned to court. Jealous of the position attained by his older brother Edward, he sought to establish his own importance at court. According to gossip, on the death of the old king Thomas was quick to weigh up the advantages of marrying one of Anne of Cleves, Princess Mary or Princess Elizabeth. But Catherine was either oblivious to this gossip or chose not to believe it.[3] It has even been suggested that Thomas Seymour proposed to Elizabeth and was rebuffed; this has been widely debated, and among Katherine's biographers differences of opinion exist as to its validity. Much of the information comes from Kat Ashley, Elizabeth's governess, who claimed that Thomas Seymour had proposed to Elizabeth prior to marrying Katherine. In her biography of Queen Elizabeth, Carolly Erickson writes, 'Everyone, perhaps even Catherine herself, had heard the rumour that Seymour had sought permission to marry Elizabeth. But only Elizabeth and Kat Ashley knew the truth, as Kat said she had it from his own mouth: Seymour had sought her, not for her royal blood and prospects, but because he truly desired her. All else aside, Elizabeth believed, she, and not her starry-eyed stepmother, had been the choice of Thomas Seymour's impetuous heart.'[4]

If true, Thomas Seymour – perhaps rejected on as many as three counts – now turned his attention to the former queen. Perhaps

Katherine was his fourth choice. He responded to her letter in March alleviating her fears of how he might regard her intentions, stating that she would soon know different. He signed the letter, 'From the body of him whose heart ye have'.[5] Secret trysts began between the pair, with the baron visiting Katherine at Chelsea. She wrote to him in April, 'When it shall be your pleasure to repair hither, ye must take some pain to come early in the morning, that ye may be gone again by seven o'clock, and so I suppose ye may come without suspect.' She signed the letter, 'By her that is and shall be your humble true and loving wife during her life'.[6] Even though they had not yet married, Katherine already regarded herself as his wife.

Since less than half a year had passed since the death of King Henry, Katherine and Thomas knew that the Privy Council would not agree for the queen dowager to marry so soon. Sometime near the end of April or beginning of May they married in secret. When the marriage became public knowledge, it caused a scandal. Some even suggested that Katherine had married because she was pregnant and that the child was in fact the king's, and therefore a part of the succession. This was of course not the case and highly unlikely if not ridiculous, but gossip was rampant.

After being censured and reprimanded by the Privy Council for marrying the queen, Seymour wrote to the Lady Mary asking her to intervene on his behalf. Mary refused 'to be a meddler in this matter, considering whose wife her grace was of late. If the remembrance of the King's Majesty will not suffer her to grant your suit, I am nothing able to persuade her to forget the loss of him who is yet very ripe in mine own remembrance.'[7] News of the marriage had shattered Mary's friendship with her stepmother; their relationship was never the same again. She also doubted Katherine's suitability as a guardian for Elizabeth, and a reply written by the latter to her half-sister demonstrates the grave concerns that Mary had expressed over Katherine's marriage: 'You are very right in saying, in your most acceptable letters, which you have done me the honour of writing to me, that, our interests being common, the just grief we feel in seeing the ashes, or rather

the scarcely cold body of the king, our father, so shamefully
dishonoured by the queen, our stepmother, ought to be common
to us also. I cannot express to you, my dear princess, how much
affliction I suffered when I was first informed of this marriage.'[8]
Yet, Elizabeth chose to remain under Katherine's care, perhaps
with ulterior motives involving Thomas Seymour.

Katherine asked her stepson the king to plead her case with the
Privy Council, which he did at the beginning of June, saying that
he had known for some time that Thomas Seymour had intended
to marry the queen, and that he had sent a letter signifying
his approval to Katherine. Thus the Privy Council grudgingly
sanctioned the marriage, giving Thomas Seymour permission to
take up residence at Chelsea with his wife and young Elizabeth,
creating a potentially volatile situation.[9]

Susan James observed that all the influence which Katherine
had worked so hard to attain during her four years of union
to Henry VIII had been sacrificed on the altar of her fourth
marriage.[10] In fact, the queen's reputation suffered so much that
her new husband angrily sought an Act in Parliament 'that men
should not have liberty to speak against the queen'. Crude jests
began to make the rounds and Katherine became a target of ribald,
scornful gossip at court and in city taverns. Any potential influence
that the queen might have commanded with the king and council
died in Thomas Seymour's bed.[11] For his part, Thomas Seymour
threatened to 'take his fist to anyone who dared to slander her'.
For Katherine, this was evidence of his love.[12]

Katherine Parr, who had demonstrated such wisdom and
diplomacy as England's queen, made a foolish decision in
choosing her fourth husband. Although Thomas was a handsome
and highly talented bachelor – and a lord admiral as well – he
is described as a rogue and schemer primarily interested in
advancing his own status at court. He was loud-mouthed and
prone to fits of rage. But worse still is the suggestion that he was
an atheist. Evangelical preacher Hugh Latimer reported that he
had been told that Seymour denied the immortality of the soul:
'I have heard say, when [the queen] ordained in her house, daily

prayer both before noon, and after noon, the admiral gets him out of the way like a mole digging in the earth.'[13] Elizabeth Norton claims that Latimer's comments about Thomas's ungodliness were slander, but Thomas was certainly less of a committed Christian than his wife, the 'driving religious influence' in the household.[14] While Katherine's decision to marry Thomas is difficult to understand, as Blaise Pascal put it, 'The heart has its reasons which reason knows nothing of.'

Katherine's marriage to Seymour led her into two difficult situations which would further tarnish her reputation. First, a highly contentious feud developed between Katherine and Anne Stanhope Seymour, Duchess of Somerset, over jewellery. Anne Stanhope had formerly been one of Queen Katherine's ladies-in-waiting, but now, married to Lord Protector Edward Seymour, her status had been elevated – at least in her own mind. The tension between the two women also created difficulties between their husbands, brothers Edward and Thomas Seymour, even though their relationship was already far from brotherly.

The Duchess of Somerset was perhaps prone to disagreements. The historian John Strype records an incident that occurred in 1549 between the duchess and the wife of John Cheke, one of King Edward's tutors: 'She, having given some offense unwarily to the Duchess or the Duchess, a very imperious woman, having taken some offense by some words spoken, or some matters concealed of, I know not what. This female fraction employed Cheke to obtain a reconciliation for his wife, and to qualify the lofty Peeress's mind towards her.'[15]

After the turmoil over their marriage had died down, Katherine and Thomas returned to court. Katherine desired that the queen's jewellery, being stored in the Treasury at London, be returned to her, especially those pieces specifically given to her by Henry. Some of the jewels were certainly her own possessions, including a gold cross and some pearl pendants left to Katherine by her mother, as well as her wedding ring, given to her by Henry. It was Katherine's legal right to wear the queen's jewels until such time as King Edward had a consort of his own, but the Duchess of

Somerset had already decided that, as wife of the Lord Protector, she should wear the jewels. The issue was brought before the Privy Council, who clearly felt it was far more advantageous to support the wishes of the Lord Protector over the dowager queen. The duchess won the argument. Her relationship with Katherine was permanently damaged. In addition, the relationship between the Seymour brothers worsened as a result; Thomas saw the whole dispute as a personal attack by his brother.

The duchess was particularly nasty toward Katherine, wanting to blacken her reputation among those who continued to hold her in high esteem. She would publicly recall how the late king had married Katherine Parr 'in his doting days, when he had brought himself so low by his lust and cruelty that no lady who stood on her honour would venture on him. And shall I now give place to her who in her former estate was but Latimer's widow, and is now fain to cast herself for support on a younger brother. If master admiral teach his wife no better manners, I am she that will.'[16]

Katherine also had no liking for the Duke of Somerset, in particular feeling aggrieved over a piece of property that belonged to her and which he was granting to someone else to gain favour. Katherine wrote to Thomas, 'My lord your brother hath this afternoon made me a little warm! It was fortunate we were so much distant, for I suppose else I should have bitten him!'[17] Throughout the later months of 1547, Edward Seymour's power only grew. He was described as the 'king of the king'. This rankled with Katherine's husband, who displayed 'hatred and rivalry against his brother' both in private and in public.[18] Realising that she no longer had any future at court, Katherine retired to the manor at Chelsea, where she was able to maintain her status as queen. According to the *Legend of Throckmorton*, 'Her house was term'd a seconde court of right, because there flocked still nobilitie. He spared no coste his ladie to delight, Or to maintaine her Princelie Royaltie.'[19]

In addition to overseeing Elizabeth's education, Katherine probably worked at completing or perhaps adding to *The Lamentation of a Sinner*, which was finally published in

November 1547. After the conflict surrounding her marriage to
Thomas, she was apprehensive about making the work public and
perhaps only did so after encouragement from her friend Catherine
Brandon and her brother William. Susan James observes, 'The
queen was reluctant to place herself once more on the public
stage by allowing the book's publication. As Henry was dead, this
reluctance must have stemmed from the notoriety that she had
endured during the summer of 1547 when her secret and precipitate
marriage to Sir Thomas Seymour became common knowledge ...
Royal lamentations by Catherine in November 1547 over sins she
had committed would have had all too specific an interpretation
for the backbiters at court and the wags in city taverns.'[20] Norton
offers that 'Catherine was persuaded by the argument that it might
help lead others to Protestantism and, according to the preface by
Catherine's friend, William Cecil, "to all ladies of estate, I wish
as earnest mind, to follow our Queen in virtue as in honour, that
they might once appear to prefer God before the world, and be
honourable in religion, who now are honourable in vanities."'[21]

In early 1547, Thomas had purchased the wardship of Lady
Jane Grey, promising her parents that he would work at getting her
married to the king. Jane was the daughter of Henry VIII's niece
Frances Brandon and her husband Henry Grey, Marquis of Dorset.
She had royal blood. After her marriage to Thomas, Katherine
welcomed the nine-year-old Jane into her household. Katherine
was now in charge of overseeing the education of both Jane and
Elizabeth. Regarding Elizabeth's education, Linda Porter observes,
'The adult Elizabeth was very much the product of Katherine Parr.
Her education, her religious beliefs, her consciousness of personal
image owed much to the stepmother who guided and loved her
during those formative years.'[22]

Katherine had known Elizabeth since she was nine years
old. Now she was fourteen and undoubtedly developing as
a woman. Thomas, also regarded as her guardian, paid an
inordinate amount of attention to Elizabeth. At first it was
innocent horseplay in which Katherine also participated, but
later it appeared to turn more serious, causing Kat Ashley,

Elizabeth's governess, to become concerned. Thomas would enter Elizabeth's bedchamber in the morning dressed only in his nightclothes, tickle her and slap her on the rear. Kat Ashley reported the incidents to Katherine, but at first she seemed unconcerned, thinking it was merely innocent fun. For Katherine, the crisis came in May 1548 when she entered a chamber and found Elizabeth and Thomas in an embrace. Katherine was furious and broken-hearted. She had been betrayed by her husband and her stepdaughter. She must have also been terrified. She had been entrusted with Elizabeth's care, and if the relationship between her husband and Elizabeth ever became public both she and Thomas would be in danger.

There has been much debate regarding the extent of the relationship between Thomas and Elizabeth. Linda Porter writes:

> There have been assertions that Seymour was a sexual predator preying on a young girl, of three-in-a-bed romps, of passion-filled trysts and an unwanted pregnancy. The reputations of Thomas, Katherine and Elizabeth were dragged through the mire by contemporaries and what took place during the space of barely a year, when Elizabeth lived with the queen and her last husband, has provided titillation ever since. The story that Elizabeth had a son by Seymour makes good television drama but is poor history.[23]

The relationship between Thomas and Elizabeth, though not innocent, was probably nothing more than a flirtatious affair. Nonetheless, if it was left to continue there is no telling what might have happened. Elizabeth, a teenager enthralled by the attention given to her by Thomas, obviously did not dissuade him from showing her affection. She could have easily complained, and the matter would have been settled.

The solution to the problem was obvious. Katherine knew that she had to send Elizabeth away. She contacted her friend Anthony Denny and his wife and asked them to invite Elizabeth to stay with them. They agreed, and Elizabeth moved out, never to see Katherine again. Following her departure, Elizabeth wrote Katherine a letter, realising both her failure and Katherine's concern for her.

> Although I could not be plentiful in giving thanks for the manifold kindness, received at your highness' hand at my departure, yet I am something to be borne withal, for truly I was replete with sorrow to depart from your highness, especially leaving you undoubtful of health; and albeit I answered little, I weighed it more deeper when you said you would warn me of all evils that you should hear of me, for if your grace had not a good opinion of me you would not have offered friendship to me that way.[24]

In March 1548, Katherine had become pregnant. This pregnancy was a surprise as Katherine had not conceived during her first three marriages. She moved out of the manor at Chelsea to the retreat at Sudeley Castle in Gloucestershire. Lady Jane Grey accompanied her.

Once Elizabeth had left their household, Katherine and Thomas set about repairing their tenuous relationship. A baby was on the way. As the time drew near, however, it became increasingly obvious that Katherine was having a difficult pregnancy. Even though their relationship had been strained, she received a kind letter from Mary wishing her well. 'I wish to hear good success of your grace's great belly, and in the meantime, shall desire much to hear of your health, which I pray almighty God to continue and increase to His pleasure as much as your own heart can desire.'[25]

Katherine gave birth to her only child, Mary Seymour, named after Katherine's stepdaughter Mary, on 30 August 1548. While everything at first seemed normal, Katherine died eight days later, on 7 September 1548, at Sudeley Castle. The cause was thought to be childbed fever, which was common due to the lack of hygiene around childbirth. She was only thirty-seven years old.

Two days before her death, Katherine had made a very interesting statement that was heard by Elizabeth Tyrwhitt and allegedly by others who attended her. Lady Tyrwhitt claimed to remember the words, but we must bear in mind that she was no fan of Thomas Seymour. Katherine said, 'My lady Tyrwhitt, I am not well handled, for those that be about me careth not for me but standith laughing at my grief and the more good I will to them, the less good they will to me.' Seymour, hearing the statement, objected. 'Why, sweetheart, I would you no hurt.' She replied to him loudly, 'No, my lord, I think so.' She immediately said in his ear, 'But my lord, you have given me many shrewd taunts.' Lady Tyrwhitt adds, 'Those words I believe she spake with good memory, and very sharply and earnestly, for her mind was unquieted.'[26]

These words, allegedly spoken on her deathbed, either give some insight into how Katherine was treated by her husband or some insight into the feelings of Lady Tyrwhitt. While the correspondence between Thomas and Katherine does reflect some shared affection, Katherine might have been masking her true feelings, and Thomas merely playing a role. Her few remaining days were rendered wretched, not only by her illness but also by her suspicion that her husband was poisoning her. We cannot know whether this was the result of her delirium or if she had in fact come to realise that Thomas's ambition was stronger than his love had ever been.[27] He appears to have primarily responded to Katherine's death by intensifying his campaign to supplant his brother.

Was Katherine poisoned by Thomas Seymour? In a 1544 correspondence with Lady Wriothesley upon the death of her young son, Katherine encourages Lady Wriothesley to put away all immoderate and unjust heaviness and to gladly and quietly submit to God's will. She says, 'For what is excessive sorrow but a plain evidence against you that your inward mind doth repine against God's doings.'[28] Erickson contrasts this with her own behaviour: 'Yet, when confronted by her own death, she complains that she has not been well treated. That she evidently had not welcomed her own imminent death as a gateway to eternal life only fuelled the gossip that Catherine had been poisoned. The circumstances were highly suspicious.'[29]

Despite all this, in her will Katherine leaves everything to Thomas, making him a very wealthy man. With everything considered, the nature of the true relationship between Katherine Parr and Thomas Seymour remains a mystery.

Katherine's daughter, Mary Seymour, was taken in by her good friend Catherine Brandon. The last record of Mary Seymour is on her second birthday, and although stories circulated that she eventually married and had children, most historians believe she died as a child.

Katherine's body was carefully wrapped in layers of a waxed cloth used to help prevent decay and encased in a lead envelope in her coffin. She was buried in the floor of St Mary's Chapel at Sudeley Castle. Lady Jane Grey, who had a deep affection for Katherine, was the chief mourner. The service was short, performed in English, as Katherine would have desired, and over in a morning. Psalms were sung in English by the choir, three lessons read, and offerings made in the alms box for the living, not the dead. Miles Coverdale preached the sermon and reminded the people that the offerings gathered were not for the benefit of the dead but for the poor only, said a prayer, and the corpse was buried, during which time the choir sang the *Te Deum* in English. This simple ceremony was the first Protestant burial of an English queen. The location of Katherine's tomb was lost for over two hundred years, only to be discovered by accident in 1784 in the ruins of the Sudeley chapel.

Thomas Seymour was allegedly shocked by the loss of Katherine and mourned for a time, but he soon returned to court, attempting to improve his standing. He set out again to marry Elizabeth, and continued to undermine his brother's authority. He foolishly attempted to kidnap the young king, and was caught and arrested. Accused of treason, Thomas Seymour was beheaded on 20 March 1549.

Lady Jane Grey became a tragic figure. In 1553, before his death at the age of fifteen, King Edward set forth a new Act of Succession. He was undoubtedly prompted by his Lord Protector John Dudley, Earl of Warwick, who had replaced a disgraced Edward Seymour. Dudley and the rest of the Protestant Privy Council did not want to see Mary on the throne, though the Third Act of Succession placed her next in line to ascend the throne. Mary had remained Roman Catholic in her loyalties and would undoubtedly reverse the English Reformation. In the new succession, Edward determined that his cousin Lady Jane Grey should be queen. After Edward's death, a reluctant Jane was proclaimed queen on 10 July 1553 and awaited coronation in the Tower of London, but popular support for Mary grew very quickly, and most of Jane's supporters abandoned her. The Privy Council suddenly changed sides and proclaimed Mary queen on 19 July 1553, deposing Jane, who reigned for all of nine days. Queen Mary had her beheaded in 1555.

After the death of Mary in 1558, Elizabeth became the Queen of England and reigned for forty-five years. Her chief advisor was William Cecil, who authored the prefatory letter to *The Lamentation*. Elizabeth, probably the greatest queen in England's history, brought peace to the land and officially established the Church of England. She was Queen Katherine's legacy. In 1563, the *Thirty-Nine Articles*, defining the doctrinal position of the Church of England, were passed by Parliament. The clergy, but not the laity, were required to subscribe. Since Elizabeth produced no heir, the tumultuous Tudor dynasty, which began when the crown was placed on the head of Henry VII in 1485, ended with the death of Elizabeth in 1603.

10

KATHERINE PARR REPRISE

Queen Katherine Parr had led a remarkable life. After two marriages, the second to a man twice her age, she had finally discovered the hope of romance in a relationship with Thomas Seymour, yet fate intervened and she caught the roving eye of King Henry. After weighing all her options, she had decided to accept the king's proposal to enjoy the 'comfort' of being queen and seeing the advancement of her family. Was she an opportunist? Of course. How many young women would pass up such an opportunity? Moreover, considering the health of the king, it could not be a long ordeal. She became his sixth and final wife. She wrote to her brother William that she was thrilled the king had chosen her. Considering everything that had taken place over those four years of marriage, she became convinced that marrying Henry was not only for her ease and luxury, but was also the will of God.

Until recently, her life, work and writings have been largely forgotten. Having embraced the defining truth of the Reformation, justification by faith, she was the first truly Protestant queen in English history. For the most part, Katherine's modern biographers fail to realise the vital importance of her discovery of justification. This is not a part of their agenda. They focus on other issues, and, lacking an interest in theology, hopelessly confuse the reform of Erasmus with the Protestant Reformation.

I suspect the primary criticism my work will receive is that I place an undue emphasis on Katherine Parr's discovery of justification by faith. An explanation is in order. Every author undertakes a literary task with an agenda in mind. It is not surprising that most of Katherine's recent biographies are written by women, some of whom may have an underlying feminist agenda. Katherine Parr is an excellent case study in this respect. She was the first woman in England to be published under her own name. Apart from Catherine of Aragon, she was the only queen to rule as queen regent and exercise authority over an austere grouping of male politicians. Her role in the education of both Edward and Elizabeth left an indelible mark on English history. Through her influence, women were, for the first time, listed as successors to the throne of England. To elevate Katherine Parr is to elevate the role of women, and rightly so. Defining Katherine initially as an opportunist is not intended to tarnish her reputation but to accentuate her courage in sharing her 'conversion narrative', rejecting both the traditional Catholic theology of the king and the 'middle way' of Erasmus. Katherine was becoming a bold reformer, doing battle on two fronts.

Without sacrificing my objectivity on the altar of personal experience, I need to say that, for personal reasons, the biblical teaching of justification by faith is very important to me. Having gone through spiritual turmoil, I came out on the other side recognising that this thing called Christianity was not about me but rather about what God had done for me though Jesus Christ. This was also the life-changing experience of Martin Luther that fuelled the entire Protestant Reformation. For a queen of England to go through the same personal conflict and arrive at the same conclusion, engaging in battle with the popular thinking of her day, is not only remarkable but amazing. How sad it is that this courageous, dynamic facet of Queen Katherine's character has been marginalised, ignored, forgotten and misunderstood.

For example, Roland Bainton, one of the foremost historians of the Reformation, dedicates a chapter to Katherine Parr in his *Women of the Reformation in France and England* yet never mentions her discovery of justification by faith. Regarding *The Lamentation of a Sinner*, Bainton writes, 'This little treatise is one of the gems of

Tudor devotional literature.' He goes on and erroneously concludes, 'What Catherine has to say about the contemporary situation is entirely in line with the policy of her late husband, and does not overtly go beyond.'[1] By embracing justification by faith and rejecting good works as contributing to salvation, Queen Katherine certainly does go 'overtly' beyond the religious policies of her husband. While the *Lamentation* was a clear departure from Erasmian piety, James McConica identifies it as 'the unmistakable record in the Erasmian vein of a deep religious experience'.[2] I wonder if these two historians carefully read and studied the treatise.

Perhaps the rationale for marginalising Katherine's discovery of justification is attributable to the religious landscape of sixteenth-century England. The mainstream English Reformation elevated the primacy of Erasmus. Roland Bainton further writes, 'England was the land where the influence of Erasmus was paramount at his death. The entire English Reformation has been characterised as Erasmian, and with justice ... since other men of influence in England like Colet and More were of like mind. None can deny the immense popularity of Erasmian works during the latter years of Henry VIII and well into the period of Elizabeth.'[3] Yet, there was also an ulterior motive in promoting Erasmus. 'Thomas Cromwell initiated an extensive program of translation in order to bolster the Henrician reform. Those works of Erasmus were chosen which by criticism of the papacy could serve to justify the breach and by liberalising of divorce could excuse the setting aside of the queen. Erasmus, of course, approved of neither.'[4] Peter Marshall adds, 'Luther was a minority interest. He may have been the best-selling author in Germany, but the Oxford bookseller John Dorne sold only eleven copies of books by him in 1520, a year in which customers bought 150 of Erasmus' work.'[5] The noted Dutch historian H. A. Enno van Gelder, in his work on the two reformations in the sixteenth century, defines the Erasmian humanist reformation as the 'major' reformation and the Lutheran reformation as the 'minor' reformation.[6]

In 1973, Anthony Martienssen wrote a full biography of Katherine Parr which was published first in England and by other notable publishers including McGraw Hill. This I believe is the first full biography of Queen Katherine since Agnes Strickland's

1853 work on the queens of England. There is no biographical information about this author. He wrote two other books, *Hitler and His Admirals* and *Crime and Police*. Upon receiving a used library copy of his Katherine Parr biography, I carefully browsed the work and readily dismissed it since he offered no references and admitted that much of what he had written was conjecture based on circumstantial evidence.[7] In addition, there are many inaccuracies. However, what is fascinating about his work is that he identifies the English Reformation as a move from traditional Roman Catholicism to the 'New Learning' of the humanism of Erasmus. He makes no reference to the Lutheran Reformation. While he does speak of Katherine's *Lamentation of a Sinner*, he makes no reference to her discovery of justification by faith or her repudiation of Erasmus. I am amazed not by what he says but by what he doesn't say.

In the same vein as Martienssen, James McConica in his *English Humanists and Reformation Politics* views the entire English Reformation through the lens of the promotion of the Erasmian humanist ideal, making scant mention of the Lutheran Reformation. Gregory D. Dodds, author of *Exploiting Erasmus, the Erasmian Legacy and Religious Change in Early Modern England*, writes, 'One of the most interesting and unlikely books to emerge from the English Reformation was the English translation of Erasmus' *Paraphrases of the New Testament*. The *Paraphrases*, along with the Bible, the *Book of Homilies*, and the *Book of Common Prayer*, became a required text of the evolving English church. It is, of course, hardly surprising that Erasmus was a popular author in the mid-sixteenth century. What is unusual is that a Catholic author whose theology was far different from the Protestantism of Luther and Calvin became an official part of the English Reformation under Edward VI and again during the reign of Elizabeth I.'[8] Erasmus' intention for his *Paraphrases* was of the same nature as Katherine's *Prayers or Meditations*. Gregory Dodds continues, 'It is important to remember that the *Paraphrases* were designed to persuade readers to imitate the life of Christ. They were sermons that were not concerned so much with doctrine as with inspiring lives of piety.'[9]

In September 1545, Nicolas Udall wrote to Katherine prefacing his translation of Luke from the *Paraphrases* of Erasmus, 'There cannot be any one man picked out, more apt than Erasmus ... whose doctrine as it is not in any point (after my poor judgment), corrupt.'[10] Peter Marshall writes, 'Erasmian ideals undoubtedly helped foster a critical perspective on traditional piety, as well as a yearning for a simpler, more direct and authentic relationship with God.'[11] If it is true that mainstream Protestantism in England was Erasmian in nature, we must view *The Lamentation of a Sinner* and Katherine's discovery of justification by faith in a totally new light. She was not merely presenting her narrative in opposition to the king's traditional Catholic theology but also to the popular religiosity of the day. While the first target of her treatise might see her arrested, the second would see her work lapse into obscurity. No Erasmian humanist would give it a serious consideration.

The Lamentation of a Sinner was the first 'conversion narrative' published in England and was the work of a queen. But this conversion narrative was not the story of a conversion from unbelief to faith, from the secular to the spiritual, but from Erasmus to Luther. Janel Mueller comments, 'In embracing Luther's (justification by faith) formulation ... KP parts company with Erasmian Christianity.'[12] William Haugaard writes, 'Katherine left the Erasmians when she assigned a primary place to faith in the justification of men.'[13] Katherine was attacking the heart of Erasmian piety, and in many ways, considering the popularity of Erasmus, she was courageously swimming against the tide.

The issues raised in *Lamentation* went beyond justification by faith. It was a full-blown frontal attack on both traditional Catholicism and Erasmian rationalism. The humanism of Erasmus emphasised human dignity and happiness as the principal components of the teachings of Jesus. Katherine's denigration of herself must have been shocking to the sensibilities of Erasmians, 'nothing at all similar to her self-abasement as a queen and Christian had thus far been presented to English readers.'[14] Erasmus rejected predestination, and Katherine taught the election of the children of God before the beginning of the world. While Erasmus encouraged the study of Scripture and desired that everyone should have the privilege of reading God's Word and discovering and living out the 'philosophy of Christ', he acknowledged that there were issues in Scripture that were outside the purview of human reason and should not become the objects of debate and division. Katherine, following the lead of Luther, installed the Holy Spirit as the interpreter of Scripture who enlightens the mind to grasp the truths of the redemptive work of Christ. Katherine would echo the thoughts of Luther to Erasmus: 'Uncertainty is the most miserable thing in the world.'[15]

Good works for Erasmus were the result of the human effort informed by Scripture and aided by the grace of God to follow the example of Christ. For Katherine, good works were not the imitation of Christ resulting from human effort but the direct consequence of justifying faith, whereby the benefits of the redemptive work of Christ were grasped. Out of faith springs all good works. They were the fruit of the Spirit. Janel Mueller comments, 'Parr cannot even envisage as a possibility the Erasmian pattern in which the soul acquires charity and other virtues by emulating the example of Christ's life.'[16] Faith was not the mere rationally grounded truth acknowledging the historical events of Scripture so that the mind could be fashioned to follow the philosophy of Christ but the result of the work of the Holy Spirit whereby the benefits of Christ crucified are apprehended. Mueller further comments, 'She repudiates his Aristotelian notion of virtue as a habit of the will based on knowledge; for Parr, human nature is inherently reprobate, and any goodness it has is "imputed" through justifying faith in the merits of "Christ crucified".'[17]

Katherine Parr was a woman of courage. She had no difficulty confronting the intellectual elite of her day, as evidenced by her response to the flamboyant Latin letter written by Sir Thomas Smith seeking her support for the University of Cambridge. After criticising Smith's pseudo-intellectualism, she admonishes him to set aside the profane learning of the Greeks at Athens and focus upon the Gospel.[18] But now she had a bigger fish to fry.

I wonder how Katherine felt when her eyes were opened to the truth and she began to see her former piety as a follower of Erasmus as empty and vain. Did she regret some of her former writings and wish that, somehow, she could remove her *Prayers or Meditations*, wherein she taught the imitation of Christ from public access? Did she regret initiating the translation of Erasmus' *Paraphrases* when she learned that King Edward had made them required reading? What was the level of her resolve, realising that she was engaging in warfare with one of the greatest minds of the sixteenth century? Even though Erasmus had died ten years earlier, many of his disciples remained. Perhaps she shared the resolve of Martin Luther who had written, 'I shall parry the eloquent Erasmus with all confidence, caring nothing for his authority, reputation, or good will.'[19]

Upon receiving a copy of the *Lamentation*, the scholar Roger Ascham wrote to William Cecil. He said nothing about Katherine's treatise but interestingly merely praised Cecil for his use of the English language: 'We have read the most holy confessions of our queen, together with your most eloquent letter. I wish that you could find it in your heart to devote some of your time to the cultivation of English, so that men might know how easily our language admits all the members of eloquence.'[20] Ascham's response is understandable. As a noted British humanist and follower of Erasmus, Ascham probably did not appreciate Katherine's rejection of Erasmian rationalism in favour of the conversion of the heart. Instead, he praises Cecil's skill with the English language. In his phrase 'most holy confessions', is there a note of sarcasm?

Would the host of Erasmians opting for the 'middle way' Reformation touted by Erasmus be willing to entertain the conversion narrative of a former queen, or would they merely set it aside and ignore it? It must have been Katherine's hope that the opening remarks of the noted William Cecil would convince the readers to take her assault on Erasmus seriously. 'See and learn what she has done,' Cecil recommended, 'then may you practice and amend what you can.' There is no evidence to suggest that Katherine further promoted her views as expressed in *The Lamentation*.

During the reign of Edward VI, *The Lamentation of a Sinner* was again published in 1548, not necessarily as a second edition but as a new edition which included chapter headings for easier reading. During the reign of Mary I, despite Katherine's friendship with the Catholic queen, *The Lamentation* was considered enough of a threat to efforts to restore England to Roman Catholicism that it was banned. During the subsequent reign of Elizabeth I, it was again made available in 1563. Even though Katherine's *Prayers or Meditations* went through thirteen printings, this is the last we hear of *The Lamentation of a Sinner*. I do question the notion[21] that it remained popular with dissenters during the Civil War period (1642–1651) when, under the leadership of Oliver Cromwell, a more radical, Puritan form of Protestantism was promoted. While the genre of 'conversion narratives' was popular during this time period, there is no evidence to suggest that one of those 'conversion narratives' was *The Lamentation of a Sinner*.

By the time of Henry's death, most of the Lutheran reformers in England had either been burned at the stake or fled the country. Upon the succession of Edward VI, Lutheran and Calvinist Protestants held out great hopes for the future of the English Reformation whereby the final vestiges of Roman Catholicism could be eradicated, and that included the primary notion of salvation by good works which was at the heart and core of the Catholic system. Edward was compared with Josiah, the biblical king of Judah, who destroyed the last remaining altars and images of Baal.[22] While Edward's education was primarily of an Erasmian humanist bent, it would be difficult to suggest that he had not read the work of his 'beloved mother' and been moved by her 'conversion narrative'.

Under the leadership of Thomas Cranmer, justification by faith alone became the 'official position' of Edwardian reform. Cranmer had attempted this inclusion in the King's Book of 1543 but was rebuffed by King Henry. Despite objections from Stephen Gardiner, who questioned the legality of bypassing both Parliament and Convocation, justification by faith was made a central teaching of the English Church.[23] In order to accomplish that feat Cranmer was probably bolstered by the conversion narrative of the former queen.

In the Church of England today, the *Thirty-Nine Articles of Religion* form the essential beliefs of the Anglican church. The articles were established by a Convocation of the Church in 1563. Articles X through XIII are statements regarding the human condition and justification by grace through faith in Christ Jesus. These are the identical truths that are clearly expressed in Katherine Parr's *Lamentation of a Sinner*. Whether these truths are proclaimed and taught from the pulpits of England today or whether the Erasmian notion of human free will having the capability to be informed by the study of Scripture, strive to follow the example of Jesus, love the neighbour, and live in peace and harmony is a question I am unable to answer. The twentieth-century ecumenical movement has attempted to restore the Erasmian notion that the importance of doctrinal truth should be sacrificed on the altar of unity and compromise. In so doing, the distinctiveness of justification by faith has been marginalised.

In debunking the notion that the Erasmian Reformation was greater than the Protestant Reformation, A. G. Dickens writes, 'Millions of people are still Lutherans, Calvinists and Anglicans but few are Erasmians or Christian humanists.'[24] This may indeed be true, but the intention of Erasmus was not to form a new church or denomination bearing his name but to influence the present structures, which his philosophy continues to do.

In his introduction to Luther's *Bondage of the Will*, J. I. Packer writes, 'We are forced to ask whether Protestant Christendom has not tragically sold its birthright between Luther's day and our own. Has not Protestantism today become more Erasmian than Lutheran? Do we not too often try to minimise and gloss over doctrinal differences for the sake of inter-party peace? Are we innocent of the doctrinal indifferentism with which Luther charged Erasmus? Do we still believe that doctrine matters? Or, do we now with Erasmus, rate a deceptive appearance of unity as more important than truth?'[25]

In July 1817, Merle d'Aubigné was ordained a minister of the established church in Geneva, but before assuming a pastorate he journeyed to Germany for the tercentenary celebration of Martin Luther's posting of the Ninety-five Theses. He was amazed that the emphasis at these celebrations was essentially on Luther's intellectual and political significance, ignoring the rediscovery of biblical truth. He was determined to do something about it.

During his forty-one years as a professor in Geneva, his resolution was realised. He produced a massive five-volume *History of the Great Reformation of the Sixteenth Century*. His work is without doubt the most comprehensive history of the Reformation. 'I want this history to be truly Christian,' he wrote, 'and to give a proper impulse to the religious spirit.'

One is not a true historian who defines the reformation initiated by Martin Luther without acknowledging the primary controverted truth that drove that reformation – justification by faith. Perhaps the revival of interest in the life of Katherine Parr will also include a new look at her *Lamentation of a Sinner*, prompting a revival in the pursuit of this cardinal doctrine of the Reformation. Perhaps there will be some who, following the example of Queen Katherine, forsake the philosophy of Erasmus in favour of the theology of Luther. Even if that be not the case, perhaps future historians will at least recognise Katherine's courage in presenting a conversion narrative that not only attacked Catholic traditionalists but also struck a decisive blow against Erasmian rationalists.

Without attempting to push a comparison, I do see similarities between the life of Martin Luther and that of Katherine Parr. Both Luther and Katherine Parr came to an understanding of justification by faith out of the personal travail of searching for righteousness and holiness before God. Luther's quest is well known. Joining the Augustinian monastery was the pinnacle of this pursuit. He embraced the monastic life with a fervour unlike anything his teachers had seen. Luther would remain in confession for hours, depriving himself almost to the point of death. He acknowledges that his horribly aggressive years as a monk, beating himself and damaging his health, shortened the years of his life. He wrote, 'If ever a monk got to heaven through monasticism, I, too, would have got there.'[26] Katherine Parr begins her *Lamentation of a Sinner* by deploring her evil and wretched former life. Whether dealing with the Apostle Paul (defining himself as the chief of sinners),[27] Martin Luther, or Katherine Parr, the process is the same.

Regarding justification by faith, Peter Marshall in his history of the English Reformation comments, 'For all its novelty, justification by faith made sense to people – some people – because it spoke to their livid experience, suggesting a way to resolve tensions and difficulties encumbering their spiritual lives. This was the story of Luther himself, burdened with a sense of sin, and convinced of the inadequacy of works of satisfaction to put himself right with God.'[28]

If such is not the case, the individual either has a high estimate of his own righteousness or a low estimate of the righteousness of God. Justification by faith is not justification 'on account of faith', but justification 'on account of' the righteousness of Christ – a fact that is often forgotten in the discussion. Faith only justifies because of the object that is grasped.

In the writings of both Luther and Parr, an early stage and a later stage must be discerned. In the early writings of Luther, remnants of Roman Catholicism are readily discernible. In fact, Luther does not reject purgatory in his ninety-five theses, but the abuses caused by the sale of indulgences. His 1535 *Commentary on Galatians* demonstrates a greater understanding than his 1519 commentary on the same epistle. The same is true of Katherine Parr. Her writings cannot be read together to define her religious sensitivities. There is a marked difference between her *Prayers or Meditations* and her *Lamentation of a Sinner*. C. Fenno Hoffman Jr is correct in saying that the one should be read as a repudiation of the other.[29]

The actions and attitudes of both Martin Luther and Katherine Parr subsequent to their conversion experience caused their opponents to question the validity of their experience. When Christians publicly proclaim their conversion and new-found relationship with Jesus Christ and later demonstrate questionable behaviour, observers are quick to criticise and raise doubts about their sincerity and the legitimacy of their faith, and perhaps even make them the objects of scorn and ridicule. Such was the case with Martin Luther. When some of his later writings were filled with obscenities and personal attacks, enemies of the Reformation were prone to use these improprieties to question his sincerity and denigrate his influence. Luther's unfortunate 1543 treatise *The Jews and their Lies* caused some to place the blame for the Holocaust at his feet.

We want our Christian heroes to acknowledge their sin and failure and embrace the redemptive work of Christ on the cross, yet we also expect them to be free of such human imperfections.

Martin Luther, like every other Christian, remained a sinner who had found his righteousness in the person of Jesus Christ, not in himself. Luther was certainly no spiritual prude who flaunted his own piety. While those who share Luther's faith might wish that he had been more restrained, as far as Luther was concerned, what you see is what you get. Luther was certainly not trusting his own piety to gain divine favour.

The same could be said about Katherine Parr. While confident of her righteousness in Christ, she knew that her faith did not eliminate the desires of the sinful nature. She wrote, 'Although the dregs of Adam do remain, that is our desires of the flesh, which indeed are sins, nevertheless, they are not imputed as sins, if we are truly joined to Christ.' And again, 'Although the children of God sometime do fall by frailty into some sin, yet that falling causes them to humble themselves, and to acknowledge the goodness of God, and to come to him for refuge and help.'[30] Katherine Parr was no spiritual prude. She had discovered that the truth of the Christian Gospel was not about her but about what God had done for her. She was free to be herself, warts and all. Because of her romance and marriage to Thomas Seymour shortly after the death of King Henry, Katherine became the object of criticism and personal attacks.

The Lamentation of a Sinner was published in November of 1547. Probably in the late spring or summer of that same year, Katherine was engaged in a furious battle with Anne Seymour, the Duchess of Somerset and wife of Edward, the brother of her husband. They battled over the question of who had the right to be adorned with the queen's jewels, and their position of honour at court. Linda Porter comments, 'The fact that Katherine hated her is inescapable.'[31] Katherine's letter to Thomas stating that she was so angry with his brother that she could have bitten him is dated May 1547.

After Katherine lost the battle with her sister-in-law, she left court that summer. She probably came to recognise that her attitudes had compromised her Christian faith and likely added some additional thoughts to her work. She might have been admonished for her behaviour, perhaps by her friend Catherine Brandon, who was rather brash and not afraid to voice her opinions. The admonition might have initially offended her. While this is all conjecture and speculation, in these next two passages it is very possible, in the light of her experience that summer, to read between the lines and conclude that she wrote them after the unfortunate encounter.

> I would to God we would all, when occasion arises, confess our faults to the world, laying aside all respect to our own position. But, alas, self-love so reigns among us that, as I have said before, we cannot spy our own faults. And if perhaps we should discover our own guilt, we either favourably interpret it as not being sin, or else we are ashamed to confess it. Yes, and we are badly offended and grieved to hear another tell us our faults in a lovingly and godly manner, making no distinction between a loving warning and malicious accusation. Truly, if we sought God's glory, as we should do in all things, we should not be ashamed to confess ourselves as deviating from God's commands and ordinances, when it is obvious that we have done so, and, in fact, daily do.[32]
>
> If any man shall be offended at this my lamenting the faults of men which are in the world, imagining that I do it either out of hatred or spite to any sort or kind of people: truly, in so doing, they do me a great wrong. For I thank God, by His grace, I hate no person; yes, I would say more, to give witness to my conscience, that neither life, honour, riches, nor whatsoever I possess here, which pertains to my own private possessions, be it never so dearly loved by me, that most willingly and gladly I would leave it, to win any man to Christ, of whatever degree or sort he was.[33]

If I am right in suggesting that the final passages in the *Lamentation* were added in response to the events of the summer involving Katherine's combative relationship with the Duchess of Somerset, we can assume that Katherine had repented of her actions and attitudes. Perhaps she even attempted to reconcile with her sister-in-law, although there is no evidence to suggest it.

There are three names associated with the *Lamentation*: William Cecil; Catherine Brandon, Duchess of Suffolk; and William Parr, brother of Queen Katherine. What follows is a brief review of the lives of these three contributors.

William Cecil, the author of the prefatory letter to the *Lamentation*, was an astute politician who had Protestant leanings. His early career was spent in service to Edward Seymour, Duke of Somerset, who was the Lord Protector of young Edward VI. During this time, he authored the preface to the *Lamentation*. With the overthrow of Seymour in October 1549, Cecil spent three months imprisoned in the Tower. Upon being released, he ingratiated himself with the new Lord Protector, John Dudley, and in 1550 became one of King Edward's secretaries of state. As it was becoming evident that the sickly Edward was approaching death, to be certain the Roman Catholic Mary did not ascend the throne and reverse the Reformation policies, Edward's lawyers created a document entitled 'My Devise for the Succession', which set aside Parliament's Third Act of Succession. The document barred both Elizabeth and Mary, the remaining children of Henry VIII, from the throne, in favour of Henry's distant relative Lady Jane Grey. Cecil resisted signing the document since it could be deemed treasonous without the support of Parliament, but at Edward's royal command he signed it. He signed not only the devise, but the letters from the council to Princess Mary on 9 June 1553.

When it became evident that Mary had the popular support of the people, the council reversed their loyalties in favour of Mary. Lady Jane Grey reigned for nine days and was later executed by the new queen. Cecil was now in a bind. He approached the triumphant Queen Mary as representative of the council and pleaded his case, claiming to have only signed the documents as a witness. He won her approval as 'a very honest man'. Cecil was willing to change his religious leanings and embraced Mary's Catholicism.

Similarly, when it became clear that Mary's chronic illnesses would soon cause her demise, Cecil began to form a relationship with her sister Elizabeth, who was next in line for the throne. On Elizabeth's accession, in 1558, Cecil was appointed her sole secretary, and he served in this role throughout her entire reign. In 1571, Cecil was created a peer as 1st Baron Burghley. While his prefatory letter speaks highly of Queen Katherine's conversion narrative, it is evident that Cecil was more of a politician than a reformer. As you read his prefatory letter, consider the context. Cecil, anticipating that Katherine's treatise will be met with scorn and ridicule considering her former behaviour, attempts to set the negative issues aside, calling upon the reader to judge the work by its own merit.

The *Lamentation of a Sinner* was 'put in print at the instant desire of the right gracious lady Katherine, Duchess of Suffolk'. Catherine Willoughby Brandon was the wife of the late Charles Brandon, Duke of Suffolk, a dear friend of Henry VIII. Having been a ward of the duke, Catherine married Brandon in her teenage years. She became one of the more interesting, outspoken proponents of the Reformation. Her disdain for traditional Catholicism is evidenced in the fact that she named her dog 'Gardiner' after the Bishop of Rochester, causing much laughter when she demanded her dog to heel. At a banquet she attended, the host suggested that each woman should choose the man she cared for most to accompany her. 'The duchess ... turned to her godfather, Bishop Stephen Gardiner, saying that since she could not have her husband for whom she most cared she would invite the bishop for whom she cared least. The barb rankled for years. One said of her: She is "a lady of sharp wit, and sure hand to drive her wit home, and make it pierce where she pleases".'[34] After the death of Charles Brandon in 1545, Catherine returned to court and joined Queen Katherine's controversial group of ladies. It is said that she exerted much influence upon the religious beliefs of the queen.

After Katherine Parr's death in August of 1548 at the birth of Mary Seymour, Thomas Seymour went to London with his new baby daughter. A few months later, he was arrested, tried and executed for treason. His wealth was confiscated by the crown, and so Mary became a penniless orphan at the age of seven months. Catherine Brandon was appointed Mary's guardian, which task she evidently did not relish: 'The duchess might well have taken over had not the babe been accompanied by a horde of retainers without stipend.'[35] She appealed to William Cecil, asking for funds. In January 1550, an Act of Parliament was passed restoring Mary to what was left of her father's property. No further claim was ever made, and Mary Seymour disappears from history.

In 1551, Catherine's two sons, both students at Cambridge, died within an hour of each other after catching the sweating sickness. As a result of this severe test of her faith, she determined to build a new life. She married again, to a member of her household named Richard Bertie, out of both love and shared religious beliefs, but she continued to be known as the Duchess of Suffolk. During the reign of Mary I, the Berties were among those exiles who left for the Continent. Peter Marshall writes, 'Catherine Willoughby Brandon, Duchess of Suffolk, set off for Germany in considerable state at the start of 1555, after her husband, Richard Bertie, secured them a safe conduct from Gardiner. The couple left accompanied by their steward and six other servants, including a brewer, a laundress, and a fool.'[36] In 1559, while still abroad, Catherine heard that the new Queen Elizabeth was dragging her heels when it came to restoring England to Protestantism. She wrote an angry letter to William Cecil: 'Catherine, Duchess of Suffolk ... let Cecil know exactly how unimpressed she was by report that the queen "tarried but the Gospel". When it came to the mass, "There is no part of it good."'[37] After their return to England, the Berties lived at Catherine's Grimsthorpe estate in Lincolnshire, and at court. Bainton concludes, 'The duchess of Suffolk, the daughter of the most devoted and devout among the ladies of Catherine of Aragon became the high priestess of early English Puritanism.'[38]

The *Lamentation of a Sinner* was published 'at the earnest request of the right honourable lord William Parr, Marquess of Northampton'. William Parr, the brother of Queen Katherine, had a fascinating life. On 9 February 1527, he married Anne Bourchier, who was only ten years old at the time. After serving as Member of Parliament for Northamptonshire, he was made Baron Parr in 1539. In 1541, Anne created a scandal when she deserted William to elope with her lover, John Lyngfield, prior of St James's Church, Tanbridge, Surrey. She would have several illegitimate children by Lyngfield. In 1543, William obtained an Act of Parliament repudiating Anne. After his sister's marriage to the king, William obtained his ex-wife's lands and titles, and on 23 December 1543 he became Earl of Essex. He subsequently married Elizabeth Brooke. After the death of Henry VIII, William was favoured as King Edward VI's 'beloved uncle'. He became a very important man at Edward's court during the protectorate of John Dudley. Parr, and especially his wife Elizabeth, were leaders in the attempt to put Lady Jane Grey on the throne after Edward's death. He was convicted of high treason, attainted, and sentenced to death on 18 August 1553 after the accession of Queen Mary. Perhaps Mary did not have the heart to execute the brother of her former dear friend Katherine Parr, for William was released in the autumn. His titles were restored to him by Elizabeth in 1559.

As you read *The Lamentation of a Sinner*, bear a few things in mind. In adapting this work, I did not attempt to impose my own style of writing but only update the English into a modern version. You may find some of the content difficult to comprehend, so, taking the advice of William Cecil in his prefatory letter, keep in mind that 'these great mysteries and graces are not properly understood, except they be surely studied.'

II

THE LAMENTATION OF A
SINNER[1]

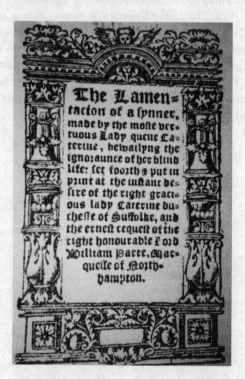

The Lamentacion of a synner, made by the moste vertuous Lady quene Caterine, bewailyng the ignoraunce of her blind life: set foorth & put in prynt at the instant desire of the right gracious lady Caterine duchesse of Suffolke, and the ernest requeſt of the right honourable Lord William Parre, marqueſſe of Northhampton.

The Lamentation of a Sinner made by the most virtuous lady Queen Katherine, bewailing the ignorance of her blind life: set forth and put in print at the instant desire of the right gracious lady Katherine, Duchess of Suffolk, and the earnest request of the right honourable lord William Parr, Marquess of Northampton.

Prefatory Letter

William Cecil, having taken much profit by the reading of this treatise, desires every Christian, by reading it, the same profit with increase from God.

Most gentle and Christian reader, if matters were confirmed by their reporters rather than the reports determined by the matters, I might justly lament our time, where evil deeds are described as good, and charitable deeds called evil. But since it is true that things are not good because they are praised, but rather, they are praised because they are good. It is not my intention to convince you to like this Christian treatise because I have chosen to praise it. But I urge you to consider it, for whatever goodness you shall ascribe to it. I am not writing to convince you to like this treatise, but to follow my example by passing judgment based on the treatise itself, not on what others say about it.

Truly our age is so disposed to use good words to describe evil fruits, and apply excellent terms to unkind works, so that charitable deeds cannot enjoy a proper description, being defrauded by the evil; and excellent works cannot be defined with worthy terms, being prevented by the unkind works. Men say as much as they can about a matter rather than how much they should say, inclining more to their own enjoyment rather than to their judgment. They try to be eloquent regardless of whether the matter is good or evil, so that neither the goodness of the cause can move them to say more, nor the evilness less.

For if the excellency of this Christian contemplation, either for its marvellous goodness or for the resulting profit for the reader, should be commended, it would be necessary for me to find new words since the old ones have already been used to describe evil works, or I could wish that the common speech of praising was suspended until suitable matters were found to use them. Such is the abundance of praising, and scarceness of deserving. Wherefore, lacking the manner in words, and not indeed the matter of granting high commendation, I am compelled to be silent and not offer my judgment. I trust that those who might have been moved to like this treatise based on my judgment, will be compelled to grant it honour based upon its own worthiness.

Any earthly man would soon be stirred to see some mystery of magic, or practice of alchemy, or perchance some enchantment of elements,[2] but you, who are baptised, have here a wonderful mystery of the mercy of God, a heavenly practice of regeneration, a spiritual enchantment of the grace of God. If joy and triumphs are shown when a king's child is born to the world, what joy is sufficient when God's child is regenerated from heaven? The one is flesh, which is born of flesh; the other is spirit, which is born of spirit.[3] The one shall in brief time wither like the grass of the earth; the other shall live in heaven beyond all time. If the finding of one lost sheep be more joyful than having the ninety and nine, what joy is it to consider the return of a stray child of almighty God, whose return teaches the ninety and nine to come to their fold?[4] Even such cause of joy is this, that the angels in heaven take comfort herein. Be therefore, joyful where a noble child is newly born. Show thyself glad where the lost sheep has won the whole flock. Be not sad, where angels rejoice.

Here you may see one (if you are so moved) a woman, (if degree may aggravate you) a woman of high estate: by birth made noble, by marriage most noble, by wisdom godly; by a mighty king, an excellent queen; by a famous Henry, a renowned Katherine. A wife to him that was a king to realms: refusing the world wherein she was lost, to obtain heaven, wherein she may be saved; abhorring sin, which made her bound, to receive grace, whereby she may be free; despising flesh, the cause of corruption, to put on the Spirit, the cause of sanctification; forsaking ignorance, wherein she was blind, to come to knowledge, whereby she may see; removing superstition, wherewith she was smothered, to embrace true religion, wherewith she may revive.

The fruit of this treatise, good reader, is your own amendment; if only this, the writer is satisfied. This good lady thought no shame to detect her sin, to obtain remission; no vileness, to become nothing, to be a member of Him, which is all things in all; no folly to forget the wisdom of the world, to learn the simplicity of the Gospel; at the last, not being displeased to submit herself to the school of the cross, the learning of the crucifix, the book of our redemption, the very absolute library of God's mercy and wisdom. This way she thought her honour increased, and her state permanent: to make her earthly honour heavenly and neglect the transitory for the everlasting. Of this, I would inform you, that profit may follow.

These great mysteries and graces are not properly understood, except they be surely studied; neither are they perfectly studied, unless they are diligently practiced; neither profitably practiced, without amending your life. See and learn what she has done then may you practice and amend what you can. So, shall you practice with ease, having a guide; and amend with profit, having a zeal. It is easier to see these than to merely learn them.

Begin at the easiest, to come to the harder. First, consider her confession, that you may learn her repentance; practice her perseverance, that you may have similar amendment; displease yourself in shunning vice, that you may please God in asking grace. Let not shame hinder your confession, which certainly did not hinder your sin. Be sure, if we acknowledge our sins, God is faithful to forgive us, and to cleanse us from all unrighteousness.[5] Obey the prophet's saying: 'Declare thy ways to the Lord.'[6] Thus far, you may learn to know yourself; but next, be as diligent to relieve yourself in God's mercy as you have been revealing yourself in your sin and repentance. For God has concluded all things under sin, so that He would have mercy upon all.[7] Who has also borne our sins in His body, upon the tree, that we should be delivered from sin, and should live to righteousness: by whose stripes we are healed.[8]

Here is our anchor; here is our Shepherd; here we are made whole. Here is our life, our redemption, our salvation, and our bliss. Let us, therefore, now feed by this gracious queen's example; and do not be ashamed to become in confession publicans, since this noble lady will be no Pharisee. And to all ladies of estate I wish as earnest mind to follow our queen in virtue as in honour: that they might once appear to prefer God before the world, and be honourable in religion, as you are now honourable in vanities. So, shall they (as in some virtuous ladies of right high estate it is viewed with great comfort) taste of this freedom of remission, of this everlasting bliss which exceeds all thoughts and understandings, and is prepared for the holy in spirit. For the which, let us, with our intercession in holiness and pureness of life, offer ourselves to the heavenly Father an undefiled host: to whom be eternal praise and glory, through all the earth, without end. Amen.

The Lamentation of a Sinner

Chapter One
A humble confession of sins to the glory of God

When I think about my evil and wretched former life, my obstinate, stony, and exceedingly evil stubborn heart, I not only neglected, yes, but condemned and despised God's holy teachings and commandments, and embraced, received, and esteemed vain, foolish, and artificial trifles. Partly by the hate I owe to sin, which has reigned in me, and partly by the love I owe to all Christians, whom I am content to edify with the example of my own shame, I am forced and constrained with my heart and words to confess and declare to the world, how ingrate, negligent, unkind, and stubborn I have been to God my Creator; and how beneficial, merciful, and gentle He has always been to me, His creature, being such a miserable and wretched sinner.

Truly, I have undertaken no small thing: first, to set forth my whole stubbornness and contempt in words, which are incomprehensible in thought, as it is said in the Psalm: 'Who understands his faults?'[9] Next, to declare the excellent benevolence, mercy, and goodness of God, which is infinite, unmeasurable. All the words of angels and men could not recount His exalted goodness. If one considers what he has received from God, and daily receives, who is not forced to confess the same? Yes, if men would not acknowledge and confess the same, the stones would cry it out.[10] Truly, I am constrained and forced to speak and write of my own confusion and shame, but to the great glory and praise of God. For He, as a loving Father, of most abundant and exalted goodness, has heaped upon me innumerable blessings; and I, contrary, have heaped many sins, despising that which was good, holy, pleasant, and acceptable in His sight, and choosing that which was delicious, pleasant, and acceptable in my sight.

And it was no marvel that I did so. For I would not learn to know the Lord and His ways, but loved darkness better than light:[11] yes, darkness seemed to me, light. I embraced ignorance as perfect knowledge; and knowledge seemed to me superfluous and vain. I had little regard for God's Word but gave myself to vanities and shadows of the world. I forsook Him, in whom is all truth, and followed the vain, foolish imaginations of my own heart. I covered my sins with the pretence of holiness. I called superstition, 'godly meaning,' and true holiness, 'error.'

The Lord did speak many pleasant and sweet words to me, and I would not hear. He called me in many ways, but through rebellion, I would not answer. My evils and miseries are so many and so great, they accuse me even to my face. Oh, how miserable and wretched I am! Confounded by the multitude and greatness of my sins, I am compelled to accuse myself.

It was an incredible unkindness, when God spoke to me and called me, that I would not answer Him? What man, so called, would not have heard? Or what man, hearing, would not have answered? If an earthly prince had spoken or called him, I suppose anybody would have willingly done both.

What a wretch and coward I am! When the Prince of Princes, the King of Kings, did speak many pleasant and gentle words to me, and called me so many and various times that they cannot be numbered; and yet, despite these great signs and tokens of love, I would not come to Him. I hid myself out of His sight. I sought and walked so long in many crooked paths that I had totally lost sight of Him.

And it is no marvel or wonder: for I had a blind guide called Ignorance, who dimmed my eyes, that I could never totally get any picture of the fair, good, straight, and right ways of His teaching, but continually followed dangerously in the foul, wicked, crooked, and perverse ways. Yes, and because there were so many following those ways, I could not imagine that I was not walking in the perfect and right way: having more regard for the number of the followers rather than to what they were following. I believed most surely, they were leading me to heaven, whereas I am certain now, they would have brought me down to hell.

I forsook the spiritual honouring of the true, living God, and worshiped visible idols and images made of men's hands,[12] believing that by them I attained heaven. Yes, truly, I made a great idol of myself; for I loved myself better than God. How many things we love or prefer in our hearts before God and receive and esteem them as idols and false gods!

How I have violated this holy, pure, and most high law and commandment concerning loving God, with my whole heart, mind, force, strength, and understanding.[13] And I, as an evil, wicked, disobedient child, gave my will, power, and senses to the contrary, making a god out of almost every earthly and carnal thing.

Furthermore, I did not consider the blood of Christ to be sufficient to wash me from the filth of my sins as He planted in His Word. Rather, I sought such riffraff the Bishop of Rome planted in his tyranny and kingdom. Through the virtue and sacredness of them, I trusted with great confidence to receive full remission of my sins.

And so, I did as much as possible to obscure and darken the great benefit of Christ's passion; and it is not possible to think of anything of greater value. No greater injury and displeasure to almighty God our Father can be done than to tread Christ underfoot, His only begotten and well-beloved Son. All other sins in the world, gathered together in one, are not as heinous and detestable in the sight of God. And no wonder, for in Christ crucified, God shows Himself to be most noble and glorious, even an almighty God, and most loving Father, in His only dear and chosen blessed Son. And therefore, I count myself one of the most wicked and miserable sinners, because I have been so much against Christ my Saviour.

Saint Paul desired to know nothing, but Christ crucified,[14] after he had been raptured into the third heaven, where he heard such secrets as were not fitting and proper to speak to men,[15] but counted all his works and doings as nothing, to win Christ.[16] And I, most presumptuously thinking nothing of Christ crucified, went about to set forth my own righteousness,[17] saying with the proud Pharisee:[18] Good Lord, I thank You, I am not like other men; I am no adulterer nor fornicator, and so forth: with such words of vainglory, extolling myself and despising others.

I worked as a hired servant for wages[19] or for reward; and not as a loving child. I should have been working only for the sake of love without respect of wages or reward. Neither did I consider how beneficial a Father I had, who did show me His love and mercy and out of His own simple grace and goodness, when I was most His enemy, He sent His only-begotten and well-beloved Son into this world of wretchedness and misery, to suffer most cruel and sharp death for my redemption. But my heart was so stony and hard, that this great benefit was never truly and lively printed in my heart, although I often rehearsed it with my words, thinking myself to be sufficiently instructed in the same, but indeed, being in blind ignorance.

Yet, I stood so well in mine own judgment and opinion, that I thought it vain to seek to increase my knowledge of the work of Christ. Paul calls Christ the wisdom of God, and the same Christ was to me foolishness;[20] my pride and blindness deceived me, and the hardness of my heart opposed the growing of truth within it. Such were the fruits of my carnal and human reason, to receive rotten ignorance instead of valuable ripe and seasonable knowledge. Such also is the malice and wickedness that possesses the hearts of men: the wisdom and pleasing of the flesh.

I professed Christ in my baptism when I began to live but as life continued, I swerved from Him even as an unbaptised heathen. Christ was innocent and void of all sin; and I wallowed in filthy sin and was free from no sin. Christ was obedient unto His Father, even to the death of the cross;[21] and I disobedient and most stubborn, even to the confusion of truth. Christ was innocent. Christ was meek and humble in heart; and I most proud and vainglorious. Christ despised the world with all its vanities; and because of the vanities, I made it my God. Christ came to serve His brethren; and I desired to rule over them. Christ despised worldly honour; and I much delighted to attain it. Christ loved the base and simple things of the world; and I esteemed the most fair and pleasant things. Christ loved poverty; and I, wealth. Christ was gentle and merciful to the poor; and I, hard-hearted and ungentle. Christ prayed for His enemies; and I hated mine. Christ rejoiced in the conversion of sinners; and I was not grieved to see them return to their sin.

By this declaration, all may understand how far I was from Christ, and without Christ: yes, how contrary to Christ, although I bore the name of a Christian. So much that, if any man had said I had been without Christ, I would have rigidly opposed them. And yet, I neither knew Christ, nor why He came. As concerning the effect and purpose of His coming, I had a certain vain, blind knowledge, both cold and dead, which may be had with all sin: as is plainly true based on this my confession and open declaration.

Chapter Two
Repentance in faith and the merits of Christ

Why should I now lament, mourn, sigh, and weep for my life, and time spent so evil? With how much humility and lowliness should I come and confess my sins to God, giving Him thanks, that it has pleased Him, out of His abundant goodness, to give me time for repentance?

In considering my sins, I know them to be so grievous, and in number, so exceeding, that I have very often deserved eternal damnation. And, for the deserving of God's wrath, so exceedingly due, I must unceasingly give thanks to the mercy of God, asking also that the same delay of punishment cause not His plague to be more severe, since mine own conscience condemns my former doings.

But His mercy exceeds all iniquity. And, if I should not thus hope: where should I seek refuge and comfort? No mortal man has power to help me; and, for the multitude of my sins, I dare not lift my eyes to heaven where the seat of judgment is. I have so much offended God. What, shall I fall in desperation?

No! I will call upon Christ, the Light of the world, the fountain of life, the relief of all the weary, and the peacemaker between God and man, and the only health and comfort of all true repentant sinners. He can, by His almighty power, save me and deliver me out of this miserable condition. He desires, by His mercy, to save even the entire sin of the world[22]. I have no hope nor confidence in any creature, neither in heaven nor earth, but in Christ, my total and only Saviour.

He came into the world to save sinners, and to heal them that are sick; for He said, 'The healthy have no need of a physician.'[23] Behold, Lord, how I come to You: a sinner, sick and grievously wounded. I am not asking for bread, but for the crumbs that fall from the children's table.[24] Cast me not out of Your presence,[25] although I deserve to be cast into hell fire.

If I should look upon my sins, and not upon Your mercy, I should despair. For in myself I find nothing to save me, but a dunghill of wickedness to condemn me. If I should hope, that by mine own strength and power, to come out of this maze of iniquity and wickedness wherein I have walked for so long, I should be deceived. For I am so ignorant, blind, weak, and feeble that I cannot bring myself out of this entangled and wayward maze. The more I seek means and ways to wind myself out of it, the more I am wrapped and entangled in it. So, I perceive my struggling to be a hindrance, and my travail to be labour spent in vain.

It is the hand of the Lord. that can and will bring me out of this endless maze of death; for, without the grace of the Lord that comes before, I cannot ask forgiveness for my sins, nor be repentant or sorry for them. There is no man who can confess that Christ is the only Saviour of the world, but by the Holy Spirit: yes, as Saint Paul says, 'No man can say 'Jesus Christ is Lord!' but by the Holy Spirit.'[26] 'The Spirit helps our infirmities, and makes continual intercession for us, with such sorrowful groanings as cannot be expressed.'[27]

Therefore, I will first require and pray to the Lord to give me His Holy Spirit: to teach me to confess that Christ is the Saviour of the world, and to utter these words, 'Jesus Christ is Lord,' and finally, to help mine infirmities, and to intercede for me. For I am most certain and sure, that no creature in heaven nor earth is of power, or can by any mean help me, but God, who is omnipotent, almighty, beneficial, and merciful, willing to help, and loving to all those who call, and put their whole confidence and trust in Him. Therefore, I will seek none other means nor advocate, but Christ's Holy Spirit, who is the only Advocate and Mediator between God and man, to help and relieve me.

Chapter Three
What true faith works in the heart of a sinner

But, now, what makes me so bold and strong, to presume to come to the Lord with such audacity and boldness, being so great a sinner? Truly, nothing but His own Word: for He says, 'Come to me all you that labour, and are burdened, and I shall refresh you.'[28] What gentle, merciful, and comfortable words these are to all sinners! What a most gracious, comfortable, and gentle saying, with such pleasant and sweet words to allure His enemies to come to Him! Is there any worldly prince or magistrate that would show such clemency and mercy to their disobedient and rebellious subjects, having offended them? I suppose they would not with such words allure them, unless to entice them whom they cannot capture, and punish them. But even as Christ is Prince of Princes and Lord of Lords, so His charity and mercy surmounts all others.

Christ says, 'If earthly fathers give good gifts to their children when they ask them, how much more shall your heavenly Father, being in substance holy and gracious, give good gifts to all those who ask Him?'[29] It is no small nor little gift that I require, neither do I think I am worthy to receive such a noble gift, being so ingrate, unkind, and wicked a child. But when I behold the kindliness, liberality, mercy, and goodness of the Lord, I am encouraged, emboldened, and stirred to ask for such a noble gift. The Lord is so bountiful and liberal that He will not allow us to be satisfied and contented with just one gift, nor to ask simple and small gifts.

Therefore, he promises and binds Himself to His Word, to give good and beneficial gifts to all them that ask Him with true faith: without which, nothing can be done acceptable or pleasing to God.[30] For faith is the foundation and ground of all other gifts, virtues, and graces. Therefore, I will say: 'Lord, increase my faith.'[31] For this is the life everlasting, Lord, that I must believe You to be the true God, and Jesus Christ whom You did send.[32] By this faith I am assured; and by this assurance, I feel the remission of my sins. This makes me bold. This comforts me. This quenches all despair. I know, O my Lord, Your eyes look upon my faith.

Saint Paul says we are justified by faith in Christ, and not by the deeds of the law.[33] For if righteousness came by the law, then Christ died in vain.[34] Saint Paul means not a dead, human, historical faith, gotten by human effort, but a supernatural, living faith which works by love, as he himself plainly states.[35]

This esteem of faith does not disparage good works, for out of this faith springs all good works. Yet, we may not impute to the worthiness of faith or good works our justification before God; but ascribe and give the worthiness of it totally to the merits of Christ's passion; and declare and attribute the knowledge and perception of those merits to faith alone. The very true and only property of faith is to take, apprehend, and hold fast the promises of God's mercy, which makes us righteous; and causes me to continually hope for the same mercy; and, in love, to do the many good works ascribed in the Scripture, that I may be thankful for the same.

Thus, I feel myself to come, as it were, in a new garment before God; and now, by His mercy, to be declared just and righteous: which before, without His mercy, was sinful and wicked; and by faith to obtain his mercy, which the unfaithful cannot enjoy. And although Saint John extolls love in his epistle, saying that God is love,[36] and He that dwells in love dwells in God:[37] truly, love makes men live like angels; and makes meek lambs out of the most furious, unbridled, and carnal men.

Yes, with how fervent a spirit should I call, cry, and pray to the Lord, to make His great love burn and flame in my heart, being so stony and evil affected, that it never would conceive nor regard the great, inestimable charity and love of God in sending His only-begotten and dear-beloved Son into this vale of misery,[38] to suffer the most cruel and sharp death of the cross for my redemption?

Yet, I never had this unspeakable and abundant love of God properly printed and fixed in my heart until it pleased God, of His simple grace, mercy, and pity, to open my eyes, making me see and behold Christ crucified to be my only Saviour and Redeemer. For then I began (and not before) to perceive and see my own ignorance and blindness because I would not learn to know Christ, my Saviour and Redeemer. But when God, of His simple goodness, had thus opened mine eyes,[39] and made me see and behold Christ, the wisdom of God, the Light of the world, through the supernatural eyes of faith: all pleasures, vanities, honour, riches, wealth, and supports of the world began to taste bitter to me.

Then I knew, when such benefits came, that it was no illusion of the devil, nor false nor human doctrine that I had received. What I formerly loved and esteemed, (even though God had forbidden us to love the world and the vain pleasures and shadows of the world[40]), I now detested. Then I began to understand that Christ was my only Saviour and Redeemer, and this same teaching to be completely divine, holy, and heavenly, infused by grace into the hearts of the faithful. This never can be attained by human doctrine nor foolish reason, although they should struggle and work for the same until the end of the world. Then I began to dwell in God by love, knowing that by the loving charity of God, through the remission of my sins, that God is love, as Saint John declares.

I do not take lightly my faith whereby I came to know God, and whereby it pleased God to justify me because I trusted in Him. But many will wonder and marvel at my statement that I never knew Christ as my Saviour and Redeemer until this time. For many have this opinion, saying, 'Who doesn't know there is a Christ? Who, being a Christian, does not confess Him as his Saviour?' And, thus they believe that their dead, human, historical faith and knowledge (which they have learned in their scholastic books) and may be had with all sin (as I said before), to be the true, infused faith and knowledge of Christ. Thus, they say that by their own experience of themselves, that their faith does not justify them. And true it is, except they have this faith, which I have described before, they shall never be justified.

Yet, it is true that, by faith alone, I am sure to be justified. This being true, many impugn this office and function of true faith because so many lack true faith. As the faithful are compelled to allow true faith, so the unfaithful can in no way claim the same. The one, feeling in himself what he claims to be true; the other, has nothing in himself to claim. I have, certainly, no special learning to completely defend this matter, but a simple zeal and earnest love for the truth, inspired by God, who promises to pour His Spirit upon all flesh: which I have, by the grace of God, whom I most humbly honour, felt in myself to be true.

Chapter Four
God's love shown in Christ-crucified

Let us therefore, now, I pray you, by faith, behold and consider the great goodness of God, in sending His Son to suffer death for our redemption when we were His mortal enemies; and after what sort and manner He sent Him.

First it is to be considered, yes, to be undoubtedly believed with a mature faith, that God sent Him to us freely: for He did give Him, and not sell Him. A more noble and rich gift He could not have given. He sent not a servant, or a friend, but His Only Son, so dearly beloved: not in delights, riches, and honours, but in crosses, poverties, and slanders; not as a lord, but as a servant. Yes, in the most vile and painful passions, to wash us: not with water, but with His own precious blood; not from dirt, but from the puddle and filth of our iniquities. He has given Him, not to make us poor, but to enrich us with His divine virtues, merits, and graces:[41] yes, and in Him, He has given us all good things, and, finally, Himself, and with such great love as cannot be expressed.

Was it not a most high and abundant love of God, to send Christ to shed His blood, to lose honour, life, and all, for His enemies? Even at the time when we had done Him the most injury,[42] He first showed His love to us, with such flames of love, that greater could not be shown. God in Christ has opened to us (although we be weak and blind of ourselves) that we may behold, in this miserable state, the great wisdom, goodness, and truth, with all the other godly perfections, which are in Christ.

Therefore, inwardly to behold Christ crucified upon the cross is our best and godliest meditation. We may also see in Christ crucified, the beauty of the soul, better than in all the books of the world. For who, with living faith, sees and feels in spirit that Christ, the Son of God, is dead for the satisfying and the purifying of the soul, shall see that his soul is appointed for the very tabernacle and mansion of the inestimable and incomprehensible majesty and honour of God.

We see also, in Christ crucified, how vain and foolish the world is;[43] and how Christ, being most wise, despised the same. We see also how blind it is; because the world knows not Christ but persecuted Him. We also see how unkind the world is, by killing Christ, at the time He showed it the most favour. How hard and obstinate was it, that would not be appeased with so many tears, such sweat, and so much bloodshed of the Son of God, suffering with so great and lofty love? Therefore, he is very blind who does not see how vain, foolish, false, ingrate, cruel, hard, wicked, and evil the world is.

We may also, in Christ crucified, weigh our sins as in a divine balance: how grievous and how weighty they are, seeing they have crucified Christ. They would never have been counterbalanced, but with the great and precious weight of the blood of the Son of God. And therefore God, of His great goodness, determined that His Blessed Son should rather suffer bloodshed than our sins should have condemned us. We shall never know our own misery and wretchedness, but with the light of Christ crucified. Then, when we feel his mercy, we shall see our own cruelty; when we see his righteousness and holiness, we see our own unrighteousness and iniquity.

Therefore, to learn to know truly our own sins is to study the book of the crucifix, by continual discussion in faith. To have perfect and plentiful love is to learn first, by faith, the love that God has towards us. We may see also, in Christ upon the cross, how great the pains of hell and how blessed the joys of heaven are; and what a sharp, painful thing it will be for those who are deprived of that sweet, happy and glorious joy.

Then this crucifix is the book, wherein God has included all things, and has most concisely written therein, all truth profitable and necessary for our salvation. Therefore, let us endeavour ourselves to study this book, that we, being enlightened with the Spirit of God, may give Him thanks for so great a benefit.

Chapter Five
Christ's great victory over His enemies

If we look further in this book, we shall see Christ's great victory upon the cross: which was so noble and mighty, that there never was, neither shall there ever be such victory. If the victory and glory of worldly princes were great, because they did overcome great hosts of men, how much more was Christ's greater, which vanquished not only the prince of the world, but all the enemies of God: triumphing over persecution, injuries, villainies, slanders, yes, death, the world, sin, and the devil; and brought to confusion all carnal wisdom.[44]

The princes of the world never fight without the strength of the world. Christ, contrarily, went to war, even against all the strength of the world. He would fight, as David did with Goliath, unarmed of all human wisdom and strategy, and without all worldly power and strength. Nevertheless, He was fully replenished and armed with the whole armour of the Spirit.[45] And in this one battle, he overcame, forever, all His enemies. There was never so glorious a spoil, neither a more rich and noble one, than Christ was upon the cross: which delivered all His elect from such a sharp, miserable captivity. He had, in this battle, many stripes, yes, and lost His life; but His victory was so much greater. Therefore, when we look upon the Son of God with a supernatural faith and light, so unarmed, naked, given up, and alone; with humility, patience, liberality, modesty, gentleness, and with the other of His divine virtues; beating down to the ground all God's enemies, and making the soul of man so fair and beautiful: I am forced to say that His victory and triumph was marvellous. And therefore, Christ deserved to have this noble title: 'Jesus of Nazareth, King of the Jews.'[46]

But if we will specifically unfold and see His great victories, let us first behold how He overcame sin with His innocence, and confounded pride with His humility, quenched all worldly love with His love, appeased the wrath of His Father with His meekness, turned hatred into love with His so many benefits and godly zeal.

Christ has not only overcome sin, but rather He has killed the same: since He has made satisfaction for it Himself, with the most holy sacrifice and offering of His precious body, in suffering most bitter and cruel death. Also, He gives to all those who love Him, so much spirit, grace, virtue, and strength, that they may resist, impugn, and overcome sin, and not consent, neither allow it to reign in them. He has also vanquished sin, because He has taken away the power of sin: that is, He has cancelled the law,[47] which was, in evil men, the occasion of sin. Therefore, sin has no power against them, who are by the Holy Spirit united to Christ; in them there is nothing worthy of damnation. And although the dregs of Adam do remain, that is, our desires of the flesh, which indeed are sins: nevertheless, they are not imputed as sins, if we are truly joined to Christ. It is true that Christ might have taken away all our immoderate affections, but He has left them for the greater glory of His Father, and for His own greater triumph. For example: When a prince, fighting with his enemies which had sometime ruled over his people, and subduing them, may kill them if he will, yet he preserves and saves them. And whereas they were lords over his people, he now makes them serve those whom they had ruled.

Now, in such a case, the prince does show himself a greater conqueror, in that he has made them to obey, who were rulers; and their subjects who served them, to be lords over them, than if he had utterly destroyed them in the conquest. For, now, he leaves continual victory to those he redeemed: whereas, if the opportunity for victory was taken away, none would remain to be the subjects. Even so, in like case, Christ has left in us these desires of the flesh, to the intent they should help us to exercise our virtues, where first they did reign over us, to the exercise of our sin. And it may be plainly seen that, whereas first they were such impediments to us, that we could not move ourselves towards God: now by Christ we have so much strength that, notwithstanding the force of them, we may assuredly walk to heaven. And although the children of God sometime do fall by frailty into some sin, yet that falling causes them to humble themselves, and to acknowledge the goodness of God, and to come to Him for refuge and help.[48]

Likewise, Christ, with His death, has overcome the prince of devils with all his host, and has destroyed them all. For, as Paul says: This is verified, that Christ should break the serpent's head, prophesied by God.[49] Although the devil tempts us, yet if by faith we are joined to Christ, we shall not perish; but rather, by his temptation, take great force and might. So, it is evident that the triumph, victory, and glory of Christ is the greater, having subdued the devil that, whereas he was prince and lord of the world, holding all creatures in captivity, now Christ uses him as an instrument to punish the wicked, and to exercise and strengthen the elect of God in Christian warfare.[50]

Christ likewise has overcome death in a more glorious manner (if it be possible), because He has not taken it away, but leaving universally all subject to the same fate. He has given so much virtue and spirit that, whereas before we passed through death with great fear, now we are bold, through the Spirit, for the sure hope of resurrection, that we receive it with joy. It is now no more bitter, but sweet; no more feared, but desired. It is not death, but life.[51]

And, also, it has pleased God that the infirmities and adversities do remain in the sight of the world; but the children of God are, by Christ, made so strong, righteous, whole and sound, that the troubles of the world are comforts of the spirit; the passions of the flesh are medicines of the soul. For all manner of things work to their service and good;[52] for they in spirit feel that God, their Father, doth govern them, and arranges all things for their benefit; therefore, they feel themselves secure. In persecution, they are quiet and peaceful; in time of trouble, they are without weariness, fears, anxieties, suspicions, miseries; and finally, all the good and evil of the world works to their service.

Moreover, they see that the triumph of Christ has been so great, that not only has He subdued and vanquished all our enemies and the power of them, but He has overthrown and vanquished them in such a manner that all things serve to our well-being. He might and could have taken them all away, but where, then, should have been our victory, palm, and crown? For we daily have struggles in the flesh, and, by the support of grace, have continual victories over sin, giving us cause to glorify God that, by His Son, He has weakened our enemy the devil and, by His Spirit, gives us strength to vanquish his offspring.[53]

So, we acknowledge daily the great triumph of our Saviour, and rejoice in our own wonders, which we can in no way impute to any wisdom of this world whereby sin increases. And where worldly wisdom governs most, there sin rules most. For as the world is the enemy of God, so also the wisdom of the world is against God. Christ has declared and exposed the wisdom of the world as foolishness.[54] And although He could have taken away all worldly wisdom, yet He has left it for His greater glory, and triumph of His chosen vessels.

For before, the world was our ruler against God, now, by Christ, we are served by it for God. While still a slave in worldly things; this is not the case when considering supernatural things. If any time men would oppose and contradict us with the wisdom of the world, yet we have, in Christ, so much supernatural light of the truth, that we make a mockery of all those who oppose the truth. Christ, also, upon the cross, has triumphed over the world. First, because He has discovered the world to be nothing: that whereas it was covered by the veil of hypocrisy and the garment of moral virtues, Christ has showed that, in God's sight, the righteousness of the world is wickedness; and He has borne witness that the works of men, not regenerated by Him in faith, are evil. And so, Christ has judged and condemned the world as nothing.

Furthermore, He has given to all His, so much light and spirit, that they know it, and disapprove the same: yes, and tread it under their feet, with all vain honours, dignities, and pleasures, not accepting the fair promises, nor the offers it presents. No, they rather scorn them. And, as for the threats and might of the world, they have nothing to fear.

Now, therefore, we may see how great the victory and triumph of Christ is, who has delivered all those the Father gave Him from the power of the devil, cancelling, upon the cross, the writing of our debts.[55] For He has delivered us from the condemnation of sin, from the bondage of the law, from the fear of death, from the danger of the world, and from all evils in this life, and in the world to come. And He has enriched us, made us noble and most highly happy, so tongues cannot express such a glorious and triumphant way. Therefore, we are forced to say: 'His triumph is marvellous!'

It is also seen and known that Christ is the true Messiah, for He has delivered man from all evils; and through Him, man has all goodness, so that He is the true Messiah. Therefore, all other helpers are vain and counterfeit saviours, seeing that, by this our Messiah, Christ, completely and only, we are delivered from all evils and, in Him, we have all goodness. It is evident and clear that this is true, because the true Christian is a Christian by Christ. And the true Christian senses inwardly, through Christ, so much goodness of God, that even troublesome life and death are sweet to him, and miseries, happy. The true Christian, through Christ, is unburdened: from the servitude of the law, having the law of grace (graven by the Spirit) inhabiting his heart, and from sin that reigned in him, from the power of the demonic spirits, from damnation, and from every evil; and is made a son of God, a brother of Christ, heir of heaven, and lord of the world. So that in Christ, and through Christ, he possesses all good things.

And know that Christ still fights in spirit in His elect vessels and shall fight even to the day of judgment. At which day shall the great enemy, death, be wholly destroyed,[56] and shall be no more. Then shall the children of God rejoice in Him, saying: 'O death, where is thy victory and sting?'[57] There shall be, then, no more trouble nor sin, no evil: but heaven for the good, and hell for the wicked. Then the victory of triumph of Christ shall be fully discovered: who (according to Paul) shall present to His Father the kingdom, together with His chosen, saved by Him.[58] It was no little favour towards His children, that Christ was chosen of God to save us, His elect, so exceedingly, by the way of the cross. Paul calls it a grace, and a most singular grace.

We may well think that He, having been to the world so valiant a captain of God, was full of light, grace, virtue, and spirit. Therefore, He might justly say: 'It is finished!' We, seeing then that the triumph and victory of our captain Christ is so marvellous, glorious, and noble and to the battle we are appointed: let us force ourselves to follow Him, by bearing our cross, that we may have fellowship with Him in His kingdom.

Chapter Six
Meditating upon the 'Book of the Crucifix'

It is most justly true that to behold Christ crucified, in spirit, is the best meditation that can be. I certainly never knew my own miseries and contentions so well, by reading books, receiving admonition, or correction, as I have done by considering the spiritual book of the crucifix. I greatly lament that I have passed so many years not regarding that divine book, but I judged and thought myself to be well instructed in the same: whereas now I am of this opinion, that if God would allow me to live here for thousand years, and I should study continually in the same divine book, I would not complete the contemplation of it.

Nor am I contented, but always have a great desire to learn and study more. I never knew my own wickedness, neither truly lamented for my sins until the time that God inspired me with His grace, that I looked in this book of the crucifix. Then I began to see perfectly, that my own power and strength could not help me, and that I was in the Lord's hand: even as the clay is in the potter's hand. Then I began to cry, and say: 'Alas, Lord, I have so wickedly offended You, and You have been to me from the beginning so gracious and so good a Father, and most especially, now you have declared and showed Your goodness to me when, in the time I have done You the most injury, to call me, and to make me to know and take You for my Saviour and Redeemer.'

Such are the wonderful works of God, to call sinners to repentance, and to have them receive Christ, His well-beloved Son, as their Saviour. This is the gift of God for all Christians to require and desire. For, unless this great benefit of Christ crucified is felt and fixed surely in man's heart, there can be no good work done, acceptable before God. For in Christ is all fullness of the Godhead[59] and in Him are hid all the treasures of wisdom and knowledge.[60] He is the water of life, whereof whosoever shall drink, shall never thirst; but it shall be in him a well of water, springing up into everlasting life.[61] Saint Paul says there is no condemnation to them who are in Christ, who walk not after the flesh, but after the spirit.[62] Moreover, he says: 'If when we were enemies, we were reconciled to God by the death of His Son, how much more, being reconciled, we shall be preserved by His death.'[63] It is no little or small benefit we have received by Christ, if we consider what He has done for us, as I have now perfectly declared.

Wherefore, I pray the Lord that this great benefit of Christ crucified may be steadfastly fixed and printed in all Christian hearts, that they may be true lovers of God, and work as children, for love, and not as servants, compelled with threats or incited with hire. The sincere and pure lovers of God do embrace Christ with such fervency of spirit, that they rejoice in hope, are bold in danger, suffer in adversity, continue in prayer, bless their persecutors; further, they are not wise in their own opinion, neither high-minded in their prosperity, neither ashamed in their adversity, but humble and gentle, always, to all men. For they know that by their faith they are all members of one body, and they have possessed all, one God, one faith, one baptism[64], one joy, and one salvation.

If these pure and sincere lovers of God were abundantly sown, there would not be so much contention and strife growing in the fields of our religion, as there is. Well, I shall pray to the Lord to take all contention and strife away, and that the sowers of sedition may have mind to cease their labour, or to sow it among the stones; and to have grace to sow gracious virtues, where they may both root and bring forth fruit, sending a godly unity and concord among all Christians, that we may serve the Lord in true holiness of life.

Chapter Seven
The miserable ignorance and blindness of humanity

The example of good living is required of all Christians, but especially for the ecclesiastical pastors, and shepherds: for they are called in Scripture, workers with God, disbursers of God's mysteries, the light of the world, the salt of the earth, at whose hands all others should take comfort, in the working knowledge of God's will, and purpose, to become children of the light, and taste of appropriate wisdom. They have, or should have, the Holy Spirit abundantly, to pronounce and set forth the Word of God, in clarity and truth. If ignorance and blindness reign among us, they should, with the truth of God's Word, instruct and set before us the truth, and direct us in the way of the Lord.

But thank the Lord, who has now sent us such a godly and learned king, in these latter days, to reign over us: that, with the virtue and force of God's Word, he has taken away the veils and mists of errors, and brought us to the knowledge of the truth by the light of God's Word, which was so long hidden and kept suppressed, that the people were nearly famished and hungered for lack of spiritual food. Such was the charity of the spiritual clergy, and shepherds. But our Moses, and most godly, wise governor and king, has delivered us out of the captivity and bondage of Pharaoh.

By Moses, I mean King Henry the eighth, my most sovereign, favourable lord and husband: who, through the excellent grace of God, is suitable to be an expressed picture of Moses' conquest over Pharaoh. And by Pharaoh, I mean the Bishop of Rome, who has been and is a greater persecutor of all true Christians than ever was Pharaoh of the children of Israel.[65]

For he is a persecutor of the Gospel and grace, a promoter of all superstition and counterfeit holiness, bringing many souls to hell with his alchemy[66] and counterfeit money, deceiving the poor souls under the pretence of holiness; but so much the greater shall be his damnation, because he deceives and robs under Christ's mantle.

The Lord keep and defend all men from his juggling and craftiness, but specially the poor, simple, unlearned souls. And this lesson I wish all men had of him, that when they begin to dislike his doing, only then they begin to like God, and certainly not before.

As for the spiritual pastors, and shepherds, I think they will cling and hold fast to the Word of God, even to death, to vanquish all God's enemies. If need requires, to lay aside all respects of honour, dignity, riches, wealth, and their private possessions, following also the examples of Christ and His chosen apostles, in preaching and teaching sincere, pure, and wholesome doctrine, and such things as make for peace, with godly lessons, wherewith they may edify others: that every man may walk after his vocation, in holiness of life, in unity and concord. Such unity is to be desired for all true Christians.

It is much to be lamented: the schisms, diversities, contentions, and disputations that have been, and are, in the world about the

Christian religion. There is no agreement or unity among the learned men. Truly, the devil has been the sower of sedition, and shall be the maintainer of it, even till God's will is fulfilled. There is no war so cruel and evil as this: for the war with swords kills only the bodies, but this war destroys many souls.

For the poor, unlearned people remain confused, and almost everyone believes and goes his own way, and yet there is but one truth of God's Word, by which we shall be saved. Happy are they who receive it; and most unhappy are they who neglect and persecute it. For it shall be easier for Sodom and Gomorrah at the day of judgment, than for them. And not without just cause, if we consider the benevolence, goodness, and mercy of God: who hath declared His love toward us, greater and more laudable, than He ever did to the Hebrews. For they lived under shadows and figures and were bound to the law. And Christ has delivered us from the bondage of the law and has fulfilled all that was prefigured in their law, and in their prophets: shedding His own precious blood to make us the children of His Father, and His brethren. He has made us free, setting us in a godly liberty. Of course, I do not mean license to sin, as many gladly interpret when the subject of Christian liberty is discussed.

Truly, it is not a good spirit that causes men to find fault with everything; and when issues are properly presented, to pervert them into an evil sense and meaning. There are in the world many speakers of holiness and good works; but very rarely and seldom is it declared what those good and holy works are. The fruit of the Spirit is almost never spoken of. Therefore, very few know what they are.

I am truly able to justify the great ignorance of the people: not in this matter alone, but in many others, which are very necessary for Christians to know, because I have much evidence of this. It causes me great sorrow and grief in my heart to speak of such a miserable ignorance and blindness among the people. Certainly, we all can say, 'Lord, Lord.'[67] But I fear that God may say to us: 'This people honours me with their lips, but their hearts are far from me.'[68] God desires nothing but the heart and says that

He will be worshipped in spirit and in truth.[69] Christ condemned all hypocrisy and false holiness, and taught sincere, pure, and true godliness. But we, worse than demented or blind, will not follow Christ's doctrine, but trust in men's doctrines, judgments, and sayings, which dim our eyes: and so, the blind leads the blind, and both fall into the ditch.[70] Truly, in my simple and unlearned judgment, no man's doctrine is to be esteemed, or preferred to Christ's and the Apostles', nor to be taught as a perfect and true doctrine, but only as it does agree with the doctrine of the Gospel.

Those who are called spiritual pastors, even though they are most carnal as is evident and clear by their fruits, are so blinded with the love of themselves and the world, that they extol men's inventions and doctrines before the doctrine of the Gospel. And when they are not able to maintain their own inventions and doctrine with any jot of the Scripture, they cruelly persecute those who don't agree with them. Are such the lovers of Christ? No! No! They are the lovers of wicked Mammon, neither regarding God nor His honour. For filthy lucre[71] has undoubtedly made them nearly mad. This miserable state of spiritual men in the world is to be greatly lamented by all sincere Christians. Yet, I cannot permit nor praise all kinds of complaints, but such as may stand with Christian love.

Chapter Eight
The fruits of true Christianity

Love suffers long, and is gentle; does not envy, chastises no man, does not throw man's faults in his teeth, but refers all things to God:[72] being angry without sin[73], reforming others without slanders, ever bearing a storehouse of mild words to pierce the stonyhearted.

I wish all Christians, that as they have professed Christ, would so endeavour to follow Him in godly living. For we have not put on Christ to live any more to ourselves, in the vanities, delights, and pleasures of the world and the flesh, permitting the desires and carnality of the flesh to have full sway. For we must walk after the

Spirit, and not after the flesh. For the Spirit is spiritual, and desires spiritual things, and the flesh carnal, and desires carnal things.[74] Those regenerate in Christ despise the world, and all the vanities and pleasures of the world.[75]

They are not lovers of themselves, for they feel how evil and weak they are, not able to do any good thing without the help of God, from whom they acknowledge all good things to proceed. They do not flatter themselves and think that everything that shines in the world is good and holy, for they know that all external and outward works that are not so glorious and fair to the world, may still be prompted by evil as well as of good. Therefore, they have very little estimate for the outward show of holiness, because they are spiritual, casting their eyes upon heavenly things and neither looking nor regarding the earthly things for they are to them vile and dismal.[76]

They have also the simplicity of the dove, and the strategy of the serpent.[77] They simply have a desire to do good to all men and to hurt no man, even though they may have opportunity. And in practice, they neither give nor minister any reason for any man to rebuke their doctrine. They also are not as a reed shaken with every wind.[78] When they are blasted with tempests and storms of the world, they remain firm, stable, and quiet, feeling in spirit that God, as their best Father, does send and allow all things for their benefit and service. Christ is to them a rule, a line, an example of the Christian life. They are never offended at anything, although occasion arises.

For like as Christ, when Peter tried to dissuade Him from going to his death, answered and said, 'Go back from me, Satan,[79] for you are offensive. As much as possible, you give me occasion with your words to make me withdraw myself from death, although I do not yield. For you cannot extinguish the burning desire I have to shed My blood for My chosen.'

Even so, the mature Christians are never offended at anything. For although the world was full of sin, they would not withdraw themselves from doing good, nor wax cold in the love of the Lord. And much less would they be moved to be evil; yes, rather they are so much more moved to do good.

The regenerated by Christ are never offended at the works of God, because they know by faith that God does all things well, and that He cannot err, neither for lack of power, nor by ignorance, nor malice. For they know Him to be almighty, and that He sees all things, and is most abundantly good. They see and feel in spirit that out of the highest perfect will, cannot but proceed most perfect works.

Likewise, they are not offended by the works of men: for, if those works are good, they are moved by them to take opportunity to follow them, and to acknowledge the goodness of God, while giving thanks and daily praising His name. But if the works of men are indifferent and may be done with either good or evil intention, they judge the best part, thinking they may be done for a good purpose, and so, they are edified. But if those works of men are so evil that they cannot in any way be taken as good, yet they are not offended, although they very well could be. No, rather they are edified, using the occasion to bear fruit, although the opposite is presented to them. Then they begin to think and say: 'If God had not preserved me with His grace, I should have committed this sin, and worse. O how much am I bound to confess and acknowledge the goodness of God!'

They also further think and say: 'He that has sinned may be one of God's elect; perhaps the Lord has allowed him to fall so that he may know himself better. I know he is one of them for whom Christ has shed His blood, and one of my Christian brethren. Truly I will admonish and rebuke him; and in case I find him desperate, I will comfort him and show him the great goodness and mercy of God, in Christ; and with godly consolations I will see if I can lift him up again.' So, you see how those regenerated by Christ, in all matters win and receive fruits.

Chapter Nine
The fruits of unfaithfulness, and the offense of the weak

On the other hand, the ignorant and immature are offended at small trivialities, judging everything to be evil, grudging and murmuring against their neighbour; and, in addition, they demonstrate such fervency so that they judged by the blind world as being great zeal-bearers for God.

But this is not the greatest evil of the ignorant. I fear they are so blind and ignorant that they are also offended by good things, and judge nothing good but that which they accept and esteem to be good, murmuring against all who do not follow their ways.

If there are any like this, I pray that the Lord give them the light of His truth, that they may increase and grow in godly strength. I suppose if such ignorant and immature had seen Christ and His disciples eat meat with unwashed hands,[80] or not to have fasted with the Pharisees, they would have been offended, seeing Him a breaker of men's traditions. While their desires incline their eyes to see through other men, they see nothing in themselves. Love, on the other hand considers no one evil, but discreetly and properly interprets all actions, taking everything justly and honestly.

Now these superstitious weaklings, if they had known Christ, and saw the way he led His life, sometimes with women, sometimes with Samaritans, with publicans, sinners, and with the Pharisees, they would have murmured against Him. Also, if they had seen Mary pour the precious ointment on Christ, they would have said with Judas: 'This ointment could have been sold and given to the poor.'[81] If they also had seen Christ with whips[82] drive out of the Temple those who bought and sold, they would have immediately judged Christ to have been anxious and moved with anger, and not by zealous love. How they would have been offended, if they had seen Him going to the Jews' feast, heal a sick man on the Sabbath day,[83] converse with the woman of Samaria,[84] yes, and show her His most divine teaching and life. They would have taken the opportunity to hate and persecute Him, as did the scribes and Pharisees. Christ, the Saviour of the world, would have been offensive and destructive to them.

There is another type of the ignorant and immature who are offended in this manner: when they see someone, who is considered and esteemed to be holy, commit sin, immediately they learn to do the same, and worse. They grow cold in doing good and confirm themselves in evil.

And then they excuse their wicked life by revealing the sin of their neighbour and thereby slander him. If any man corrects them, they say: 'Such a man did this, and worse.' So, it is evident that such individuals would deny Christ, if they saw others do the same.

If they went to Rome and saw the abominations of the priests, which is reported to reign among them, and they saw one sin who was reputed and assumed to be holy, their faith would be lost: but not the true faith in Christ which they never possessed. But they would lose the human opinion they had of the goodness of the priests. For if they had faith in Christ, the Holy Spirit, who would be mighty in them, would witness to them, that in case all the world would deny Christ, they would remain firm and stable in the true faith.

The Pharisees also took opportunity by the evil of others to grow haughty and proud, taking themselves to be men of greater perfection than any other because of their virtue, as they did when they saw the publican's confession. And so, they are offended with every little thing, judging evil, murmuring against their neighbour; and, for that reason, they are reputed by many as being more holy and good, but, indeed, they are more wicked.

The most wicked persons are offended even at themselves; for at their little stability in goodness, and of their detestable and evil life, they take occasion to despair. They should instead commit themselves more to God, asking mercy for their offenses, and immediately giving thanks, that it hath pleased God, out of His goodness, to put up with them for such a long time.

But what more can be said? The evil men are even offended at the works Of God. They see God put up with sinners. Therefore, they think that sin does not displease Him. And because they see that the good are not rewarded with riches, they often imagine that God does not love them. It seems to them God is partial, because He hath elected some, and some reproved. They use that as an occasion to do evil saying, 'Whatsoever God hath determined, shall take place'

If they also see the good men oppressed, and the evil men exalted, they judge God unjust, taking occasion to do evil, saying:

'Since God favours the evil men, let us do evil enough, so that He does us good.' If, then, the wicked be offended even at God, it is no wonder if they are offended by those who follow and walk in His paths and ways.

Chapter Ten
Slandering the Word of God

Now I will speak, with great sadness and heaviness in my heart, of a sort of people who are in the world, that are called 'professors of the Gospel' and by their words declare and show, they are deeply affected by the same. But I am afraid, some of them have built upon the sand, as Simon Magus[85] did, making a weak foundation. I mean, they don't make Christ their chief foundation, professing His doctrine out of a sincere, pure, and zealous mind. Either, because they are called 'gospellers,' they seek to gain some credit and good opinions from the sincere and appreciative of Christ's doctrine, or to find out some fleshly liberty, or to be contentious disputers, finders, or rebukers of other men's faults, or else, finally, to please and flatter the world. Such 'gospellers' are an offense and a slander to the Word of God, and make the wicked rejoice and laugh at them, saying: 'Behold, I pray you, their fair fruits. What love, what discretion, what godliness, holiness, or purity of life is amongst them? Be they not great avengers, foul gluttons, slanderers, backbiters, adulterers, fornicators, swearers, and blasphemers?'

Yes, they stagger and tumble in all these sins; these are the fruits of their doctrine. And thus, it is seen how the Word of God is spoken of as evil, through licentious and evil living.

And yet the Word of God is all holy, pure, sincere, and godly, being the teaching and motivation for all holy and pure living. It is the wicked who pervert all good things into evil, for an evil tree cannot bring forth good fruit. And when good seed is sown in a barren and evil ground, it yields no good crop, and so it is with the Word of God. For when it is heard and known of wicked men, it brings forth no good fruit; but when it is sown in good ground, I mean the hearts of good people, it brings forth good fruit abundantly:[86] so that the lack and fault is in men, and not in the Word of God.

I pray God that all men and women may have grace to become good ground for the fruits of the Gospel, and to only forsake all the wrangling over it. For only speaking of the Gospel does not make men good Christians, but merely good talkers, unless their facts and works agree with the same. Their speech is good, because their hearts are good.[87]

So much talk of the Word of God, without practicing the same in our living, is evil and detestable in the sight of God. It is lamentable to hear that there are many in the world who do not properly digest the reading of Scripture, and commend and praise ignorance, and say that much knowledge of God's Word is the origin of all dissension, schisms, and contention, and makes men haughty, proud, and presumptuous by reading of the same.

This manner of saying is no less than a plain blasphemy against the Holy Spirit. For the Spirit of God is the author of His Word, and so the Holy Spirit is made the author of evil: which is the greatest blasphemy and, as the Scripture says, a sin that shall not be forgiven in this world, neither in the one to come.[88]

All of us have the duty, to procure and seek all the ways and means possible, to have more knowledge of God's Word set forth abroad in this world, and to not allow ignorance, and opposition to the knowledge of God's Word to stop the mouths of the unlearned with subtle and crafty persuasions of philosophy and sophistry. This produces no fruit, but a great distress to the minds of the simple and ignorant because they will not know which way to turn.

It is an extreme wickedness to charge the holy, sanctified Word of God with the offenses of men, to allege the Scriptures to be perilous learning because certain readers fall into heresies. These men might be forced, by this kind of argument, to forsake the use of fire because fire burned their neighbour's house, or to abstain from meat or drink because they see many gluttons. O blind hate! They slander God for man's offense, and excuse the man who offends, and blame the Scripture, which they cannot improve.

Yes, I have heard of some who very well understood the Latin language who, when they have heard educated men persuade concerning the credit and belief of certain 'unwritten verities'[89] as they call them, which are not expressed in Scripture, and are yet taught as apostolic doctrine and necessary to be believed. They contend that educated men have more 'epistles' written by the apostles of Christ than we have in the canon of the Old and New Testament. These unwritten verities are only known by the clergy. I was greatly grieved to hear this and think that any person could have such a blind, ignorant opinion.

Some simple explanations are to be praised, but this simplicity, devoid of truth, I can neither praise nor condone. And thus, it may be seen how we who are unlettered remain confused, without God and His grace to lighten our hearts and minds with a heavenly light and knowledge of His will. For of ourselves, we are given to believe men more than God. I pray that God would send the Spirit of God abundantly to all learned men, that their doctrine may bring forth the fruits thereof.

I suppose there was never a greater need for good doctrine to be set forth in the world than in this age: for the carnal children of Adam are so wise in their generation that, if it were possible, they would deceive the children of light. The world loves his own, and therefore their facts and works are highly esteemed by the world. But the children of God are hated because they are not of the world. For their habitation is in heaven, and they despise the world as a most vile slave. The fleshly children of Adam are so political, subtle, crafty, and wise in their kind that the elect should be deluded, if it were possible. For in outer appearance, they are clothed with Christ's garment with a fair show of all godliness and holiness in their words. But they have so shorn, trimmed, and twisted Christ's garment and so disguised themselves, that the children of light, beholding them with a spiritual eye, account and take them for mere men who have sold their Master's garment, and have stolen a piece of every man's garment. Yet, by their subtle art and crafty wits, they have so put those patches and pieces together that they make the blind world and carnal men believe it is Christ's very mantle.

Chapter Eleven
The Virtues of God's Children

But the children of light know better. For they are led by the Spirit of God to the knowledge of the truth; and therefore, they discern and judge all things properly, and know from where they come: even from the bishop of Rome and his members, the chief source of all pride, vainglory, ambition, hypocrisy, and false holiness.

The children of God are not ashamed, although the world hate them. They believe they are in the grace and favour of God, and that He, as a best Father, does govern them in all things, putting away from them all vain confidence, and trust in their own doings. For they know, by themselves, they can do nothing but sin. They are not so foolish and childish, not to give God thanks for their election, which was before the beginning of the world.[90] For they believe most surely, they are of the chosen: for the Holy Spirit does witness to their spirit that they are the children of God, and therefore they believe God rather than man.[91] They say with Saint Paul: 'Who shall separate us from the love of God? Shall tribulation, anguish, persecution, hunger, nakedness, peril, or sword? As it is written: For Your sake, we are killed all day long, and are counted as sheep appointed to be slain. Nevertheless, in all these things, we overcome through Him that loveth us. For I am sure that neither death, nor life, nor angels, nor rule, neither power, neither things present, neither things to come, neither quantity or quality, neither any creature, shall be able to depart us from the love of God, which is in Christ Jesus our Lord.'[92]

They are not arrogantly inflamed by this godly faith, nor do they become loose, idle, or slow in doing godly works, rather, they are so much more fervent in doing most holy and pure works, which God has commanded them to walk in.[93] They wander not in men's traditions and inventions, leaving the most holy and pure precepts of God undone, which they know they are bound to observe and keep.

Also, they work not like hirelings for wages, or reward, but as loving children, without respect of money, gain, or position.

They are in such liberty of spirit, and joy so much in God, that their inward consolation cannot be expressed with tongue. All fear of damnation is gone from them, for they have put their whole hope of salvation in His hands, who will and can perform it. Neither have they any post or pillar to lean upon, but God and His smooth and unwrinkled Church.[94] For He is to them All in all things, and to Him they lean, as a most sure, square pillar, in prosperity and adversity, not doubting His promises and covenants, for they believe most certainly they shall be fulfilled.

Also, the children of God are not curious in searching the high mysteries of God, which are not proper for them to know. Neither do they go about with human and carnal reasons to interpret Scripture, persuading men, by their subtle wits and carnal doctrine, that much knowledge of Scripture makes men heretics, unless they dilute it with human doctrine, philosophy, and logic: and thus, be seduced according to the traditions of men, after the ordinances of the world, and not after Christ. Saint Paul does most diligently admonish us, which arts are not convenient and proper to rival Scripture.[95] For the Scriptures are so pure and holy that no perfection can be added to them. For even as fine gold doth excel all other metals, so doth the Word of God excel over all men's doctrines.

I ask the Lord to send the learned and unlearned such abundance of His Holy Spirit, that they may obey and observe the most sincere and holy Word of God. And show the fruits thereof, which consists chiefly in love and godly unity: that, as we have professed one God, one faith, and one baptism,[96] so we may be all of one mind and one accord, putting away all biting and gnawing; for, in backbiting, slandering, and misrepresenting our Christian brethren, we do not show ourselves to be the disciples of Christ, whom we profess.[97]

In Him was extraordinary love, humility, and patience, suffering most patiently all ignominy, rebukes, and slanders, praying to His Eternal Father for His enemies with most fervent love: and in all things, when He prayed on the Mount, did submit His will to His Father's.[98] A goodly example and lesson for us to follow in all times and seasons, as well as in prosperity as in adversity: to have no will but God's will, committing and leaving to Him all our cares and griefs, and to abandon all our strategies and inventions, for they are most vain and foolish, and, indeed, very shadows and daydreams.

But we are yet so carnal and fleshly that we come headlong, like unbridled colts, without bridle or bit. If we had the love of God printed in our hearts, it would hinder us from running astray. And until it please God to send us this bit to hold us in, we will never run in the right direction, although we may never speak and talk so much of God and His Word.

The true followers of Christ's teaching always have a respect and an eye to their vocation.

If they are called to the ministry of God's Word, they preach and teach it sincerely, to the edifying of others, and show themselves, in their living, followers of the same. If they are married men, having children and family, they nourish and bring them up, without bitterness and harshness, in the doctrine of the Lord; in all godliness and virtue, They commit the instruction of others, who are not under their care, to the improvement of God and His ministers, who are chiefly kings and princes, bearing the sword even for that purpose, to punish evildoers.

If they are children, they honour their father and mother, knowing it to be God's commandment, and that He has thereto attached a promise of long life.

If they are servants, they obey and serve their masters with all fear and reverence, even for the Lord's sake, neither with murmuring nor grudging, but with a free heart and mind.

If they are husbands, they love their wives as their own bodies, after the example as Christ loved the church, and gave Himself for it, to make it to Him a bride, without spot or wrinkle.[99]

If they are married women, they learn of Saint Paul, to be obedient to their husbands, and to keep silence in the congregation, and to learn from their husbands, at home.[100] Also, they wear such apparel as befits holiness and suitable usage, with soberness: not being accusers or detractors, not given too much to the eating of delicacies and drinking of wine. But they teach honest things, to make the young women sober-minded, to love their husbands, to love their children, to be discreet, chaste, domesticated, good, obedient unto their husbands, that the Word of God be not evil spoken of.

Truly, if all sorts of people would look to their own vocation, and order the same according to Christ's teaching, we should not have so many eyes and ears beholding other men's faults as we have. For we are so busy and glad to find and spy out other men's doings, that we forget and have no time to weigh and ponder our own: which we ought to first reform after the Word of God, and then we shall be better at helping another with the straw in his eyes.[101]

But, alas, we are so much given to love and to flatter ourselves, and so blinded with carnal affections, that we can see and perceive no fault in ourselves. And therefore, it is required and necessary for us, to pray with one heart and mind to God, to give us a heavenly light and knowledge of our own miseries and calamities, that we may truly see them and acknowledge them before Him.

Chapter Thirteen
Living changed lives

If any man shall be offended at this my lamenting the faults of men which are in the world, imagining that I do it either out of hatred or spite to any sort or kind of people: truly, in so doing, they do me a great wrong. For I thank God, by His grace, I hate no person; yes, I would say more, to give witness to my conscience, that neither life, honour, riches, nor whatsoever I possess here, which pertains to my own private possessions, be it never so dearly loved by me, that most willingly and gladly I would leave it, to win any man to Christ, of whatever degree or sort he was.

And yet this is nothing in comparison to the love that God hath shown me, in sending Christ to die for me: no, if I had all the love of angels and apostles, it should be but like a spark of fire compared to a great heap of burning coals. God knows my intentions and mind. I have lamented my own sins and faults to the world. I trust nobody will judge I have done it for praise or the thanks of any person, since rather I might be ashamed than rejoice in rehearsing them. For if they know how little I esteem and weigh the praise of the world, that opinion would soon be removed and taken away.

For I thank God, that by His grace, I know the world to be a blind judge, and the praises thereof vain and of little consequence, and therefore I seek not the praises of the same, neither to satisfy it in no other way than I am taught by Christ to do, according to Christian love.

I would to God we would all, when occasion arises, confess our faults to the world, laying aside all respect to our own position. But, alas, self-love so reigns among us that, as I have said before, we cannot spy our own faults. And if perhaps we should discover our own guilt, we either favourably interpret it as not being sin, or else we are ashamed to confess it. Yes, and we are badly offended and grieved to hear another tell us our faults in a lovingly and godly manner, making no distinction between a loving warning and malicious accusation.

Truly, if we sought God's glory, as we should do in all things, we should not be ashamed to confess ourselves as deviating from God's commands and ordinances, when it is obvious that we have done so, and, in fact, daily do.

I pray God our own faults and deeds condemn us not, at the last day, when every man shall be rewarded according to his doings. Truly, if we do not redress and amend our living, according to the teaching of the Gospel, we shall receive a terrible sentence by Christ, the Son of God, when He shall come to judge and condemn all transgressors and breakers of His precepts and commandments, and to reward all His obedient and loving children.

We shall have no lawyer to make a plea for us, neither can we have the day delayed; neither will the just Judge be corrupted with affection, bribes, or reward; neither will He hear any excuse or delay; neither shall this saint or that martyr help us, be they ever so holy; neither shall our ignorance save us from damnation. But, yet, wilful blindness and obstinate ignorance shall receive greater punishment, and not without just cause. Then shall it be known who has walked in the dark, for all things shall appear manifest before him. No man's deeds shall be hidden, no, neither words nor thoughts.

The poor and simple observers of God's commandments shall be rewarded with everlasting life, as obedient children to the heavenly Father. And the transgressors, adders and diminishers of the law of God, shall receive eternal damnation for their just reward. I ask God that we may escape this fearful sentence, and be found such faithful servants and loving children, that we may hear the happy, comfortable, and most joyful sentence, ordained for the children of God, which is: 'Come hither, you blessed of my Father, and receive the kingdom of heaven, prepared for you before the beginning of the world.'[102]

Unto the Father, the Son, and the Holy Spirit, be all honour and glory, world without end. Amen.

Finis.

Colophon

Imprinted at London, in Fleet Street, at the sign of the Sun, over against the Conduit, by Edward Whitchurch, the fifth day of November, in the year of our Lord, 1547.
Cum privileged ad imperilment soul.
(With exclusive rights to print)

12

TEXTUAL SOURCES

The Lamentation of a Sinner was a unique document in sixteenth-century England. It was the first 'conversion narrative', and nothing like it had appeared before. The shock value was twofold. For England's former queen to so abase herself and bemoan her former state must have been a source of embarrassment – and indeed anger, since the esteem of the monarchy has the residual effect of inspiring the populace. Can one imagine the repercussions of any member of today's royal family publishing such a document for all the world to read and consider? What if Meghan Markle, Duchess of Suffolk, wrote a lamentation of her former life as an actress and spoke of her discovery of God's great forgiveness? What would be the response? It would be front-page news. The duchess would become the object of scorn and ridicule. Imagine the discussion in the local pubs. In Katherine's case, I would not be surprised if even those who shared her theology, loyal Englishmen like Cranmer and Latimer, wished that the queen had been more restrained in confessing her utter ignominy.

For those whose interests went beyond gossip-mongering to the higher plane of philosophy and theology, the fact that Queen Katherine had not only rejected traditional Catholic beliefs but also lampooned Erasmus, the primary voice of the English Reformation, must have been disconcerting. Katherine prayed that 'this great benefit of Christ crucified may be steadfastly fixed and printed in all Christian hearts'. I believe Derek Wilson is correct in saying, 'Like innumerable Christians who have experienced a dramatic conversion, Catherine felt the need to tell the world about it.'[1] Those who were proud of their Erasmian piety must have been offended. 'Is she saying that she has something we don't have?' 'Is she claiming that she is going to heaven, and we are not?' 'Is she now a better Christian than we are?' Such is the typical response to conversion narratives where the writer is insinuating, 'I used to be like you until my eyes were opened, and I saw the light.'

One cannot help but wonder what some of the specific responses were to Katherine's *Lamentation*. We know humanist Roger Ascham basically ignored it. According to Martienssen, Stephen Gardiner referred to it as 'this most abominable book'.[2] Nicholas Udall had praised the theology of Erasmus as being nearly perfect, and in the *Lamentation* he found Katherine pointing out all its imperfections. Cuthbert Tunstall, Bishop of London, was a relative and dear friend of the Parr family. He had assisted in overseeing the education of young Katherine. He had encouraged Erasmus to write against Luther, and now he reads the *Lamentation*. You can hear him say, 'Dear Katherine has gone overboard.' Francis Goldsmith, who in 1544 praised Queen Katherine's piety, must have been shocked when he read her confession of shame. Of course, Katherine's husband Thomas Seymour must have been thrilled that his wife had again put herself in the firing line, and this time over religion, a subject he seemed to disdain. Princess Mary had written Katherine a kind letter upon hearing of her pregnancy, but never mentioned the *Lamentation*. In a few years, after ascending the throne, she would banish it.

In evaluating *The Lamentation of a Sinner*, it is good to consider the possible sources behind it. Was Queen Katherine one of those rare original thinkers who came up with her treatise without the benefit of literary benefactors, or was she merely rearranging the thinking of someone who influenced her religious beliefs?

The study of a document to discover the possible sources is called *intertextuality*. There are basically two types of intertextuality: *iterability* and *presupposition*. Iterability refers to the repeating of certain – possibly unique – phrases, references or allusions in earlier documents indicating a possible source. Presupposition refers to the assumptions a text might make about its source even if not explicitly stated. The danger in engaging in the practice of intertextuality is that one attempts to find connections that exist perhaps only in the mind of the examiner. There is also the issue of objectivity. What are you trying to prove by dissecting a work and seeking to discover the real sources behind it? Is there an agenda?

While many of Katherine's biographers note in passing possible sources for her work, the only author who has engaged in an in-depth intertextual study of *The Lamentation of a Sinner* is the University of Chicago scholar Dr Janel Mueller. In doing my study, her massive work *Katherine Parr: Complete Works and Correspondence* has been the most helpful, especially her footnoting of the *Lamentation*. Dr Mueller is recognised as the foremost expert in Katherine Parr research. The depth of her study is phenomenal. While her conclusions are objective in nature, she does have a stated feminist agenda.

My interest in discovering sources is limited to the sections in the *Lamentation* where Katherine alludes to her discovery of justification by faith and draws conclusions, especially as to the nature of justifying faith. The definition and description of 'faith' as an element in justification was, and probably still is, the primary controverted issue between Rome and the theologians of the Reformation.

It is an obvious assumption that Katherine Parr's discovery of justification by faith finds its source in the earlier discovery of Martin Luther. This is a valid presupposition, even though it is not explicitly stated. While there were hints of this radical teaching in the works of St Augustine and others, Luther's discovery was unique and resulted from the exegetical study of the Bible, specifically Romans 1:17: 'For therein is the righteousness of God revealed.' It was a grammatical issue. Is the phrase 'righteousness of God' (*dikaiosune theou*) a subjective or an objective genitive?

If subjective, righteousness was the possession of God whereby He was just and properly punished those who were unjust. This was the typical interpretation of Rome, and Luther hated the phrase.

Upon further inspection, especially as related to Romans 1:16, which identified the 'therein' as the Gospel or 'good news', Luther entertained the possibility that it could be objective and mean that God is the source or giver of righteousness. Going through other phrases from the New Testament that presented the objective genitive, such as 'peace of God', 'wisdom of God' and 'strength of God', he began to become excited. If true, this was indeed the good news of Romans 1:16. Comparing this with other verses from Paul, especially Romans 3:21–22, it was consistent. As he put it, 'heaven opened up to me'. Yes, the just shall live by faith, trusting in the merits of Christ whereby the sinner is declared righteous. The fuel for the fire of the Reformation came into being. Like Katherine Parr, Luther, having made this discovery, wanted to tell the world about it, and he did. What is ironic is that Luther used the Greek translation of Erasmus to make this discovery – a discovery that was a fatal blow to Erasmian piety.

Was Katherine Parr aware of Luther's teaching of justification by faith? Of course. How could she not have been? The issues surrounding this subject were well known. Thomas Cranmer had attempted to include justification in the King's Book of 1543 but was quickly rebuffed by Henry VIII. It is safe to say that Cranmer, desiring to bring Katherine around to his way of thinking, had shared justification by faith with her, but according to her writings in 1544 and 1545 she had not embraced it. She had no desire to embrace a way of thinking contrary to that of her husband. Sometime in early 1546, circumstances were such that she sought the Lord, her eyes were opened to the truth, and she shared her conversion in *The Lamentation of a Sinner*, thus producing a document that can becomes an object for intertextual evaluation.

After comparing content, style and structure, Dr Mueller concludes that the sources behind *The Lamentation* are the noted Protestant divines Thomas Cranmer and William Tyndale, and the preaching of Hugh Latimer. She does admit that 'even my eclectic English Protestant model will not finally explain every identifying feature of Parr's authorial voice', and she goes on to say, 'At the level of overall form, it is historically as well as literarily suggestive that Parr's *Lamentation* bears more resemblance to Tyndale's *Obedience of a Christian Man* (1528) than to any other prose tract I know from the period.'[3] This may indeed be true, and the 'English Protestant model' does provide primary source material for Katherine's *Lamentation*, yet when examining the singular section pertaining to the subject of justification by faith, I find many corollaries to the Lutheran Confessions, especially Philip Melanchthon's 1537 *Apology of the Augsburg Confession*. Peter Marshall writes that a large number of Lutheran books had come into the possession of English people.[4] He goes on to say, 'On Sunday, 12 May 1521, copies of Luther's books were consigned to the flames in a splendid ceremony at the cross outside St. Paul's Cathedral.'[5] Of course, this was fifteen years earlier. A ban on heretical books had been issued again in 1530 and in 1546. The primary question is, did Katherine Parr have access to the writings of Luther and the Lutheran Confessions?

We know that Katherine and her ladies had in their possession banned books. The morning after being informed of her imminent arrest, Katherine informed her ladies to hide them. When the apartment was later searched by Gardiner and Wriothesley they found no incriminating evidence. What banned books had been in their possession? Since Katherine had recently embraced the theology of Luther, it is not a stretch of the imagination to conclude that some of those books were Lutheran in nature.

There is one issue that I find particularly intriguing. According to biographer Dr Linda Porter, on New Years of 1546, Princess Elizabeth presented Queen Katherine with a translation of the first chapter of Calvin's *Institutes of the Christian Religion*.[6] As far as I am aware, no other biographer of Katherine Parr includes this noteworthy event, which is well documented. It is rather amazing that the young princess had in her possession a copy of a work regarded by many as more radical than Luther. If Princess Elizabeth possessed such a document, it is not a major leap to suggest that Queen Katherine had access to the writings of Luther and the Lutheran Confessions.

There is one example of iterability, the repetition of unique phrases and allusions, in the *Lamentation of a Sinner* that is both fascinating and puzzling and a possible link to the writings of Martin Luther. I have placed the key words in italics. Katherine writes, 'And not without just cause, if we consider the benevolence, goodness, and mercy of God: who hath declared His love toward us, greater and more laudable, than He ever did to the *Hebrews*. For they lived under *shadows and figures* and were bound to the *law*.' In his *Lectures on Romans*, specifically Romans 9:28, Martin Luther writes, 'For before this Word of faith, the Word of the Spirit was revealed, everything was in *shadow and figure* because of the slowness of the *Jews*.' He goes on to write, 'The entire Scripture deals only with Christ everywhere, if it is looked at inwardly, even though on the face of it, it may sound differently by the use of *shadows and figures*. Hence, he also says that Christ is the end of the *Law*.'[7]

Is it coincidental that both Martin Luther and Katherine Parr used the same imagery of 'shadows and figures' to define the condition of the Jews who remained under the law? This phrase is not found in the New Testament. Perhaps it can be located in the writings of Cranmer and Tyndale. If not, it seems that Queen Katherine had access to Luther's notes from his *Lectures on Romans*, but this assumption has added difficulties. Apparently, Luther never intended to publish these notes. They were written for his own use in the lecture hall. Nevertheless, he seems to have preserved them carefully, intending perhaps to use them again for future lectures. This purpose never materialised. Melanchthon took over the Roman's lectures when he arrived at the university in 1518. Some surmise that Philip Melanchthon, who is known to have lectured on Romans five times, may have used Luther's notes for his work.[8] While it is an intriguing possibility that Katherine's reference to the Hebrews merely seeing 'figures and shadows' is taken from Luther's discourse on Romans, it is open to debate. It could be that Melanchthon sent his 'good friend' Henry VIII copies of Luther's notes which fell into the hands of Queen Katherine, but this is mere conjecture with no basis in recorded fact.

In the *Lamentation*, Katherine repeatedly refers to the 'Book of the Crucifix'. In her essay 'Complications of Intertextuality: John Fisher, Katherine Parr, and "The Book of the Crucifix"',[9] Dr Janel Mueller finds a connection to a much earlier sermon by Bishop John Fisher in which he employs that phrase, but the context is totally different. Fisher's use of the phrase 'Book of the Crucifix' has nothing to do with a 'book' or reading as such but portrays a graphic image of the suffering and bleeding body of Jesus on the cross. According to Dr Mueller, Katherine Parr is referring to a 'printed Bible in which the reader apprehends the truth of sacrifice, mercy, love, and salvation as the inspired Word of God'.[10]

The phrase 'the Book of the Crucifix' appears to have been unique to Queen Katherine, especially in the way she used the phrase. This is not to be equated with the Gospel, the message of God's grace, mercy, and salvation in Christ Jesus, but defines the full council of God as reflected in the suffering and death of Jesus on the cross. The 'Book of the Crucifix' does not only show us the great mercy of God but reveals to us the depth of our sin, which is somewhat of a unique application. Consider these passages from the *Lamentation*: 'It is most justly true that to behold Christ crucified, in spirit, is the best meditation that can be. I certainly never knew my own miseries and contentions so well, by reading books, receiving admonition, or correction, as I have done by considering the spiritual book of the crucifix.' 'I never knew my own wickedness, neither truly lamented for my sins until the time that God inspired me with His grace, that I looked in this book of the crucifix.' 'Therefore, to learn to know truly our own sins is to study the book of the crucifix, by continual discussion in faith.' 'We may also, in Christ crucified, weigh our sins as in a divine balance: how grievous and how weighty they are, seeing they have crucified Christ. They would never have been counterbalanced, but with the great and precious weight of the blood of the Son of God.'

This is reminiscent of Martin Luther's 'Meditation on Christ's Passion'. Luther wrote this treatise in 1519. By 1524, a total of twenty-four editions had been printed. Whether Katherine had a copy of this treatise is a matter of conjecture. The content is similar to her 'Book of the Crucifix'.

Luther writes, 'They contemplate Christ's passion aright who view it with a terror-stricken heart and a despairing conscience. This terror must be felt as you witness the stern wrath and the unchanging earnestness with which God looks upon sin and sinners, so much so that he was unwilling to release sinners even for his only and dearest Son without his payment of the severest penalty for them ... It must be an inexpressible and unbearable earnestness that forces such a great and infinite person to suffer and die to appease it. And if you seriously consider that it is God's very own Son, the eternal wisdom of the Father, who suffers, you will be terrified indeed. The more you think about it, the more intensely will you be frightened.'[11] Did this influence Katherine's use of the suffering and death of Christ as revelatory of her sinful condition? Perhaps.

It is suggested that Katherine's bemoaning her sinful condition finds its source in Marguerite Navarre's *The Mirror of the Sinful Soul*. We know this poem was translated by an eleven-year-old Princess Elizabeth and presented as a gift to her stepmother Katherine Parr on New Years of 1545. Linda Porter writes concerning the *Lamentation*, 'Though written as prose, not poetry, the work owes a good deal to Marguerite of Navarre's already famous personal statement of belief. There may even have been an element of competition. When Elizabeth began her translation of *The Mirror of the Sinful Soul* (perhaps at her stepmother's prompting) it may also have occurred to Katherine that she might attempt a similar piece of literature. Could not an English queen rival a French one in this way?'[12] This is rather patronising of Katherine's intentions. It's hard to conceive of competition over the issue of who is the biggest sinner. While Susan James suggests the same source, she adds the caveat, 'Yet oddly enough, the open sensuality which is so apparent in Marguerite's writings and which Catherine embraced so eagerly in earlier works is largely missing from *Lamentation of a Sinner*.'[13] Derek Wilson rejects the connection: 'Catherine's spiritual manual was personal, original, and owed much less to earlier writings than her former books.'[14] Janel Mueller observes that the difference between the two works is that *The Mirror* is allegorical, analogical, unliteral, subjective and has no real-world setting whereas the *Lamentation* presents a life-changing conversion experience as personal history set in this world.[15]

Katherine attributed the knowledge of her sinful condition to meditating upon Christ crucified. There is no reason to look for other sources. She writes, 'I never knew my own miseries and contentions so well, by reading books.' She was probably referring to Navarre's work.

Of all the controverted issues that distinguished the Lutheran Reformation from the dictates of Roman Catholicism, the most important and widely discussed had to do with the nature of faith within the context of justification. Martin Luther wrote, 'Hence there was very great need to treat of and to restore this teaching concerning faith in Christ in order that anxious consciences should not be deprived of consolation but know that grace and forgiveness of sins are apprehended by faith in Christ.'[16]

The concept of faith can take on a wide variety of meaning. There is a general faith that says, 'I believe there is a God.' Of course, the Bible says the devil also believes there is a God and trembles.[17] Faith can be directed at the providence of God. The Book of Psalms is filled with the imagery that God will rescue, save, deliver, defend, etc. That the Bible is the Word of God becomes an object of faith. Faith believes that the facts recorded in the Bible are true. In considering the all-important teaching of justification by faith, the central teaching of the Reformation, defining the nature of this thing called 'faith' was vital.

The fullest treatment of this issue is found in Article IV of the 1537 *Apology of the Augsburg Confession* authored by Philip

Melanchthon. While Luther's 'right-hand man', Melanchthon was also a noted humanist scholar and regarded by King Henry as a friend. Melanchthon had dedicated his 1535 edition of his seminal work *Loci Communes* (Common Places in Theology) to King Henry. In response, Henry sent him 200 gold florins, with a very gracious letter, in which he calls Melanchthon his 'dearest friend'. I believe it is very possible that Queen Katherine had in her possession a copy, perhaps written in Latin, of Melanchthon's *Apology*.

Of all the content in the *Lamentation*, I was most impressed by the statements that Katherine makes within a single paragraph concerning the definition, nature and results of justifying faith. Katherine is not developing her themes but making brief, matter-of-fact statements. It appears to demonstrate that she was referencing some authoritative document, such as the *Apology*. This is the paragraph:

Saint Paul says we are justified by faith in Christ, and not by the deeds of the law.[18] For if righteousness came by the law, then Christ died in vain.[19] Saint Paul means not a dead, human, historical faith, gotten by human effort, but a supernatural, living faith which works by love, as he himself plainly states.[20] This esteem of faith does not disparage good works, for out of this faith springs all good works. Yet, we may not impute to the worthiness of faith or good works our justification before God; but ascribe and give the worthiness of it totally to the merits of Christ's passion; and declare and attribute the knowledge and perception of those merits to faith alone. The very true and only property of faith is to take, apprehend, and hold fast the promises of God's mercy, which makes us righteous; and causes me to continually hope for the same mercy; and, in love, to do the many good works ascribed in the Scripture, that I may be thankful for the same.

Katherine succinctly deals with several controverted issues. The first issue is to distinguish justifying faith from mere historical knowledge.

Katherine writes, 'Saint Paul means not a dead, human, historical faith, gotten by human effort, but a supernatural, living faith which works by love, as he himself plainly states.' She later adds, 'And, thus they believe that their dead, human, historical faith and knowledge (which they have learned in their scholastic books) and may be had with all sin (as I said before), to be the true, infused faith and knowledge of Christ.'

In his *Apology*, Melanchthon writes, 'Our opponents imagine that faith is only historical knowledge and teach that it can exist with mortal sin. And so, they say nothing about faith by which, as Paul says so often, men are justified, because those who are accounted righteous before God do not live in mortal sin. The faith that justifies, however, is no mere historical knowledge, but the firm acceptance of God's offer promising forgiveness of sins and justification.'[21]

As a potential source for Queen Katherine's disparaging of mere historical faith, Janel Mueller offers the work of William Tyndale. In his 1532 *Answer to More* (Thomas More), Tyndale makes a distinction between 'historical' faith and 'feeling' faith.[22] Using the account of Jesus' confrontation with the woman at the well in John 4, he says that when the people of Samaria heard the woman tell them about her encounter with Jesus, they had 'historical faith'. When they heard the words of Jesus for themselves, they had 'feeling faith'. Neither Melanchthon nor Katherine are speaking about 'feeling faith' and would reject Tyndale's distinction. While 'feelings' may be the consequence of faith, for Katherine and Melanchthon they most certainly were not the essence of faith. Faith is not 'feeling' but the actions of the will.

The second issue is to define faith as the active apprehension of the promises of God. Katherine writes, 'The very true and only property of faith is to take, apprehend, and hold fast the promises of God's mercy, which makes us righteous.' Melanchthon writes, 'Paul clearly shows that faith does not simply mean historical knowledge but is a firm acceptance of the promise (Rom. 4:16): "That is why it depends on faith, in order that the promise may be guaranteed." For he says that only faith can accept the promise. He therefore correlates and connects promise and faith.'[23] Both Katherine and Melanchthon join faith and promise – a very important Lutheran distinctive.

The next issue is to make clear that faith is not to be considered a good work which justifies. Katherine writes, 'Yet, we may not impute to the worthiness of faith or good works our justification before God; but ascribe and give the worthiness of it totally to the merits of Christ's passion; and declare and attribute the knowledge and perception of those merits to faith alone.' Melanchthon writes, 'And so at every mention of mercy we must remember that this requires faith, which accepts the promise of mercy. Similarly, at every mention of faith we are also thinking of its object, the promised mercy. For faith does not justify or save because it is a good work in itself, but only because it accepts the promised mercy.'[24]

The final issue has to do with the relationship between faith and good works. This is a highly controverted issue. King Henry had rejected Luther's understanding of justification by faith because Luther, as Henry perceived him, did not place enough emphasis on good works as being a necessary ingredient in salvation. I believe that the primary discussion between Henry and Katherine in the latter half of 1546 that almost got Katherine arrested was focused on this subject. Katherine writes, 'This esteem of faith does not disparage good works, for out of this faith springs all good works.' Later in her treatise she writes, 'Unless this great benefit of Christ crucified is felt and fixed surely in man's heart, there can be no good work done, acceptable before God.' Melanchthon for his part writes, 'But we are talking about a faith that is not an idle thought, but frees us from death, brings forth a new life in our hearts, and is a work of the Holy Spirit. Therefore, this cannot exist with mortal sin, but whenever it appears it brings forth good fruits, as we shall point out later.'[25]

Both Katherine and Melanchthon are of the same mind when it comes to the value of good works done apart from Christ. Katherine later writes, 'Christ has showed that, in God's sight, the righteousness of the world is wickedness; and He has borne witness that the works of men, not regenerated by Him in faith, are evil.' Melanchthon writes, 'Therefore men really sin even when they do virtuous things without the Holy Spirit; for they do them with a wicked heart, and (Rom. 14:23) "whatever does not proceed from faith is sin".'[26]

Katherine often referred to receiving the *benefits* of God's grace. For example, she writes, 'Through the hearing of His Word and promises, God has also promised to create faith in the heart of the hearers to receive the *benefits* of His great and many promises.' Roland Bainton sees a possible connection to the work of an Italian evangelical. He writes, 'But *The Benefit of Christ's Death* was precisely the title of the favourite compendium of the piety of the Italian evangelicals! It appeared in Italy in 1513 with the title *Del Beneficio di Iesu Cristo Crocifisso*, and in an English translation in 1548. Catherine may not have seen the English. She could handle the Italian.'[27] I think this is a stretch. It is very much a part of Lutheran theology to speak of faith as grasping the benefits of the finished work of Christ. Faith does not *cause* the forgiveness of sins but claims the *benefits* of forgiveness gained through the shed blood of Jesus on the cross. Her use of *benefits* is consistent with her understanding of faith.

Since I have not taken the time to peruse all the works of Thomas Cranmer or William Tyndale relative to these subjects, I am open to the possibility that they may be the source. Even at that, neither Cranmer nor Tyndale would have come up with these unique doctrinal distinctives apart from either the Lutheran Confessional writings or perhaps Calvin's *Institutes of the Christian Religion*, which also deal with portions of the subject matter. I'm sure that if we carefully perused Katherine's *The Lamentation of a Sinner*, we might be able to identify a variety of sources. I have focused on the content germane to my agenda: sin, justifying faith, and good works.

I have attempted to place Queen Katherine's life, her discovery of justification by faith, and her seminal work the *The Lamentation of a Sinner* into the history and religious milieu of the sixteenth-century English Reformation. I hope to some degree I have been successful. It has been a fascinating study filled with mystery, intrigue and scandal.

I believe the *Lamentation of a Sinner* is one of the hidden gems of the Reformation. William Cecil writes, 'These great mysteries and graces are not properly understood, except they be surely studied; neither are they perfectly studied, unless they are diligently practiced; neither profitably practiced, without amending your life.'

For those who wish to take the next steps defined by practising and amending, I have attached the appendix that follows.

Appendix

PRACTISING AND AMENDING

This appendix is added for those who wish to pursue in greater detail the affirmations contained in the *Lamentation of a Sinner*. Queen Katherine Parr speaks to us today, sharing with us, for our growth and edification, the most important truths in the Christian's faith and life. These are central truths in the theology of the Reformation as clearly set forth by both Martin Luther and John Calvin, its two stalwarts.

It would obviously be possible to glean thoughts from any of the theologians of the Reformation and expound upon them. What is unique in this case is that these thoughts come to us from an English queen who, according to one of her biographers, did not regard herself as a theologian.[1] In addition, the thoughts are being gleaned from an obscure, hidden gem of the Reformation.

Katherine Parr began her conversion journey where every person must begin. Without the recognition of sin, there is no need for forgiveness. Without acknowledging that within ourselves we have no personal righteousness that can stand in the light of the perfect righteousness of God, we have no need for the righteousness of Christ. Katherine had undoubtedly read these words from the first chapter of Calvin's *Institutes of the Christian Religion*, a translation that had been given to her by Princess Elizabeth, 'But should we once begin to raise our thoughts to God, and reflect what kind of Being he is, and how absolute the perfection of that righteousness and wisdom and virtue to which, as a standard we are to be conformed, what formerly delighted us by its false show of righteousness, will become polluted with the greatest iniquity.'

Self-accusation and the discovery of justification by faith go together. She writes:

Partly by the hate I owe to sin, which has reigned in me, and partly by the love I owe to all Christians, whom I am content to edify with the example of my own shame, I am forced and constrained with my heart and words to confess and declare to the world, how ingrate, negligent, unkind, and stubborn I have been to God my Creator; and how beneficial, merciful, and gentle He has always been to me, His creature, being such a miserable and wretched sinner ... My evils and miseries are so many and so great, they accuse me even to my face. Oh, how miserable and wretched I am! Confounded by the multitude and greatness of my sins, I am compelled to accuse myself.

The Bible is very clear in its estimate of human life. We are the children of wrath,[2] totally unable by nature to grasp the things of the Spirit of God.[3] We were shaped in iniquity and born in sin[4] and the imaginations of our hearts are evil.[5] Within our human flesh, there dwells no good thing. Even though we may desire to do good and to be good, we are unable to accomplish our lofty ideals because our nature is wrong. We are in bondage to the law of sin and death.[6] The Bible says that there is nothing good within us. 'All have sinned and fallen short of the Glory of God.'[7] John Calvin writes, 'What can sinners, alienated from God, produce save that which is abominable in his sight?'[8]

Putting it very simply, from God's point of view our lives are a mess! We need self-accusation, not self-esteem. We need grace, not acceptance and understanding. We need to be rescued from ourselves, not supported by a group of fellow sinners. Most Christians confess that they are sinners, but they are not a very 'bad' sinners. Either their sense of sin or their understanding of the righteousness of God is not great enough to cause them to despair and hunger for a deeper understanding of the God's grace.

In his classic book *Guilt and Grace*, Paul Tournier observes, 'This can be seen in history; for believers who are the most desperate about themselves are the ones who express most forcefully their confidence in grace ... Those who are the most pessimistic about man are the most optimistic about God; those who are the most severe with themselves are the ones who have the most serene confidence in divine forgiveness ... By degrees the awareness of our guilt and of God's love increase side by side.'[9]

German theologian Werner Elert comments on Martin Luther's understanding of the necessity of self-accusation, 'The righteousness imparted through justification presupposes, of course, the 'self-accusation' of the sinner. Accordingly, Luther counts it among the effects of Christ's suffering 'that man comes to a knowledge of himself and is terrified of himself and is crushed. To have Christ as Saviour is to need him.'[10]

The seventeenth-century philosopher and theologian Blaise Pascal wrote, 'For if we could face ourselves, with all our faults, we would then be so shaken out of complacency, triviality, indifference, and pretence that a deep longing for strength and truth would be aroused within us. Not until man is aware of his deepest need is he ready to discern and grasp what can meet his deepest need.'[11] As Queen Katherine put it, 'Confounded by the multitude and greatness of my sins, I am compelled to accuse myself.' To accuse yourself of sin is the first step on the road to discovering the truth of the God's grace, mercy and forgiveness in Jesus Christ.

In accusing herself of sin, Katherine does not stipulate the period in her life when her 'evils and miseries' were so great, but we can from, her own words, discern the specific occasion. She was an opportunist when she married King Henry and coveted the luxuries of being queen. She writes,

Christ was meek and humble in heart; and I most proud and vainglorious. Christ despised the world with all its vanities;

and because of the vanities, I made it my God. Christ came to serve His brethren; and I desired to rule over them. Christ despised worldly honour; and I much delighted to attain it. Christ loved the base and simple things of the world; and I esteemed the most fair and pleasant things. Christ loved poverty; and I, wealth. Christ was gentle and merciful to the poor; and I, hard-hearted and ungentle. Christ prayed for His enemies; and I hated mine. Christ rejoiced in the conversion of sinners; and I was not grieved to see them return to their sin.

Within the theology of the Reformation, the preaching of Law and Gospel is the norm. The Law convicts us of our sin. The Gospel offers the promise of forgiveness. The Law can confront us in many ways, not just through the preaching of the moral dictates in the Bible. Possibly, as a result of her work on the *Paraphrases* of Erasmus, especially the Gospel of Matthew, Katherine was convicted of her sin by comparing the life of Christ with her life. The enormity of her sin became further evident when she meditated upon the 'Book of the Crucifix' and saw the great price that had been paid for her forgiveness. As she put it, 'We may also, in Christ crucified, weigh our sins as in a divine balance: how grievous and how weighty they are, seeing they have crucified Christ.' The cross of Jesus Christ is both Law and Gospel. On the one hand, it shows us the enormity of our sin, while on the other hand the grace, mercy and forgiveness of God.

Outwardly, Katherine Parr appeared to be a pious person and was praised for it, but she defined herself as a Pharisee who prayed, 'Good Lord, I thank You, I am not like other men; I am no adulterer nor fornicator, and so forth: with such words of vainglory, extolling myself and despising others.' The issue was not her external behaviour, but the attitudes of her heart. She writes, 'But my heart was so stony and hard, that this great benefit was never truly and lively printed in my heart, although I often rehearsed it with my words, thinking myself to be sufficiently instructed in the same, but indeed, being in blind ignorance.'

There is a tremendous lesson here. As we examine our lives, we are prone to judge our goodness based on our external actions. We are 'good' because we do not engage in the immoral acts evident in the lives of other people, but what about the attitudes and desires of the heart? This was Katherine's issue. She was guilty of a false piety, but she was not alone. Many were following that way, as she says: 'Yes, and because there were so many following those ways, I could not imagine that I was not walking in the perfect and right way: having more regard for the number of the followers rather than to what they were following. I believed most surely, they were leading me to heaven, whereas I am certain now, they would have brought me down to hell.'

Katherine writes that 'there were so many following those ways'. Which 'ways' is she referring to? Katherine, together with a host of others, was a follower of Erasmus. While Erasmus called people back to the Bible, which is to his credit, the piety he promoted was what he called the 'philosophy of Christ'. Erasmus, arguing for the freedom of the will, believed that the individual, informed by Scripture, could, assisted by the grace of God, choose to follow and imitate Christ. In the nutshell, Erasmus' preoccupation was with being a good person. This resulted in a false piety. She 'embraced, received, and esteemed vain, foolish, and artificial trifles'. So, Katherine defined herself as a Pharisee.

The self-accusation of Queen Katherine went against the tide of popular humanist thinking, not only in the sixteenth century but also in our age. We are faced with a new brand of humanism derived from the field of psychology and 'baptised' into the thinking of many churches. We have a 'feel good' brand of Christianity where the emphasis upon the sinful human condition becomes a detriment to self-esteem, the alleged cure-all for human needs. The desire of many pastors is to see their people exiting the doors of the church feeling good about themselves. John Calvin wrote, 'I am not unaware how much more plausible the view is, which invites us rather to ponder on our good qualities than to contemplate what must overwhelm us with shame – our miserable destitution and ignominy. There is nothing more acceptable to the human mind than flattery ... Whoever, therefore, gives heed to those teachers who merely employ us in contemplating our good qualities ... will be plunged into the most pernicious ignorance.'[12]

Prior to arriving at an accurate assessment of her human condition, Queen Katherine felt no need for increasing her knowledge of Christ. 'Yet, I stood so well in mine own judgment and opinion, that I thought it vain to seek to increase my knowledge of the work of Christ.'

There are many who might faithfully attend church every Sunday, say their table prayers, perhaps read devotional material and pray before going to sleep at night. They are secure in their judgements and opinions. They think they have this thing called Christianity figured out. To attend Bible classes or to seriously study the Word of God would be for them a vain exercise. After all, what else is there? But if you would ask them to explain the Gospel of Jesus Christ, the defining truth of the Christian faith, they know very little or anything. There is a great deal of confusion today about what it means to be a Christian.

This confusion is widespread. If you don't believe me, try asking some of the people with whom you work or interact daily what it means to be a Christian. See what kind of answers you get. You might be very surprised. While of course a very few would correctly define Christianity by the gift of God's grace and mercy as offered in the Gospel, others would focus on the Ten Commandments or would appeal to church membership, being baptised and confirmed. Still others would identify a Christian by love, or by 'the Golden Rule'. I knew one man who identified a Christian as someone who was not a Jew. There are many opinions, and those who voice them are often very certain of their judgements, but for the most part, they are ignorant of the very identity they claim.

The rapid growth of Islam today is not difficult to understand. Muslims know exactly what they believe, are committed to it, and put it into practice. On a trip to Egypt, our guide was Muslim, On the bus, we asked him what he believed. Without hesitation, he explained the five pillars. There is one God, Allah, and Mohammed is his prophet; pray five times a day; fast during Ramadan; give alms; and take a journey to Mecca. Upon a second trip, we had the same guide. He met us at the airport. He hurriedly approached me in an excited state, exclaiming, 'Don, Don, I'm a *haji*! I'm a *haji*!' meaning he had taken his trip to Mecca, and he couldn't wait to tell me about it. The struggle for the Muslim to live out his faith and build a community is called *jihad*. If you focus upon the sayings of Muhammad in the Quran during his time in Mecca, *jihad* can also mean 'holy war' or 'death to the infidels'. It is not possible, given the present conditions, for Christianity to compete with Islam. Muslims are committed to what they believe while most Christian have no idea what they believe.

Yet, there are times when we pull out all the trappings of our Christian identity, whether it be the death of a former president or the marriage of a member of the royal family. Hymns are sung, beautiful choral selections are presented, and pious platitudes are spoken by the officiants, yet the people generally remain ignorant.

There was a time in her life when Queen Katherine, by the performance of her Christian duties, was secure in her religious judgements and opinions and thought it meaningless to increase her knowledge of Christ. Because she performed her religious duties, she even considered herself better than others. She writes, 'And I, most presumptuously thinking nothing of Christ crucified, went about to set forth my own righteousness, saying with the proud Pharisee: Good Lord, I thank You, I am not like other men; I am no adulterer nor fornicator, and so forth: with such words of vainglory, extolling myself and despising others.'

The focus of Erasmian piety was upon being a good person. Of course, not everyone is a good person. There are some bad people who do some real bad things such as committing adultery or fornication. By examining the behaviour of the 'bad' people, it is only reasonable to conclude that those who do not engage in such 'sinful' practices are better than they are. So, having established the quality of her own righteousness, Katherine condemned the actions of others. With the Pharisees, she could thank God that she wasn't like those other 'bad' people.

Katherine wished that everyone would follow her example and acknowledge their sins and failures but realised that it was perhaps too much to ask. She writes, 'I would to God we would all, when occasion arises, confess our faults to the world, laying aside all respect to our own position. But, alas, self-love so reigns among us that, as I have said before, we cannot spy out our own faults. And if perhaps we should discover our own guilt, we either favourably interpret it as not being sin, or else we are ashamed to confess it.'

Dr Paul Tournier wrote in his book *Guilt and Grace*, 'In a healthy person … this defence mechanism has the precision and universality of a law of nature … We defend ourselves against criticism with the same energy we employ in defending ourselves against hunger, cold or wild beasts, for it is a mortal threat.'[13]

Martin Luther wrote, 'The righteous man is one who accuses himself first … On the contrary, those who set up their own righteousness and excuse themselves for their sins (like Saul, like Adam and Eve) do not judge themselves or accuse themselves but think they are doing well and are pleased with themselves and love themselves and their own life in this world.'[14]

We all seek to justify our actions, pass the buck and blame other people or circumstances for our failures so that we will appear to be in the right. While we are very quick to pass judgment upon the actions of others, if a judgment is levelled against us, we will seek ways and means and devise various schemes to defend ourselves, even though in our hearts we know we are in the wrong. I am sure that all of you have been in situations in which you have contrived some rather far-fetched explanations to defend your questionable behaviour. While every Christian is theoretically willing to say, 'Of course I'm a sinner – nobody is perfect', when it comes to placing blame for specific incidents of sin, the same self-confessed sinner will try every means possible to avoid having the finger of accusation pointed at him.

In order to escape from such thinking, we must ask God to examine our hearts and reveal to us our real condition. We pray with King David, 'Search me, O God, and know my heart.'[15] Katherine wrote, 'But, alas, we are so much given to love and to flatter ourselves, and so blinded with carnal affections, that we can see and perceive no fault in ourselves. And therefore, it is required and necessary for us, to pray with one heart and mind to God, to give us a heavenly light and knowledge of our own miseries and calamities, that we may truly see them and acknowledge them before Him.'

Katherine's mind was changed about her condition as a result of looking into the Book of the Crucifix or meditating upon the cross of Christ. As the star and crescent is the symbol of Islam and the star of David is the symbol of Judaism, the cross is the symbol of Christianity. Probably the most popular piece of jewellery is the cross. Cemeteries are filled with crosses to mark Christian graves. On top of every church steeple stands a cross. Somewhere in the house of every family purporting to be Christian a cross is on display. Before engaging in athletic competition, you often see participants marking themselves with the sign of the cross.

Within first-century Rome, the cross was the instrument for execution. If the execution of Jesus of Nazareth under the Roman procurator Pontius Pilate had taken place in any other time period, the Christian symbol would be different, perhaps an axe, a noose, an electric chair or a hypodermic needle. It would be hard to imagine wearing such an item around your neck or putting one on display in your home. Yet the fact remains that displaying a cross is displaying an instrument for execution.

By displaying a cross, you are making the statement that someone had to die for you, and that someone was Jesus, the Son of God. This is not only indicative of the grace of God whereby your sins are forgiven, but also of the depth of your sin which required such a sacrifice. Katherine writes, 'We may also, in Christ crucified, weigh our sins as in a divine balance: how grievous and how weighty they are, seeing they have crucified Christ.'

Having your eyes opened to see the depth of your sin is not a desirable experience, but such an eye-opening knowledge is a necessary prelude for coming to know and understand the good news of the Gospel. Martin Luther wrote, 'If you want to engage profitably in the study of Holy Scripture and do not want to run head-on into a Scripture closed and sealed, then learn, above all things, to understand sin aright.'[16]

If you read of the experiences of other Christians who progressed in their knowledge of God's life-changing grace, you will note the combination of a deep sense of sin and failure together with a deep appreciation for God. Figures like Paul the Apostle, John Calvin, Martin Luther and even Katherine Parr were not afraid to speak of their sinful nature and even boast of their weaknesses, because they knew of the grace of God. Their writings reflect a profound level of spiritual depth and insight.

Don't be afraid to confront yourself head-on and thereby uncover your sinful condition. Your pride may argue against what the Holy Spirit is trying to show you. You may struggle and squirm when he turns on the light and exposes your thoughts, attitudes, self-centeredness, priorities, and ambitions in the light of the cross. Stripped of every pretence of righteousness, you will stand before God seeing yourself as he sees you. This is the real you, prepared to be touched by the transforming grace of God. Therefore, we pray, 'Search me, O God!'

In her 1545 *Prayers or Meditations*, Katherine bemoans her sinful condition but is not yet ready to give up and seek God's solution in Christ Jesus. She still holds out the hope that by her own efforts she can amend her sinful ways and ascend to God. Such hope based on human effort inevitably leads to failure and frustration, as the Apostle Paul writes in Romans 7: 'The good I want to do, I don't do, and the evil I don't want to do, I find myself doing.' No matter how hard we try, we are unable to get out from under our guilt and shame. Katherine wrote:

For in myself I find nothing to save me, but a dunghill of wickedness to condemn me. If I should hope, that by mine own strength and power, to come out of this maze of iniquity and wickedness wherein I have walked for so long, I should be deceived. For I am so ignorant, blind, weak, and feeble that I cannot bring myself out of this entangled and wayward maze. The more I seek means and ways to wind myself out of it, the more I am wrapped and entangled in it. So, I perceive my struggling to be a hindrance, and my travail to be labour spent in vain.

Katherine's struggle is reminiscent of the struggle Martin Luther went through to ease his troubled conscience. He prayed, fasted, confessed, took a pilgrimage to Rome, beat himself and wore a hair shirt, believing that if he continually itched he could avoid the temptation to sin. It is interesting to note that Henry's first wife, Catherine of Aragon, in her later years wore a hair shirt.[17] But through all his labours in the monastery, he could find no peace with God or assurance of his forgiveness and favour with God. He comments, 'If this life (in the monastery) had lasted longer, I would have martyred myself to death with vigils, praying, reading and other labour.'[18] Katherine refers to all these so-called spiritual disciplines as 'papal riffraff' and writes, 'Furthermore, I did not consider the blood of Christ to be sufficient to wash me from the filth of my sins as He planted in His Word. Rather, I sought such riffraff the Bishop of Rome planted in his tyranny and kingdom. Through the virtue and sacredness of them, I trusted with great confidence to receive full remission of my sins.'

Katherine does not explain the nature of this 'papal riffraff' as Luther does, but in her first work, *Psalms or Prayers*, published anonymously at the end of 1544, she wrote, 'Forgive me all my sins, O Lord God almighty, for Thy own sake put out of Thy sight my heinous offenses, for according to Thy goodness, Thou hast promised forgiveness of sins ofttimes to them that do penance.'[19] Penance involves confession to a priest and performing certain acts compensating for sin. She did not consider the blood of Christ sufficient to take away her sins.

Katherine Parr was at the place where many Christians find themselves. She has come to realise her lost and sinful condition. She has struggled with the issues, seeking answers in the practices of Rome and spirituality of Erasmus, but has found no peace.

She concludes that all her struggles were really a hindrance and all her labour in vain. What should she do? She concludes:

> It is the hand of the Lord. that can and will bring me out of this endless maze of death; for, without the grace of the Lord that comes before, I cannot ask forgiveness for my sins, nor be repentant or sorry for them. There is no man who can confess that Christ is the only Saviour of the world, but by the Holy Spirit: yes, as Saint Paul says, 'No man can say "Jesus Christ is Lord!" but by the Holy Spirit.'[20] The Spirit helps our infirmities, and makes continual intercession for us, with such sorrowful groanings as cannot be expressed.

By speaking of the 'grace of the Lord that comes before', or prevenient grace, Katherine, obviously, is not using the term as used in later Methodism or Arminianism to define the prevenient grace that enables a person to decide to be saved. As we will see, she is using it as the enlightening work of the Holy Spirit to open blind eyes to the truth of the Word of God. While this was taught by Augustine, it was also a basic understanding of Luther, who advised regarding the proper approach to Scripture, 'You should completely despair of your own sense and reason, for by these you will not attain the goal ... Rather kneel down in your private little room and with sincere humility and earnestness pray God through His dear Son, graciously to grant you His Holy Spirit to enlighten and guide you and give you understanding.'[21] We will return to this subject again.

After reading *The Lamentation of a Sinner* there is one undeniable conclusion: Queen Katherine Parr knew her Bible. Within this brief treatise, there are nearly ninety quotations of or references to verses in Scripture. This must have been a major point of contention between Queen Katherine and her husband King Henry when they engaged in their discussions and debates. While Henry undoubtedly had a knowledge of Scripture, it was probably lacking when compared to that of his wife. She was able to underline every point with a quotation of Scripture, leading

Henry to declare, 'You are become a doctor, Kate, to instruct us, as often times we have seen, and not to be instructed or directed by us.'

Katherine realised that the answer to her problem was not found in 'papal riffraff' or in the 'Philosophy of Christ' as taught by Erasmus. She would not escape from her 'maze of iniquity and wickedness' through her own human efforts to establish her own piety or to imitate Christ, but in the sure and certain truths and promises of the Word of God. She writes, 'Therefore, he promises and binds Himself to His Word, to give good and beneficial gifts to all them that ask Him with true faith: without which, nothing can be done acceptable or pleasing to God.'

God binds himself to His Word. A principle of the Reformation was *Sola Scriptura*, or Scripture alone. The only solution to the human dilemma is found in the clear and certain truths found in Scripture. By appealing to Scripture and the work of the Holy Spirit Katherine is separating herself from Erasmus and his bare bones 'philosophy of Christ' by presenting a theology of the Cross.

While the primary issue that Luther and Erasmus debated was the freedom of the will, behind this debate was the larger issue of the use of Scripture. Erasmus was not a theologian and had no desire to establish doctrinal truths drawn from Scripture. He submitted himself to the interpretation of Scripture as established by the church and the church fathers. Erasmus detested dissension because it went against the teachings of Christ. The Bible for Erasmus was not clear and any discussion or debate regarding its meaning would lead to contention. It is strange that the man who gave us the Greek New Testament would turn his mind and heart against the doctrines contained in it. To study Scripture for Erasmus was to learn the basic 'philosophy of Christ' and to endeavour to follow that philosophy in piety and holy living which, of course, required the freedom of the will aided by the grace of God. There were those who examined the life of Erasmus and wondered if he was practising what he was preaching.

Luther, on the other hand, contended for the perspicuity or clarity of Scripture. He said that the Holy Spirit is no sceptic, and the things He has written in our hearts are not doubts or opinions, but assertions - surer and more certain than sense and life itself. Luther, based on his own search and spiritual turmoil, contended that man, born in sin and an enemy of God, was unable to live a life pleasing to God. Even his best effort was sin. It was in the Scripture that God provided the answer. It was not in the imitation of the life of Christ but in the crucifixion and resurrection of Christ where the forgiveness of sins, righteousness and a new life were to be found.

By focusing her attention on the 'book of the crucifix', Katherine rejected Erasmus in favour of Luther.

Katherine bemoaned the conditions in her day in which the common people were ignorant of the Word of God. She wrote, 'For the poor, unlearned people remain confused, and almost everyone believes and goes his own way, and yet there is but one truth of God's Word, by which we shall be saved.'

The words of Katherine succinctly define the conditions that exist in our own day. While Martin Luther instructed people to memorise the Book of Romans, it is sad but true that many today can't find the Book of Romans in their Bibles. As R. C. Sproul put it in his book *The Prayer of the Lord*, 'I think the greatest weakness in the church today is that almost no one believes that God invests His power in the Bible. Everyone is looking for power in a program, in a methodology, in a technique, in anything and everything but that in which God has placed it—His Word. He alone has the power to change lives for eternity, and that power is focused on the Scriptures.'[22]

In 1787, decrying the conditions that existed in the Church of England, William Wilberforce wrote in his book *Real Christianity*, 'And yet, for all that we have the Bible in our houses, we are ignorant of its contents. No wonder that so many Christians know so little about what Christ actually taught; no wonder that they are so mistaken about the faith that they profess.'[23]

What is strange is that most Christians would agree that if they read and studied the Bible more it would influence their lives. In a Bible class one Sunday I asked the question: 'How many of you wish that you had more joy and peace and that you were more loving, kinder, gentler people?' Every hand went up. I was not surprised. I asked further, 'How many of you believe that it is the will of God for you to be more loving and to have more joy and peace?' Again, every hand went up. I asked one more question: 'How many of you believe that if you spent more time reading and studying the Bible that it would make a difference and produce more of those qualities'?' Again, the response was unanimous. So, what is the problem?

The issue is not with God. In his Word, God promises the forgiveness of sins, righteousness, freedom from guilt, and the certainty of eternal life. Through the hearing of His Word and promises, God has also promised to create faith in the hearts of the hearers to receive the benefits of His great and many promises. Katherine could come boldly to God seeking His mercy and forgiveness because of His promises. She writes, 'But, now, what makes me so bold and strong, to presume to come to the Lord with such audacity and boldness, being so great a sinner? Truly, nothing but His own Word: for He says, "Come to me all you that labour, and are burdened, and I shall refresh you."'[24]

God offers many great promises in his Word yet, when it comes to the forgiveness of sins, justification and the certainty of eternal life, many remain in darkness because they are ignorant of God's Word. They claim that they do not understand the Bible. They harbour the mistaken belief that studying the Bible is reserved for pastors, Bible students and theologians.

In Queen Katherine's day, the common people wanted to read the Bible in their own language. *The Great Bible*, the first authorised English translation, was published in 1539 but restricted for use in the local churches and often chained to the wall. Other English Bibles were smuggled into England and became available to the common people. As a result, heresies, private interpretations and disputes arose. In his final address to Parliament in 1545, Henry VIII decried the fact that Scriptures were being used as 'a railing and a taunting stock against priests and preachers'.

In May 1543, Parliament had passed *The Act for the Advancement of True Religion*, which restricted the reading of the Bible to clerics, noblemen, the gentry and richer merchants. Women of the gentry and nobility were only allowed to read the Bible in private. The Act forbade the reading of the Bible in English by 'women, artificers, apprentices, journeymen, serving-men of the rank of yeoman and under, husbandmen and laborers'. Yet, in many quarters, including Queen Katherine's ladies' Bible study in her privy chamber, the Act was largely ignored.

Katherine was a staunch advocate for the common people to have access to the Word of God:

> All of us have the duty, to procure and seek all the ways and means possible, to have more knowledge of God's Word set forth abroad in this world, and to not allow ignorance, and opposition to the knowledge of God's Word to stop the mouths of the unlearned with subtle and crafty persuasions of philosophy and sophistry. This produces no fruit, but a great distress to the minds of the simple and ignorant because they will not know which way to turn.[25]

The Bible was not written for the intellectual elite or trained theologians and clergymen. The words of the Bible are not so deep and profound that a common person is unable to understand them. God most certainly would not offer his promises and benefits to this world in words that could not be understood.

The Apostle Paul wrote his epistles to people whom we would regard as primitive. He essentially says this in 1 Corinthians 1:26: 'Brothers, think of what you were when you were called. Not many of you were wise by human standards; not many were influential; not many were of noble birth.' Would the Apostle write letters to Christians they were unable to comprehend? That would be foolishness.

Yet there is something truly unique about the words of the Bible, which does leave the impression that they are beyond the understanding of the average person. But this has nothing to do with whether a person is a part of the intellectual elite or has a theological education. The words of the Bible, while not difficult, are inspired by the Holy Spirit. The Bible does not merely communicate stories, human thoughts, memories, and instructions. If you want to understand the words and promises of God, you cannot read the Bible in the same way you would read a novel or a history text. While the words of the Bible in and of themselves are not difficult, they are words that were written under the direct influence of the Holy Spirit. God himself communicates to us through the words of the Bible. The Holy Spirit inspired the very words and thoughts that were recorded by these sacred writers. The Bible itself witnesses to the divine inspiration of the writers. Peter tells us that 'men spoke from God as they were carried along by the Holy Spirit'.[26] Paul writes to Timothy, 'All Scripture is God-breathed.'[27] For this reason, the words of the Bible are God's powerful words, with the power to have an impact on people's lives. The Bible is a supernatural book. It produces supernatural results.

When God created the heavens and the earth, he merely spoke the words. When our Lord Jesus healed people of their afflictions, he merely spoke the words. God works through words. The words of the Bible are God's powerful supernatural words.

The Apostle Paul describes the words of the Gospel of Jesus Christ as being 'the power of God'.[28] The Greek word which is translated as power is *dunamis*, from which we derive the English word 'dynamite'. We might say that the words of the Bible are 'dynamite', words which release the very power of God. For this to take place, the Holy Spirit had to inspire the human writers.

Therefore, if you do not understand the Bible, this does not mean that there is something theologically technical and lofty about the words of the Bible, nor does it mean that there is something wrong with you. What it does mean is that your natural mind is not in tune with the mind of the Spirit. You need to be enlightened. If the human authors of the Bible were inspired by the Holy Spirit, must it not follow that the readers of the Bible, if they are to understand, must be enlightened by the same Holy Spirit?

Prior to engaging in a study of God's Word and discovering His great and many promises, we must pray for the Holy Spirit. Martin Luther spoke of those who come to the Word of God without praying for the guidance of the Holy Spirit as rushing in like 'pigs with dirty feet'. John Calvin wrote, 'Hence, in order that the Word of God may gain full credit, the mind must be enlightened, and the heart confirmed from some other quarter.'[29] Katherine writes:

> Therefore, I will first require and pray to the Lord to give me His Holy Spirit: to teach me to confess that Christ is the Saviour of the world, and to utter these words, 'Jesus Christ is Lord,' and finally, to help mine infirmities, and to intercede for me. For I am most certain and sure, that no creature in heaven nor earth is of power, or can by any mean help me, but God, who is omnipotent, almighty, beneficial, and merciful, willing to help, and loving to all those who call, and put their whole confidence and trust in Him. Therefore, I will seek none other means nor advocate, but Christ's Holy Spirit, who is the only Advocate and Mediator between God and man, to help and relieve me.

Praying that the Holy Spirit will open our eyes to the truth that is revealed in the Bible is a very important but often neglected practice. We should approach the Word of God with the recognition that we are dealing with God's Word. The Bible is unlike any other book. As we discussed before, the Bible is a supernatural book which cannot be grasped by mere natural reason. It is the purpose of the Holy Spirit to take the work of our Lord Jesus and deliver it to us. He did this by first inspiring the Apostles to record the redemptive acts of our Lord Jesus, His death and resurrection, and then to explain to us the significance of those events in terms of our life and eternal salvation. The historical events and the meaning of those events are recorded in the Bible. While we can grasp the history with our natural understanding and confess the words of the historic Creeds of the Church, and have what Katherine defined as an 'historical faith', yet the meaning of those events as proclaimed in the Gospel (forgiveness, atonement, redemption, reconciliation, justification) are truths unable to be grasped by unaided human reason.

This message of the Gospel, of which the Apostle Paul was not ashamed,[30] is a mystery. He refers to the preaching of the Cross of Christ as a stumbling block to the Jews and foolishness to the Greeks. The Gospel is 'God's secret wisdom, a wisdom that has been hidden'. This message, according to the Apostle, has been revealed to us by the Spirit of God, and it is only through the Holy Spirit that we are able to comprehend it. As Paul writes, 'The man without the Spirit does not accept the things that come from the Spirit of God, for they are foolishness to him, and he cannot understand them.'[31]

Without an emphasis upon the enlightening work of the Holy Spirit, the Gospel remains unknown and 'good Christian people' resort to trusting their own good works for their salvation. This is not a minor defect in the proclamation of the Church but is a matter of life and death. William Wilberforce lamented the conditions that existed in the Church of England in the eighteenth century.

The disposition so prevalent in the bulk of nominal Christians, to form a religious system for themselves, instead of taking it from the word of God, is strikingly observable in their scarcely admitting, except in the most vague and general sense, the doctrine of the influence of the Holy Spirit. If we look into the Scriptures for information on this particular, we learn a very different lesson. We are in them distinctly taught, that 'of ourselves we can do nothing;' that 'we are by nature children of wrath,' and under the power of the evil spirit, our understandings being naturally dark, and our hearts averse from spiritual things; and we are directed to pray for the influence of the Holy Spirit to enlighten our understandings, to dissipate our prejudices, to purify our corrupt minds, and to renew us after the image of our heavenly Father.[32]

What was the result of Queen Katherine praying for the Holy Spirit?

> Yet, I never had this unspeakable and abundant love of God properly printed and fixed in my heart until it pleased God, of His simple grace, mercy, and pity, to open my eyes, making me see and behold Christ-crucified to be my only Saviour and Redeemer. For then I began (and not before) to perceive and see my own ignorance and blindness because I would not learn to know Christ, my Saviour and Redeemer. But when God, of His simple goodness, had thus opened mine eyes, and made me see and behold Christ, the wisdom of God, the Light of the world, through the supernatural eyes of faith: all pleasures, vanities, honour, riches, wealth, and supports of the world began to taste bitter to me.[33]

Queen Katherine's eyes were opened so that she could see and behold Christ. John Calvin defined enlightenment as taking place 'when the Spirit, with a wondrous and special energy, forms the ear to hear and the mind to understand'.[34]

The human mind is a strange and mysterious thing. It has tremendous capabilities. It can know, understand, feel, think, reason, determine, remember, invent and discover. Great minds can grasp incredible concepts and solve complicated problems. Yet for less trained minds, certain concepts are beyond their limits. I remember trying to explain the workings of a computer to my eighty-five-year-old father. He interrupted my explanation by saying, 'Donald, forget it. It's beyond me!'

There are times when the mind is 'enlightened', or a person has what psychologists call an 'aha experience'. Something finally clicks, and what previously had been cloudy, and obscure is now clear and able to be understood. According to the dictionary, to enlighten means 'to give to the mind revealing or broadening knowledge', or 'to give the light of truth'. Enlightenment is the illumination of the mind by which the 'eyes of the understanding' are opened. Thus, a problem finds a solution. A puzzling concept is finally understood. A good idea begins to emerge. Cartoonists usually depict enlightenment by drawing the picture of a lit lightbulb over the head of a character.

The disciples of our Lord Jesus had the same problem in understanding the teachings of their Master. They were often confused as to his ministry and purposes, even though he clearly explained himself, using all kinds of parables and illustrations. Their minds had to be opened. Their eyes had to be enlightened. The disciples were having difficulty receiving the words of Jesus because they were not spiritually in tune with him. Their minds did not comprehend the spiritual truths that Jesus spoke. They were not equipped to hear and receive what Jesus was talking about. Something inside them had to be adjusted before they could understand.

Think of it in this way: a radio station transmits words and sounds into the air. Some of the words are AM words while others are FM words. This defines the way the words or sounds are modulated or regulated as they are transmitted. Some are regulated by their amplitude or size. This is called AM. Others are regulated by their frequency. This is called FM. To receive these words and hear them, you must have a 'receiver'. Some receivers will accept FM words and others will accept AM words. If you have an AM radio you cannot receive FM sounds. They are not compatible. In the same way, the Bible speaks of two dimensions in this world. There is a 'natural' dimension and a 'spiritual' dimension'. The natural dimension relates to basic human life. The biblical Greek word that is translated as 'natural' is *psychikos*, meaning 'pertaining to the human mind'. From this word we get 'psychology', which is a study of the natural human mind. The truths of history or science or mathematics are natural truths. They are grasped by the natural capabilities of the human mind.

The words of the Bible are not a part of that natural dimension but are a part of the spiritual dimension. While there is of course a natural dimension to the Bible in that it deals with facts of history and is written in human language, for spiritual knowledge and understanding to be gained and spiritual benefits to be received from the Bible, such as the knowledge of the forgiveness of sins and justification, the mind of the reader must be enlightened, or illuminated, by the Holy Spirit. Without his gracious enlightenment, we are doomed to say, 'I don't understand the Bible. It's beyond me.'

After Jesus rose from the dead, on Easter evening he caught up with two of his disciples who were heading home to Emmaus after celebrating the Passover in Jerusalem. But even though they were followers of Jesus, they did not recognise him. They were very upset by the events that had taken place in Jerusalem. Their Lord and Master had been put to death, and they were discussing these events. Jesus, who was a stranger to them, explained to them from the Old Testament that these events were necessary. It was God's intention for his Messiah to suffer and to die. When they arrived at Emmaus, since it was evening, they invited this Stranger to spend the night with them. At the supper table Jesus broke the bread and gave it to them. At that point their eyes were opened. They saw him. They recognised him as being Jesus. He then disappeared from their sight. In some miraculous fashion, Jesus caused the eyes, the minds, and the hearts of these disciples to become spiritual 'receivers'. They said to each other, 'Were not our hearts burning within us while he talked with us on the road and opened the Scriptures to us?'

This same type of eye-opening experience took place with all the disciples of Jesus immediately before he ascended into heaven. Jesus gathered his disciples together and taught them from the Scriptures that it was necessary for him to suffer and die so that repentance and the forgiveness of sins would be preached to all people. In Luke 24:45 we read this simple yet startling verse: 'Then he opened their minds, so they could understand the Scriptures.' He opened their minds! It was a miracle! Jesus enabled his disciples to understand, and it produced great results.

Queen Katherine lamented her lost and sinful condition, accusing herself of sin. She longed to be set free but could find no peace. Realising that the only answer to her dilemma was in the Word of God, she prayed for the Holy Spirit and her eyes were supernaturally opened to the truth about Christ. What a simple yet profound reality! She writes, 'Then I began to understand that Christ was my only Saviour and Redeemer, and this same teaching to be completely divine, holy, and heavenly, infused[35] by grace into the hearts of the faithful. This never can be attained by human doctrine nor foolish reason, although they should struggle and work for the same until the end of the world.'

The teaching of the Gospel – that Jesus Christ is our only Saviour and Redeemer – as Queen Katherine put it, is 'completely divine, holy and heavenly'. It is not of human origin and can never be 'attained by human doctrine nor foolish reason'. When a Christian begins to understand that Christ is the only Saviour and Redeemer, such knowledge is totally the work of the Holy Spirit 'infused by God's grace into the hearts of the faithful'.

Katherine refers to the Word of God as the 'Book of the Crucifix'. Everything is about Christ crucified, as the Apostle Paul put it: 'For I resolved to know nothing while I was with you except Jesus Christ and him crucified.'[36] 'Then this crucifix is the book, wherein God has included all things,' she wrote, 'and has most concisely written therein, all truth profitable and necessary for our salvation. Therefore, let us endeavour ourselves to study this book, that we, being enlightened with the Spirit of God, may give Him thanks for so great a benefit.'

Katherine questioned whether the blood of Christ was enough to forgive her sins and for good reason. Have you ever wondered how it is possible for the suffering and death of Jesus on the Cross to be enough to forgive the sins of the entire human race, past, present and future? After all, there are those in the past who, on the surface, have probably endured greater suffering at the hands of their enemies than that experienced by Jesus. Think of what Anne Askew went through – being tortured on the rack until her arms and legs became disjointed and to be burned alive at the stake. In your mind, set up a set of the scales of justice. On the one side place all the sins of humanity, past, present and future, and on the other side place the shed blood of Christ on the Cross. How is it possible that the shed blood of Christ is enough to balance the scales? Katherine answers that question: 'We may also, in Christ crucified, weigh our sins as in a divine balance: how grievous and how weighty they are, seeing they have crucified Christ. They would never have been counterbalanced, but with the great and precious weight of the blood of the Son of God.' We can be certain that the suffering and death of Jesus on the cross is more than sufficient to forgive our sins because, as Katherine put it, the scales are balanced with the 'precious weight of the blood of the Son of God'.

Christians are often prone to take lightly the subject of the forgiveness of sins. If a person fails or experiences guilt, someone will be quick to say, 'God will forgive you.' The question is, why should God forgive you? The answer to that question is usually, 'Because He loves me.' There is truth in that answer. The Bible says that God so loved the world that He gave his only Son.[37] While love is what motivated God to forgive the sins of the world, love is not the cause or the reason why God forgives. God forgives because His justice has been satisfied.

Consider the relationship between love and justice.

Let's say a judge, seated on the bench, is asked to sentence a young man who was convicted of committing a crime and deserved to be punished, and that *young man happened to be his son*. Would love and justice be in conflict? While the love of the father for his son would not want to see him punished, the judge, who is just, would be forced to impose the punishment. Justice would have to be satisfied. Sin is an atrocity in the eyes of God. The Apostle Paul writes, 'The wrath of God is being revealed from heaven against all the godlessness and wickedness of people, who suppress the truth by their wickedness.'[38]

Within the biblical context, the word 'atonement' means to appease or to set aside the wrath of God. Atonement for sin requires the shedding of blood. In describing the sacrificial system of Israel, the Old Testament says, 'For the life of a creature is in the blood, and I have given it to you to make atonement for yourselves on the altar; it is the blood that makes atonement for one's life,'[39] and as the New Testament Epistle to the Hebrews echoes, 'without the shedding of blood there is no forgiveness'.[40] The Apostle Paul writes, 'God presented him as a sacrifice of atonement, through faith in his blood.'[41]

Katherine had written, 'I did not consider the blood of Christ to be sufficient to wash me from the filth of my sins as He planted in His Word.' But now, having had her eyes opened to the Gospel, she writes, 'He sent not a servant, or a friend, but His Only Son, so dearly beloved: not in delights, riches, and honours, but in crosses, poverties, and slanders; not as a lord, but as a servant. Yes, in the most vile and painful passions, to wash us: not with water, but with His own precious blood; not from dirt, but from the puddle and filth of our iniquities.'

I'm sure that such references to the blood of Christ are offensive to the sensibilities of some folks. God seems to be described as a 'blood-thirsty' God and not the sweet, kind deity we might prefer. But think about it. If God had imposed some lesser requirement for atonement to take place it would not be an accurate depiction of the attributes of God. The severe requirements for atonement underline the utter holiness and justice of God, and His disdain for sin. God takes your sin very seriously.

Katherine writes that that 'Christ was my only Saviour and Redeemer'. The word 'redemption' means to buy back or to ransom. The blood of Jesus Christ redeemed us from sin, death and the power of the devil. The Apostle Paul writes, 'In him we have redemption through his blood, the forgiveness of sins, in accordance with the riches of God's grace that he lavished on us with all wisdom and understanding.'[42] In his explanation of the Second Article of the Apostles' Creed in his *Small Catechism*, Martin Luther writes concerning Jesus, 'Who has redeemed me, a lost and condemned person, purchased and won me from all sins, from death, and from the power of the devil; not with gold or silver, but with His holy, precious blood and with His innocent suffering and death.'[43]

This sacrifice of Jesus on the cross would be once and for all, unlike the sacrifices in the Old Testament. The writer to the Hebrews declares, 'He did not enter by means of the blood of goats and calves; but he entered the Most Holy Place once for all by his own blood, having obtained eternal redemption.'[44]

Jesus is the lamb of God who takes away the sins of the world.[45] The shed blood of Jesus, the sinless Son of God, on the cross is more than sufficient to forgive our sins. If anyone should ask you, 'How do you know that your sins are forgiven?' Simply reply, 'Because the blood of Christ has been shed on the cross for my forgiveness.'

As I pointed out in the introduction, my original interest in Katherine Parr's *The Lamentation of a Sinner* was the result of reading an article that stated that she had embraced the Lutheran doctrine of justification by faith. Derek Wilson writes, 'Catherine walked the path that Luther and countless others had trodden from utter despair at their sinfulness and alienation from God to the realisation that only faith justifies them.'[46] Katherine wrote, 'Saint Paul says we are justified by faith in Christ, and not by the deeds of the law. For if righteousness came by the law, then Christ died in vain. Thus, I feel myself to come, as it were, in a new garment before God; and now, by His mercy, to be declared just and righteous: which before, without His mercy, was sinful and wicked.'

The doctrine or teaching of justification by faith is the most important truth. Martin Luther wrote: 'If the article of justification is lost, all Christian doctrine is lost at the same time.'[47] John Calvin wrote in his *The Institutes of the Christian Religion*, 'The doctrine of justification is now to be fully discussed, and discussed under the conviction that it is the principal ground on which religion must be supported, so it requires greater care and attention. For unless you understand first of all what your position is before God, and what the judgment which he passes upon you, you have no foundation on which your salvation can be laid, or on which piety toward God can be reared.'[48]

Katherine Parr understood justification. She felt as if she came in a new garment before God, and now, by His mercy, was declared just and righteous. The hymnwriter[49] put it, 'Jesus, Thy blood and righteousness. My beauty are, my glorious dress; 'midst flaming worlds, in these arrayed, with joy shall I lift up my head.' Justification is God declaring a sinner to be righteous.

While I dealt with this issue in the chapter defining textual sources, let us consider in greater detail this vital truth.

If you want to throw out a question that will cause some heated discussion, ask, 'When you stand before God on judgment day, is it necessary that you have a perfect righteousness?' I guarantee that most will say 'No,' and underline their answer by adding, 'Nobody is perfect.'

'No,' you respond. 'That is not true. There is one person who walked the face of this earth who was absolutely perfect in thought, word, and deed and his name is Jesus, and Jesus demanded the same righteousness and perfection of his disciples.'

Consider the following verses.

Jesus said, 'For I tell you that unless your righteousness surpasses that of the Pharisees and the teachers of the law, you will certainly not enter the kingdom of heaven.'[50] In response to that question, the disciples asked, 'Who will ever be saved?' Jesus replied, 'With man it is impossible, but with God all things are possible.' He said, 'Be perfect, therefore, as your heavenly Father is perfect.'[51] According to Jesus, the divine standard for righteousness is the very righteousness and holiness of God himself.

As James wrote, 'For whoever keeps the whole law and yet stumbles at just one point is guilty of breaking all of it.'[52] If you are hanging from a cliff by a chain made up of one hundred links and one link breaks, it is no consolation to say that ninety-nine of them didn't break.

In the *Apology of the Augsburg Confession*, Philip Melanchthon wrote that there are men who imagine that we can keep the law in such a way as to do even more than it requires, but Scripture cries out everywhere that we are far away from the perfection that the law requires.[53]

If the standard for righteousness before God is absolute perfection, how will we ever attain it? Can you imagine making that New Year's resolution? 'From now on I will be perfect.' Most Christians today are unwilling to even entertain such a demand or requirement. I saw a bumper sticker that read, 'Not Perfect, Just Forgiven.' Obviously, the person who attached the bumper sticker did not understand justification.

If there was ever a person who deeply struggled with the issue of sin and righteousness it was Martin Luther. He asked, 'How could a sinful person stand confidently before a perfectly righteous and holy God?' He declared that he hated the God who demanded perfect holiness from a person who was born in sin.

Luther knew and understood the forgiveness of sins and participated daily in 'Confession and Absolution', but he was not at peace. He tried everything to become righteous before God. He joined a monastery and attempted to quiet his conscience by beating himself or wearing a 'hair-shirt'. In 1512, he visited Rome and climbed on his knees the *Scala Sancta*, 'the holy stairs'.[54] No matter what he did, he could find no peace.

Luther described himself as a good monk who kept his orders so strictly that he could say that if ever a monk could get to heaven through monastic discipline it would have been him. All his companions in the monastery who knew him would agree. If his devotions had gone on much longer, he would have martyred himself to death, with vigils, prayers, reading and other works. He said,

> I tried to live according to the Rule with all diligence, and I used to be contrite, to confess and number my sins, and often repeated my confession, and sedulously performed my allotted penance. And yet my conscience could never give me certainty, but I always doubted and said, 'You did not perform that correctly. You were not contrite enough. You left that out of your confession.' The more I tried to remedy an uncertain, weak and afflicted conscience with the traditions of men, the more each day found it more uncertain, weaker, more troubled.[55]

In his classic work *Here I Stand*, Roland Bainton wrote regarding Luther and the Confession of Sins,

> He confessed frequently, often daily, and for as long as six hours on a single occasion ... Luther would repeat a

confession and, to be sure of including everything, would review his entire life until the confessor grew weary and exclaimed, 'Man, God is not angry with you. You are angry with God. Don't you know that God commands you to hope?' In his later years, he believed he had caused permanent damage to his intestines due to his overly scrupulous monastic disciplines.[56]

No matter what he did, he could find no peace, until one day he made an enormous discovery that fuelled the Protestant Reformation and changed the world.

On 31 October 1517, Martin Luther nailed his Ninety-five Theses to the church door in Wittenberg. This date is celebrated as the beginning of the Lutheran Reformation. Yet, the content of the Ninety-five Theses does not reflect the theology that emerged in the later confessional writings as the very impetus and heart of the Reformation. The Theses themselves were merely points of discussion and dealt primarily with the subject of the sale of indulgences and the power of the Pope to remit the penalties of those in purgatory. Luther's theology as reflected in the Ninety-five Theses is certainly not 'Lutheran'.

The real 'shot across the bow' that fuelled the Reformation and changed the face of European Christendom occurred in what has been called Luther's Tower Experience. Luther makes it clear in several places that this Tower Experience, not the posting of the Ninety-five Theses, was the pivotal event of his life.

In 1519,[57] Luther was living in a heated room in the tower of the Black Cloister in Wittenberg, Germany, a monastery of the Augustinian hermits. Later, when all the monks had voluntarily left, it became Luther's home. It was here that he wrestled with the subject of righteousness, especially the phrase 'righteousness of God', found in Romans 1:17. Paul writes in Romans, 'For I am not ashamed of the Gospel of Christ: for it is the power of God unto salvation to everyone that believeth; to the Jew first, and also to the Greek. For therein is the righteousness of God revealed from faith to faith: as it is written, "The just shall live by faith."'[58]

Luther hated the phrase 'the righteousness of God' in Romans
1:17 because he interpreted it, as did Catholic scholastic theologians,
as the active righteousness of God whereby God is just in punishing
sinners. He said, 'I did not love, yes, I hated the righteous God
who punishes sinners, and secretly, if not blasphemously, certainly
murmuring greatly, I was angry with God.' He meditated upon
this phrase and its context day and night, and, as he put it, 'beat
importunately upon Paul at that place'. Finally, the light dawned,
and he writes:

At last, by the mercy of God, meditating day and night,
I gave heed to the context of the words, namely, 'In it the
righteousness of God is revealed, as it is written, "He who
through faith is righteous shall live."' There I began to
understand that the righteousness of God is that by which
the righteous lives by a gift of God, namely by faith. And this
is the meaning: the righteousness of God is revealed by the
gospel, namely, the passive righteousness with which merciful
God justifies us by faith, as it is written, 'He who through
faith is righteous shall live.' Here I felt that I was altogether
born again and had entered paradise itself through open
gates. There a totally other face of the entire Scripture showed
itself to me. Thereupon I ran through the Scriptures from
memory. I also found in other terms an analogy, as, the work
of God, that is, what God does in us, the power of God, with
which he makes us strong, the wisdom of God, with which he
makes us wise, the strength of God, the salvation of God, the
glory of God. And I extolled my sweetest word with a love as
great as the hatred with which I had before hated the word
'righteousness of God'. Thus, that place in Paul was for me
truly the gate to paradise. [59]

The Apostle Paul applies this to his own life:

If anyone else thinks he has reasons to put confidence in the
flesh, I have more: circumcised on the eighth day, of the people

of Israel, of the tribe of Benjamin, a Hebrew of Hebrews; in regard to the law, a Pharisee; as for zeal, persecuting the church; as for legalistic righteousness, faultless. But whatever was to my profit I now consider loss for the sake of Christ. What is more, I consider everything a loss compared to the surpassing greatness of knowing Christ Jesus my Lord, for whose sake I have lost all things. I consider them rubbish, that I may gain Christ and be found in him, not having a righteousness of my own that comes from the law, but that which is through faith in Christ – the righteousness that comes from God and is by faith.[60]

Paul passed judgment upon everything that was a part of his former life and exchanged it for the perfect righteousness of Jesus Christ. He writes, 'God made him who had no sin to be sin for us, so that in him we might become the righteousness of God.'[61] This verse is defined as 'the great exchange'. Jesus takes my sin and gives me, as a gift received by faith, His righteousness, or the righteousness of God. We can be at peace with God! The Apostle Paul declares, 'Therefore, since we have been justified through faith, we have peace with God through our Lord Jesus Christ.'[62]

Martin Luther uncovered the central New Testament teaching of justification by grace through faith because of Christ alone. This is the truth that changed everything and fuelled the Protestant Reformation. It became and continues to be the primary controverted issue between Roman Catholics and the churches of the Reformation.

Rome teaches the infusion of the righteousness of Christ, deposited at Baptism as an investment. Through participation in Sacraments, this righteousness is supposed to develop and grow. At death, if perfection or sainthood is not attained, the sinner is destined for purgatory where the human sinful condition is burned away and only the righteousness of Christ remains. As one priest explained it to me, the gold is placed in the oven to be refined, and when the refiner can see his image in the gold, the individual is ready for the beatific vision or heaven and joins the communion of saints. It is this doctrine of Rome that Erasmus was unwilling to reject.

I found it particularly interesting that in 1545 Parliament granted King Henry authority over the chantries. A chantry was a specified amount of money given to the Church, often designated in a person's will, to require a priest to offer specific Masses for the soul of the deceased in purgatory. Some church buildings had side chapels for the Masses to be spoken. Henry shut down the chantries and confiscated the money, because he needed it. In the Roman Catholic system whereby righteousness is attained, purgatory is necessary. By moving against the chantries, Henry appeared to be moving closer to the Reformation.

Yet, after his death, Masses and dirges were held for his soul, and Thomas Cranmer, who had held his hand in death, did not play a part.[63]

For Luther, the issue was not infusion but imputation. Because of the perfect righteousness of Jesus and his willingness to suffer and die on the Cross, bearing the sins of humanity, God objectively, outside of us, imputes the righteousness of Christ to sinners who, upon coming to faith through the hearing of the Gospel, receive the benefits of that great salvation.

As I pointed out in a previous chapter, in reading *The Lamentation of a Sinner*, I was most impressed by Queen Katherine's understanding of the relationship between justification and faith. This relationship is easily distorted, causing faith to become *causative* of our justification before God or believing that you are justified before God *on account of* your faith. Faith thus becomes a good work or our contribution to the process. Katherine wrote, 'The very true and only property of faith is to take, apprehend, and hold fast the promises of God's mercy, which makes us righteous; and causes me to continually hope for the same mercy; and, in love, to do the many good works ascribed in the Scripture, that I may be thankful for the same.' Katherine goes on to say, 'Yet, we may not impute to the worthiness of faith or good works our justification before God; but ascribe and give the worthiness of it totally to the merits of Christ's passion; and declare and attribute the knowledge and perception of those merits to faith alone.'[64]

Queen Katherine's clear definition of the nature and function of justifying faith is profound, especially since there is a great deal of confusion in the minds of Christians today when it comes to the subject of faith. I have heard people referred to as 'great men or women of faith', yet many of these same people lack the assurance of their righteousness before God. The term 'faith based' is applied to religious institutions or organisations. Faith implies being certain of something even where there is no evidence or proof.

There is a 'general faith in God'. In the minds of some, a Christian is one who believes in God. There is no scientific proof for the existence of God, but it is both reasonable and logical to conclude that such a Being exists. The Bible never sets out to prove the existence of God but assumes it to be true. The Bible begins, 'In the beginning, God...' The Apostle Paul says, 'What may be known about God is plain to them, because God has made it plain to them. For since the creation of the world God's invisible qualities – his eternal power and divine nature – have been clearly seen, being understood from what has been made, so that men are without excuse.'[65]

It is not a profound expression of religious fervour for a person to confess to believe in God. James writes, 'You believe that there is one God. Good! Even the demons believe that – and shudder.'[66] A general faith or belief in God is not what the Bible speaks of as 'saving faith'. The motto of the United States is 'In God We Trust'. While the United States purports to be a God-fearing nation, this does not identify us as being a Christian nation. There is a separation between Church and State.

In England, there is no separation between Church and State. Following in the footsteps of King Henry, the queen is the head of the Church. England is, by definition, a Christian nation, but what does that mean? Subscription to the *Thirty-Nine Articles*, defining the doctrinal position of the Anglican Church, is required for the clergy, but it is not a requirement for the people. One does not have to subscribe to the *Thirty-Nine Articles* to become a citizen of the United Kingdom.

I would surmise that most within the United States and England who claim to be Christian have what is called an 'historical faith'. They believe, as they were taught, that the events recorded in Scripture, specifically the New Testament events about the life of Jesus, His birth, death, resurrection and ascension are true. Even if church attendance may be infrequent, they still celebrate Christmas and Easter. Calvin writes, 'Multitudes undoubtedly believe that God is, and admit the truth of the Gospel history and the other parts of Scripture, in the same way they believe the record of past events, or events which they have actually witnessed',[67] but this is certainly not saving faith.

In the *Lamentation of a Sinner*, Queen Katherine dealt with the issue of 'historical faith'. She wrote:

> But many will wonder and marvel at my statement that I never knew Christ as my Saviour and Redeemer until this time. For many have this opinion, saying, 'Who doesn't know there is a Christ? Who, being a Christian, does not confess Him as his Saviour?' And, thus they believe that their dead, human, historical faith and knowledge (which they have learned in their scholastic books) and may be had with all sin (as I said before), to be the true, infused faith and knowledge of Christ. Thus, they say that by their own experience of themselves, that their faith does not justify them. And true it is, except they have this faith, which I have described before, they shall never be justified.

When Kathrine says, 'Thus, they say that by their own experience of themselves', I wonder to whom she might be referring? With whom, other than her husband the King, did she debate and discuss these issues? Were there others who opposed her understanding of faith? Perhaps Henry had said to her, 'Kate, I have faith but by my own experience, my faith does not make me righteous before God.' Did Katherine have the courage to refer to her husband's faith as a 'dead, human, historical faith'? Perhaps she did. As we saw earlier, Henry was not very happy that he was being taught by his wife.

As Katherine said, the scholastic scholars taught that faith could exist 'with all sin'. In his *Commentary on Galatians*, Martin Luther dealt with this issue: 'Who could stand for the teaching that faith, the gift of God that is infused in the heart by the Holy Spirit, can coexist with mortal sin? If they were speaking about acquired or historical faith and about a natural opinion derived from history, they could be endured; indeed, they would be right if they were speaking about historical faith. But to believe this way about infused faith is to admit openly that they understand nothing at all about faith.'[68]

'Saving faith' is not directed at the historical events of the death and resurrection of Jesus but at the *benefits* received from those events. It is one thing to say, 'I believe Jesus died and rose again.' It is something quite different to say that *because* Jesus died and rose again my sins are forgiven. I am righteous before God, and I have eternal life in heaven.

Obviously, you cannot believe in Jesus and claim the forgiveness of sins unless you know that Jesus died on the cross and shed his blood for your salvation. The Apostle Paul writes, 'How, then, can they call on the one they have not believed in? And how can they believe in the one of whom they have not heard? And how can they hear without someone preaching to them?'[69] The starting point for faith is the knowledge of the historical events.

Perhaps from childhood you were taught the truth about Jesus and his, life, death and resurrection. You believe it and agree with it. You speak the words of the Apostles' Creed, 'I believe in the forgiveness of sins.' But there is still one thing lacking: trust. The confident assurance that because Jesus died for you, *your* sins are forgiven, *you* are righteous before God, and *you* have eternal life. Faith is not some non-descript emotion about God or the mere acknowledgment of historical events. Faith is very specific. Faith grasps and apprehends the promises of God as Queen Katherine so clearly pointed out.

There was no love lost between Henry VIII and Martin Luther. To begin with, Luther had written a fiercely angry, sarcastic and at points obscene response to Henry's *Defence of the Seven Sacraments*, a document of which Henry was quite proud. Henry responded in kind, calling Luther several non-complimentary names. Luther, thinking he was moving Henry toward the Reformation, offered a very humble apology; Henry refused it and made Luther an object of derision. When it came to the King's Great Matter, Luther stated that the king should not under any circumstances be permitted to divorce his wife, Catherine of Aragon. Luther later concluded that God did not wish his gospel to be touted by this king who had such a bad reputation.[70]

Henry resolutely rejected Luther's understanding of justification by faith since he felt that Luther disparaged good works. Imagine, if you can, the situation when Henry's 'beloved Kate' embraced justification by faith and was neither ashamed nor afraid to share it.

We know that Katherine and Henry engaged in discussions and debates about religion. Quoting from John Foxe *Acts and Monuments*, Linda Porter writes, 'She had become bold enough "to debate with the king touching religion". Henry, who always had a very high opinion of his own views on such matters, bore Katherine's disputations quietly, despite the pain from his legs: "In cases of religion as occasion served, she would not confine herself to reverent terms and humble talk, entering with him into discourse, with sound reasons of scripture."'[71]

One evening, probably early in 1546, Bishop Stephen Gardiner overheard a conversation between Henry and Katherine in which Katherine was arguing a specific point of religion. After Henry bade his wife good night and Katherine left, the king complained to Gardiner, 'A good hearing it is,' he fumed, 'when women become such clerks, and much to my comfort to come in mine old age to be taught by my wife!' Gardiner replied, 'His Majesty should easily perceive how perilous a matter it is to cherish a serpent within his own bosom.' According to Martin Luther, we know Gardiner despised the teaching of justification by faith. Luther wrote regarding him, 'He intends to maintain against the whole world that the thesis, "We are justified by faith," is wrong.'[72] Within that context, I wonder what Katherine was trying to teach Henry that would cause him to bristle, and Gardiner to refer to her as a 'serpent within his own bosom'?

While Katherine recognised Henry's role as head of the Church of England, she was becoming quite bold in her commitment to the Gospel. She responded to the Cambridge faculty in February 1546 by accusing them of being 'ashamed of the Gospel'. Regarding the subject of doctrine, she wrote in the *Lamentation*, 'Truly, in my simple and unlearned judgment, no man's doctrine is to be esteemed, or preferred to Christ's and the Apostles', nor to be taught as a perfect and true doctrine, but only as it does agree with the doctrine of the Gospel.' This would have been seen as a major slap at Henry, whose *Six Articles* was clearly the doctrine of men and not in agreement with the Gospel.

I don't think it is a major stretch of the imagination to surmise that Katherine had the courage to openly discuss the doctrine of justification with her husband, particularly the relationship between faith and good works, since this was the main issue that prompted Henry's rejection of justification by faith. Katherine, who was probably already working on *The Lamentation of a Sinner*, had written:

> This esteem of faith does not disparage good works, for out of this faith springs all good works. Yet, we may not impute to the worthiness of faith or good works our justification before God; but ascribe and give the worthiness of it totally to the merits of Christ's passion; and declare and attribute the knowledge and perception of those merits to faith alone. The very true and only property of faith is to take, apprehend, and hold fast the promises of God's mercy, which makes us righteous; and causes me to continually hope for the same mercy; and, in love, to do the many good works ascribed in the Scripture, that I may be thankful for the same ... For, unless this great benefit of Christ crucified is felt and fixed surely in man's heart, there can be no good work done, acceptable before God.

In their debate and discussion, these were probably the very arguments Katherine used to counter Henry's objection to justification. Katherine's understanding of good works was identical to that confessed by Luther and the reformers in the *Augsburg Confession*: 'Our teachers teach in addition that it is necessary to do good works, not that we should trust to merit grace by them but because it is the will of God. It is only by faith that forgiveness of sins and grace are apprehended, and because through faith the Holy Spirit is received, hearts are so renewed and endowed with new affections as to be able to bring forth good works.'[73]

Katherine's teaching on good works and the Christian life goes contrary to popular thinking, not only in her day, but also in our day. Good works are often defined as good acts that are performed such as generously giving to the Church, supporting various charities or donating your time for a beneficial project. While all these things are well and good and should be encouraged, for Katherine, her emphasis and the emphasis in the *Augsburg Confession*, is not upon the good works themselves but upon the heart. 'But I fear that God may say to us: "This people honours me with their lips, but their hearts are far from me." God desires nothing but the heart and says that He will be worshipped in spirit and in truth. Christ condemned all hypocrisy and false holiness, and taught sincere, pure, and true godliness.'

Katherine was critical of the emphasis upon good works – not the performance of them but how they were defined. 'There are in the world many speakers of holiness and good works; but very rarely and seldom is it declared what those good and holy works are. The fruit of the Spirit[74] is almost never spoken of. Therefore, very few know what they are.' She realised that the mere performance of various acts of charity and good deeds could be motivated by pride, as was the case of the Pharisees who performed their good works openly to receive the praise of men. Katherine wrote, 'The Pharisees also took opportunity by the evil of others to grow haughty and proud, taking themselves to be men of greater perfection than any other because of their virtue, as they did when they saw the publican's confession.

And so, they are offended with every little thing, judging evil, murmuring against their neighbour; and, for that reason, they are reputed by many as being more holy and good, but, indeed, they are more wicked.'

Therefore, Christians should have no desire to perform outward good works to demonstrate their holiness, or, as she put it, 'They do not flatter themselves and think that everything that shines in the world is good and holy, for they know that all external and outward works that are not so glorious and fair to the world, may still be prompted by evil as well as of good. Therefore, they have very little estimate for the outward show of holiness.'

Getting to the very heart of the issue, Katherine writes, 'I wish all Christians, that as they have professed Christ, would so endeavour to follow Him in godly living. For we have not put on Christ to live any more to ourselves, in the vanities, delights, and pleasures of the world and the flesh, permitting the desires and carnality of the flesh to have full sway. For we must walk after the Spirit, and not after the flesh. For the Spirit is spiritual, and desires spiritual things, and the flesh carnal, and desires carnal things.'

The Apostle Paul says, 'So then, just as you received Christ Jesus as Lord, continue to live in him, rooted and built up in him.'[75] While Katherine accurately defines the biblical understanding that living the Christian life and doing good works proceeds from the heart as a result of putting on Christ, following Him and walking after the Spirit, she acknowledges that conflict remains.

And although the children of God sometime do fall by frailty into some sin, yet that falling causes them to humble themselves, and to acknowledge the goodness of God, and to come to Him for refuge and help ... Therefore, sin has no power against them, who are by the Holy Spirit united to Christ; in them there is nothing worthy of damnation. And although the dregs of Adam do remain, that is, our desires of the flesh, which indeed are sins: nevertheless, they are not imputed as sins, if we are truly joined to Christ.

The *Lutheran Confessions* affirm this: 'But in this life Christians are not renewed perfectly and completely. For although their sins are covered up through the perfect obedience of Christ, so that they are not reckoned to believers for damnation, and although the Holy Spirit has begun the mortification of the Old Adam and their renewal in the spirit of their minds, nevertheless the Old Adam still clings to their nature and to all its internal and external powers.'[76] John Calvin writes, 'I insist not that the life of the Christian shall breathe nothing but the perfect Gospel, though this is to be desired, and ought to be attempted. I insist not so strictly on evangelical perfection, as to refuse to acknowledge any man who has not attained it. In this way, all would be excluded from the church.'[77]

The undeniable evidence of the Christian life is conflict. Even though we have come to believe in Christ as our Lord and Saviour and the Holy Spirit has graciously opened our eyes to the truth of his Gospel, assuring us that we are forgiven and righteous in the sight of God, out sinful nature is always at odds with our new spiritual life in Christ Jesus. We desire to live in Christ and walk after the Spirit, but we daily fail and sin against God. Many or our thoughts, words and actions are contrary to the will of God.

Katherine Parr must have known this quite well, especially after her controversial marriage to Thomas Seymour and her battle with her sister-in-law Anne Stanhope, Duchess of Somerset, as to who had the right to wear the queen's jewels. But unlike many of us, Katherine was very willing to confess and acknowledge her sins and failures. At the end of *The Lamentation of a Sinner*, Katherine writes, 'But, alas, we are so much given to love and to flatter ourselves, and so blinded with carnal affections, that we can see and perceive no fault in ourselves. And therefore, it is required and necessary for us, to pray with one heart and mind to God, to give us a heavenly light and knowledge of our own miseries and calamities, that we may truly see them and acknowledge them before Him.'

The Word of God assures us, 'If we claim to be without sin, we deceive ourselves and the truth is not in us. If we confess our sins, he is faithful and just and will forgive us our sins and purify us from all unrighteousness. If we claim we have not sinned, we make him out to be a liar and his word has no place in our lives.'[78]

Queen Katherine understood that the dynamic of the Christian life and the performance of good works was not the result of human effort and design. The Christian life was the production of the fruit of the Spirit brought about by living and walking in the Spirit. Paul writes to the Ephesians, 'Be filled with the Spirit. Speak to one another with psalms, hymns and spiritual songs. Sing and make music in your heart to the Lord, always giving thanks to God the Father for everything, in the name of our Lord Jesus Christ.'[79] And to the Colossians he writes, 'Let the peace of Christ rule in your hearts, since as members of one body you were called to peace. And be thankful. Let the word of Christ dwell in you richly as you teach and admonish one another with all wisdom, and as you sing psalms, hymns and spiritual songs with gratitude in your hearts to God. And whatever you do, whether in word or deed, do it all in the name of the Lord Jesus, giving thanks to God the Father through him.'[80]

There is one final teaching of Queen Katherine that we need to consider. It is the controversial and contentious teaching of election or predestination.

Luther's posting of the Ninety-five Theses to the church door in Wittenberg produced much discussion and debate. Luther wanted the opportunity to defend what he had written. His father confessor and superior in the Augustinian order, Johann Staupitz, provided him that opportunity at the April 1518 meeting of the general chapter of the Augustinians of Germany in Heidelberg, historically referred to as the Heidelberg Disputation. Staupitz asked Luther to avoid the more controversial topics of the Ninety-five Theses, and instead to simply talk about sin, free will, and grace. Luther obliged, preparing and presenting twenty-eight theological and twelve philosophical theses, with brief explanations. He defined these statements as 'paradoxes'.

Luther made the controversial statements that the 'works of men, let them be as fair and good as they may, are yet evidently nothing but mortal sins', that 'free will since the fall of man is but an empty word' and that 'a man who dreams he can attain to grace by doing all that is in his power, adds sin to sin, and is doubly guilty'. In 1520, in his treatise on *The Freedom of the Christian Man*, Luther declared that good works, if done with an eye to gaining credit with God, are damnable sins. Luther's comments stood in opposition to the Church's declaration regarding the value of good works and the merit gained.

Somebody had to deal with the radical statements of this German monk; they could not go unchecked. That somebody, in the eyes of the Pope, was the renowned scholar Desiderius Erasmus of Rotterdam. Even though the new Pope, Adrian, asked him to do so, Erasmus wasn't interested. He was no theologian and had no intention of engaging in some theological battle. It was not a part of his nature to do so. Erasmus desired peace at all costs. Cuthbert Tunstall, a former friend of the Parr family and the one who helped oversee the education of Queen Katherine, was now the Bishop of London. He wrote to Erasmus concerning Luther, 'The Pope calls upon you to refute him. No more pernicious heresy was ever voiced than his. What greater glory can ever come to a scholar than to have refuted heresy.'[81] It was King Henry himself who encouraged Erasmus to deal with the subject of free will. Henry vehemently opposed Luther's rejection of good works as being meritorious. Finally, Erasmus relented. In 1525, he presented his *De libero Arbitrio* or *Concerning the Freedom of the Will*. One year later, Luther responded to Erasmus with his classic work *De Servo Arbitrio* or *The Bondage of the Will*.

A major topic in their debate was election or predestination, which Erasmus totally rejected since it violated human free will. Regarding predestination, Erasmus 'branded the doctrine as simply monstrous. God is a tyrant if he condemns man for what he cannot help. To damn some and save others who are no better is unfair.'[82] For Erasmus, man aided by the grace of God can choose God or reject God and his grace. Luther, based on the fallen nature of man, rejected that notion. Man had no choice in the matter. It is God who, before the foundation of world, elected those who would be saved.

The teaching of predestination was a central part of the theology of the Swiss reformer John Calvin. Calvin taught a 'double predestination' whereby God had elected unconditionally those who were being saved and, in his sovereignty, elected others for damnation. This produced what has been described as the five points of Calvinism: man is totally depraved; God elects unconditionally; atonement is limited to the elect; for the elect, the grace of God proclaimed in the Gospel is irresistible; and those who are elected will persevere until the end.

While it appears from *Bondage of the Will* that Luther and Calvin were of one mind, that was not the case. Luther applied God's election or predestination to the believer, but not to the unbeliever. Recognising that the Bible often refers to those who reject Jesus and the Gospel, Luther concluded that if people are not saved and wind up in hell, it is their own fault. Luther writes, 'If God does not desire our death, that fact that we perish must be charged to our own will. This is correct, I say, if you speak of the God who is preached; for he does want all men to be saved, because he comes to all by the Word of salvation, and the will that does not receive Him is at fault.'[83] Of course, Luther is illogical. If the children of God are saved because they are elected, it would follow that those who are not saved have not been elected. Alternatively, if those who are not saved have rejected by their own will the Gospel, those who are saved have accepted by their own will the Gospel. But Luther had no interest in creating a logical system; he simply allowed Scripture to speak, and if it appeared illogical then it was simply a mystery. For Luther, the doctrine of predestination was for the comfort of the believer, not to answer the question *cur alii, alii non* ('why some and not others'). Luther believed that contention over the subject of predestination was a temptation of the devil.[84]

A later Lutheran confessional writing, the *Formula of Concord*, states, 'Predestination or the eternal election of God, is concerned only with the pious children of God in whom he is well pleased. It is the cause of their salvation, for He alone bring it about and ordains everything that belongs to it.'[85] Further, 'The reason why all who hear the Word of God do not come to faith and therefore receive the greater damnation is not that God did not want them to be saved. It is their own fault ... They resisted the Holy Spirit who wanted to work within them.'[86]

Now, with that being said, what did Queen Katherine teach about this subject? This is a very important consideration for two reasons. Many have suggested that the English Reformation was Erasmian in nature. Those who followed Erasmus' 'philosophy of Christ', believing that they had the free will, aided by the grace of God, to follow Christ and be a good person would obviously reject Luther's predestination and accept Erasmus' freedom of the will. Thus, if Katherine accepted election it would be a blatant rejection of Erasmus. Secondly, since her husband the king had requested Erasmus to write against Luther's rejection of free will, Katherine's acceptance of election would be in direct opposition to her husband.

So, let's hear what Katherine has to say.

'There was never so glorious a spoil, neither a more rich and noble one, than Christ was upon the cross: which delivered all His elect from such a sharp, miserable captivity.'

'So, it is evident that the triumph, victory, and glory of Christ is the greater, having subdued the devil that, whereas he was prince and lord of the world, holding all creatures in captivity, now Christ uses him as an instrument to punish the wicked, and to exercise and strengthen the elect of God in Christian warfare.'

'And know that Christ still fights in spirit in His elect vessels and shall fight even to the day of judgment.'

'It was no little favour towards His children, that Christ was chosen of God to save us, His elect, so exceedingly, by the way of the cross. Paul calls it a grace, and a most singular grace.'

'He that has sinned may be one of God's elect; perhaps the Lord has allowed him to fall so that he may know himself better.'

In the next brief statement, echoing the thoughts from Luther's Heidelberg paradoxes, Katherine not only rejects the possibility that man, using his free will, can follow the teachings of Christ but quotes from Ephesians 1:4: 'For he chose us in him before the creation of the world.' She writes, 'For they know, by themselves, they can do nothing but sin. They are not so foolish and childish, not to give God thanks for their election, which was before the beginning of the world.'

Katherine, by teaching on election, rejected the Erasmian notion of free will and, in opposition to both Erasmus and her husband the king, rejected the possibility of good works contributing anything to one's salvation. It was totally the work of God. But which 'brand' of predestination did she embrace: Luther or Calvin?

There is one brief but very interesting quotation dealing with this question. Katherine is lamenting the attitudes and actions of those whom she describes as 'ignorant and immature'. She writes, 'And because they see that the good are not rewarded with riches, they often imagine that God does not love them. It seems to them God is partial, because He hath elected some, and some reproved. They use that as an occasion to do evil saying, "Whatsoever God hath determined, shall take place."'

While this is a reference to 'double predestination', Katherine is not affirming it but indicating the problem that arises when some embrace it. They have no concern. Whatever God has determined will come to pass. Thomas Cranmer's influence upon Katherine would not have led her into the Calvinist camp. Article seventeen of the *Thirty-Nine Articles* presents primarily a Lutheran understanding of predestination. It is for the comfort of God's chosen people. While Katherine speaks of the many enemies of the Gospel, she never indicates that their attitudes demonstrate that they are not a part of the elect.

Katherine believed in the clarity of Scripture pertaining to life and salvation, but she acknowledges that 'the children of God are not curious in searching the high mysteries of God, which are not proper for them to know. They do not dilute Scripture with 'human doctrine, philosophy, and logic.'

There is much we can learn from Queen Katherine: know your Bible, especially those sections from the epistles that direct you to live and walk in Christ Jesus; confess that through Christ Jesus you are forgiven and righteous before God; you are one of God's elect children; when you fail, confess your sins and failures to God and receive His great forgiveness.

Katherine Parr was a remarkable woman. The final wife of the infamous King Henry VIII, she became the gentle companion and confidant of an often angry, irascible and vicious monarch with whom she undoubtedly shared the Good News of the Gospel. She ruled England for six months while Henry was in France. She reunited Henry's family. Through her influence, women were, for the first time, listed as successors to the throne of England. She left an indelible mark upon young Elizabeth, who would later rule England for forty-five years. She was the first woman to be published in England under her own name. Yet of all her accomplishments, her greatest legacy remains a small treatise, unknown and buried in obscurity for hundreds of years, in which she profoundly sets forth the primary teachings of the Christian faith in opposition to traditional Roman Catholicism and Erasmian piety – *The Lamentation of a Sinner.*

BIBLIOGRAPHY

Dickens, A. G., *The English Reformation* (New York: Schocken Books, 1964)

Anonymous, *The British Reformers* (Philadelphia: Presbyterian Church Board of Publication, 1842)

Bainton, Roland H., *Erasmus of Christendom* (Peabody: Hendrickson Publishers, 1969)

-----------, *Here I Stand* (Nashville: Abingdon Press, 2013)

-----------, *Women of the Reformation: In France and England* (Minneapolis: Fortress Press, 1973)

Calvin, John, *The Institutes of the Christian Religion* (Grand Rapids: Eerdmans, 1983)

d'Aubigne', Merle, *History of the Great Reformation of the Sixteenth Century* (New York: Robert Carter, 1842)

Dubrow, Heather and Streier, Richard (eds), *The Historical Renaissance: New Essays on Tudor and Stuart Literature and Culture* (Chicago: University of Chicago Press, 1988)

Elert, Werner. *The Structure of Lutheranism* (St. Louis: Concordia Publishing House, 1962)

Elizabeth I, *Elizabeth I: Collected Works 1st Edition* (ed. Marcus, Mueller, Rose) (Chicago: University of Chicago Press, 2000)

Erickson, Carolly, *The First Elizabeth* (New York: St. Martin's Press, 1983)

Gregory D. Dodds, *Exploiting Erasmus, The Erasmian Legacy and Religious Change in Early Modern England* (Toronto: University of Toronto Press, 2009)

Foxe, John, *Fox's Book of Martyrs* (CreateSpace Independent Publishing Platform, 2017)

Gregory, Philippa, *The Taming of the Queen* (New York: Touchstone, 2016)

Haigh, Christopher, *English Reformation* (Oxford: Oxford University Press, 1993)

Hannay, Margaret P. (ed.) *Silent but for the Word: Tudor Women as Patrons, Translators, and Writers of Religious Works* (Kent: Kent State University Press, 1985)

Haugaard, William P., 'Katherine Parr: The Religious Convictions of a Renaissance Queen', *Renaissance Quarterly* 22, no. 4 (1969)

Hoffman, C. Fenno, Jr., 'Catherine Parr as Woman of Letters', *Huntington Library Quarterly* 23, no. 4 (1960)

Hume, Martin, *The Wives of Henry VIII and the Parts They Played in History* (London: Eveleigh Nash, 1905)

James, Susan, *Catherine Parr* (Gloucestershire: The History Press, 2008)

Jones, Whitney R. D., *Erasmus the Reformer* (London: Methuen, 1994)

Katz, David S., *The Jews in the History of England 1485–1850* (Oxford: Oxford University Press, 1996)

Kaufman, Rosalie, *Agnes Strickland's Queens of England*. Vol. I. of III, Abridged (Boston: Estes, 1882)

Ledderhose, Karl Friedrich, *The Life of Philip Melanchthon* (Philadelphia: Lindsay & Blakiston, 1855)

Prole, Lozania, *Henry's Last Love* (London: Corazon Books, 2017)

Luther, Martin, *Commentary on Romans* (tr. J. T. Mueller) (Grand Rapids: Zondervan Publishing House, 1954)

----------, *Luther's Works* (Philadelphia: Fortress Press, 1999)

----------, *Small Catechism* (St. Louis: Concordia Publishing House, 1986).

Marshall, Peter, *Heretics and Believers: A History of the English Reformation*. (New Haven: Yale University Press, 2017)

Martin, Randall, *Women Writers in Renaissance England* (Oxfordshire: Routledge; 2010)

Martienssen, Anthony, *Queen Katherine Parr* (London: Martin Secker & Warburg, 1973)

Matzat, Don, *Christ-Esteem* (Eugene: Harvest House Publishers, 1990)

----------, *The Lord Told Me, I Think* (Eugene, Harvest House Publishers, 1996)

----------, *Truly Transformed* (Eugene: Harvest House Publishers, 1992)

----------, *Ten Steps* (Independently Published KDP, 2018)

McConica, James, *English Humanists and Reformation Politics* (Oxford: Clarendon Press, 1965)

Metaxas, Eric, *Martin Luther* (New York: Penguin Random House, 2017)

Mueller, Janel, *Katherine Parr, Complete Works and Correspondence* (Chicago: University of Chicago Press, 2014)

Norton, Elizabeth, *Catherine Parr* (Gloucestershire: Amberley Publishing, 2009)

Bibliography

Packer, J. R. and Johnston, O. R., *Martin Luther on the Bondage of the Will* (New York: Fleming H. Revel, 1957)

Parr, Katherine, *The Lamentation of a Sinner* (ed. Don Matzat) (Independently published KDP, 2017)

Plass, Ewald W., *What Luther Says* (St. Louis: Concordia Publishing House, 1994)

Porter, Linda, *Katherine the Queen* (New York: St. Martin's Press, 2010)

Read, Conyers, *Mr Cecil and Queen Elizabeth* (London: Jonathan Cape, 1953)

Revell, Anna, *Henry VIII* (Independently published, 2018)

Roberts, David E., *Existentialism and Religious Belief* (New York: Oxford University Press, 1959)

Sansom, C. J., *Lamentation* (New York: Little, Brown and Company, 2014)

Smalley, Beryl, *The Study of the Bible in the Middle Ages* (Notre Dame: University of Notre Dame Press, 1978)

Sproul, R. C., *The Prayer of the Lord* (Ligonier: Reformation Trust Publishing, 2009)

Starkey, David, *Six Wives* (New York: Harper Collins Publishers, 2009)

Summers, Claude J. and Pebworth, Ted Larry, *Representing Women in Renaissance England* (Columbia: University of Missouri Press, 1997)

Steinmetz, David C., *Luther in Context* (Grand Rapids: Baker, 2002)

Strype, John, *Life of the Learned Sir John Cheke* (Oxford: Clarendon Press, 1821)

Tappert, T. G., *The Book of Concord* (Philadelphia: Fortress Press, 1959)

----------, *Theological Quarterly*, Vol. 23 (published by the Lutheran Synod of Missouri, Ohio and other States, 1919)

Tournier, Paul, *Guilt and Grace* (New York: Harper and Row, 1959).

Van Gelder, H. A. Enno, *The Two Reformations in the 16th Century* (The Hague, 1961)

Weir, Alison, *Anna of Kleve, The Princess in the Portrait* (New York: Random House, 2019)

----------, *The Six Wives of Henry VIII* (New York: Harper Collins Publishers, 1991)

Wilberforce, William, *Real Christianity* (Holland, Ohio: Dreamscape Media, 2018)

Wilson, Derek, *The Queen and the Heretic* (Oxford: Lion Hudson, 2018)

Withrow, Brandon G., *Katherine Parr* (Philadelphia: P&R Publishing, 2009)

Zahl, Paul, *Five Women of the English Reformation* (Grand Rapids: Eerdmans, 2011)

NOTES

Introduction

1. A. G. Dickens, *The English Reformation,* New York, Schocken Books, 1964, pp. 59-60
2. Ewald Plass, *What Luther Says,* Concordia Publishing House, 2011. P. 703
3. Edward Mote (1834), pastor at Horsham, Sussex.
4. Derek Wilson, *The Queen and the Heretic.* Lion Hudson, 2018. Kindle Edition, Location 2971
5. Brandon G. Withrow, *Katherine Parr, A Guided Tour of the Life and Thought of a Reformation Queen* P&R Publishing, 2009. p. 12.
6. Anonymous, *The British Reformers,* Philadelphia, Presbyterian Board of Publication, 1842. P. 184.
7. Katherine Parr, *The Lamentation of a Sinner* (Adapted with Introduction by Don Matzat) Independently published, 2017.
8. C. J. Sansom, *Lamentation,* Little, Brown and Company, 2014, p. 65.
9. Linda Porter, *Katherine the Queen: The Remarkable Life of Katherine Parr, the Last Wife of Henry VIII).* St. Martin's Press, 2011. p. 241.
10. Elizabeth Norton, *Catherine Parr,* Amberley Publishing, 2011. Digital Location 2305.
11. Agnes Strickland's *Queens of England,* Vol. 1. Boston: Estes & Lauriat, 1853, p. 436.
12. Alison Weir, *The Six Wives of Henry VIII.* Grove Atlantic, 2007, pp 547-548.
13. Susan James, *Catherine Parr,* The History Press, 2009. Digital Location 3767.
14. Janel Mueller: *Katherine Parr, Complete Works and Correspondence,* University of Chicago Press, 2011, p. 442.
15. Ibid., p. 297.

16. Conyers Read, *Mr Secretary Cecil and Queen Elizabeth*, Jonathan Cape, 1955, pp.39.
17. Derek Wilson, *The Queen and the Heretic*, Digital Location 1649.
18. Ibid.
19. Janel Mueller, et. al. *The Cambridge History of Early Modern English Literature,* p. 297.
20. C. Feno. Hoffman Jr., "Catherine Parr as Woman of Letters." *Huntington Library Quarterly* 23, no. 4 (1960): 349-67.
21. Porter, *Katherine the Queen*, p. 349.
22. Katherine Parr, *The Lamentation of a Sinner,* Amazon, KDP Publishing, 2017. Pp. 27-28

1. *The Tumultuous Tudors*

1. After the battle, Richard's corpse was taken to Leicester and buried. His remains were lost for more than five hundred years. In 2012, an archaeological excavation in the city council car park, which had once been the site of Greyfriars Priory Church, uncovered a skeleton. The University of Leicester identified the skeleton as that of Richard III. His remains were reburied in Leicester Cathedral on March 26, 2015
2. Roland Bainton. *Women of the Reformation: In France and England*, Fortress Press, 1973, Digital Locations 1698-1700.
3. Appointed to rule Scotland because her son James V was a minor.
4. Starkey, David. *Six Wives*. HarperCollins e-books. Kindle Edition, Location 858.
5. Starkey, *Six Wives*. Location 879.
6. Weir, Alison. *The Six Wives of Henry VIII*. Grove Atlantic, p. 34.
7. It is interesting to note that in 2002, five hundred years after the death of Arthur, ground-probing radar was used to discover his grave below the limestone floor of Worcester Cathedral. The tomb was opened in hopes of discovering the cause of his death, but the efforts were inconclusive.
8. Starkey, *Six Wives*, Location 1899.
9. Weir, Alison. *The Six Wives,* p. 56.
10. Starkey, *Six Wives,* Location 2210.

2. *The King's Great Matter*

1. Starkey, *Six Wives*, Location 2219
2. Ibid., P. 232
3. A queen *consort* is the wife of a reigning king as opposed to a queen *regeant* who is a queen in her own right.
4. Quoted in Strickland, *Queens of England*, pp.366-368

5. Weir, *Six Wives*, p. 77

6. Peter Marshall, *Heretics and Believers, a History of the English Reformation,* Yale University Press, 2017, p 127.

7. Weir, *Six Wives*, pp. 76-77

8. Metaxas, Eric. *Martin Luther: The Man Who Rediscovered God and Changed the World.* Penguin Publishing Group, 2017, pp. 378-379.

9. *Theological Quarterly,* published by the Lutheran Synod of Missouri, Ohio and other States, Vol. 23, 1919. p. 255.

10. The Peasant's War was a widespread popular revolt in some German-speaking areas in Central Europe from 1524 to 1525. It was the largest revolt in Europe prior to the French Revolution.

11. Metaxas, *Martin Luther,* p. 379

12. Quoted in Metaxas, *Martin Luther,* p. 378

13. Weir, *Six Wives*, p. 139.

14. Porter, *Katherine the Queen*, p. 183

15. Starkey, *Six Wives,* p. 161.

16. The duties discharged by ladies-in-waiting included secretarial tasks; reading correspondence to her mistress and writing on her behalf; wardrobe care; supervision of servants and other "queenly" duties.

17. Weir, *Six Wives*, p. 194.

18. Marshall, *Believers and Heretics,* p. 166.

19. Strickland, Agnes. *Queens of England*, Vol. 1. Boston: Estes & Lauriat, p. 369.

20. Ibid., p.171.

21. Weir, *Six Wives*, p. 195

22. Starkey, *Six Wives,* p. 344.

23. Metaxas, *Martin Luther*, p. 357.

24. Ibid., p. 357.

25. Weir, *Six Wives*, p. 216.

26. Anthony Martienssen, *Queen Katherine Parr*, Martin Secker & Warburg, London, 1973, p. 46.

27. Weir, *Six Wives*, p. 196.

28. Starkey, *Six Wives*, Digital Location 16866.

29. Weir, *Six Wives,* p. 224.

30. Ibid., p. 215

31. "King Henry 8 – Rabbis and his Divorce," 15 December 2012, *The Stranger Side of Jewish History,"* strangeside.com/king-henry-8-rabbis-and-his-divorce (Accessed 22 May 2019). Source: David S. Katz, *The Jews in the History of England 1485-1850,* Oxford University Press, 1996.

32. Mary, daughter of Henry and Catherine of Aragon.

33. Martin Luther, *Luther's Works*, vol. 50: Letters III, Philadelphia: Fortress Press, pp. 32-33.
34. Marshall, *Believers and Heretics*, p. 181.
35. Starkey, *Six Wives*, p. 463
36. Weir, *Six Wives*, p. 250.
37. Carolly Erickson, *The First Elizabeth*, St. Martin's Press, 1983, p. 12.
38. Weir, *Six Wives*, p. 222.
39. Ibid., p. 251.

3. 'Divorced, Beheaded, Died...'

1. Weir, *Six Wives*, p. 258.
2. Ibid., p.293.
3. Starkey, *Six Wives*, p. 553.
4. Strickland, *Queens of England*, Vol. 1, p. 399.
5. Norris was the "groom of the stool," placing him in the most intimate relationship with the King.
6. Starkey, *Six Wives*, pp. 564-565.
7. John Foxe, *The Acts and Monuments of the Christian Church*, Vol.6 The Reign of King Henry VIII. – Part I, pp. 319-320.
8. Ibid.
9. James, *Catherine Parr*, Digital location 5575.
10. Starkey, *Six Wives*, Digital location 10194
11. Ibid., Kindle location 9226.
12. Weir, Six Wives, p. 369.
13. Starkey, *Six Wives*, Kindle location 10623.
14. Ibid., pp. 302-303
15. Porter, *Katherine the Queen*, p. 70
16. The Schmalkaldic League was a military alliance of Lutheran princes within the Holy Roman Empire officially established on February 27, 1531, by Philip I, Landgrave of Hesse, and John Frederick I, Elector of Saxony, the two most powerful Protestant rulers in the Holy Roman Empire.
17. *Luther's Works*, vol. 50 Letters III, Introduction to Luther's 1539 Letter to Elector John Frederick, Philadelphia: Fortress Press 1999, p. 190.
18. Karl Frederich Ledderhose, *The Life of Philip Melanchthon*, Lindsay & Blakiston,1855, Digital Locations 1550-1552.
19. Ibid.
20. *Luther's Works*, Letters III, Philadelphia: Fortress Press, 1999, pp. 202-203.
21. Weir, *The Six Wives*, p. 384.
22. Strickland, *Queens of England*, Vol. 1, p. 413. While Strickland quotes this, the validity of the statement has been debated.

23. Weir, *Six Wives*, p. 406.
24. Alison Weir. *Anna of Kleve, The Princess in the Portrait,* Random House Publishing Group, 2019. p. 491.
25. Weir, *Six Wives,* p. 410
26. Prole, Lozania. *Henry's Last Love*: (Lives and Loves of the Royals Book 5) Corazon, 2017. Digital Location 368.
27. Ibid., p. 412
28. Starkey, *Six Wives,* Kindle location 11264.
29. Luther, *Luther's Works*, Vol 50, Letters, p. 202.
30. Weir, *Six Wives*, p. 416
31. Starkey *Six Wives*, p. 686.
32. Wilson, *The Queen and the Heretic*, Digital Location 1121.
33. Starkey, Six Wives, p. 728
34. Strickland, *Queens of England*, Vol. 1, p. 440.
35. Weir, *Six Wives*, p. 498

4. Before Henry

1. Strickland, *Queens of England,* Vol. 1, p. 436.
2. James, *Catherine Parr,* Digital location, 51
3. Ibid., Digital location 128.
4. Ibid., Digital location 346.
5. Porter, *Katherine the Queen*, p. 16.
6. James, *Catherine Parr,* Digital Location, 359.
7. Ibid., Digital Location 1039.
8. Starkey, *Six Wives,* p. 694.
9. Porter, *Katherine the Queen*, p. 27
10. The Book of Hours is a Christian devotional book popular in the Middle Ages. With added content and comments, it was like a diary.
11. Mueller, *Complete Works and Correspondence*. P. 38
12. Starkey, *Six Wives*. p. 659.
13. Martienssen, *Queen Katherine Parr*, p. 20
14. Strickland, *Queens of England*, Vol. 1. P. 431.
15. Porter, *Katherine the Queen*, p. 37
16. Strickland, p. 431.
17. It was not strange that marriage contracts were made involving young children, but co-habitation did not take place until both parties were sixteen.
18. Strickland, *Queens of England*, Vol. 1, Digital Location 3833-3834.
19. Weir, *The Six Wives*, p. 488.
20. Norton, *Katherine Parr*, Digital location 392-393

21. Porter, *Katherine the Queen*. P. 54.
22. Norton, Elizabeth. *Catherine Parr*, Digital Location, 442.
23. Starkey, *Six Wives*, Digital Location 12101.
24. James, *Catherine Parr*, Digital Location 947.
25. Ibid., Digital Location 10012-13.
26. Weir, *The Six Wives*. p. 490.
27. Norton, *Catherine Parr*, Digital location 805-806
28. Starkey, *Six Wives*, Digital Location 12128.
29. Wilson, *The Queen and the Heretic*, Digital Location 505-506.
30. Quoted in Porter, *Katherine the Queen*, p. 60.
31. Norton, *Catherine Parr*, Digital location 228.

5. Why Marry Henry?

1. Wilson, *The Queen and the Heretic*, Digital Location 1134.
2. Norton, *Catherine Parr*, Digital Location 1306
3. The king's bodyguards were known as The Honourable Band of Gentlemen Pensioners.
4. Wilson, Derek. *The Queen and the Heretic*, Digital Location 1217.
5. Susan James, *Catherine Parr: Henry VIII's Last Love,* History Press, Digital Locations 1384-1385).
6. Erickson, *The First Elizabeth*, p. 66
7. Porter, *Katherine the Queen*, p. 122.
8. Starkey, *Six Wives,* Digital Location 1239.
9. Weir, *Six Wives*, p. 494.
10. Norton, *Catherine Parr*, Digital location 1312.
11. Starkey, *Six Wives*, Digital Location 12329.
12. Weir, *Six Wives*, p. 490.
13. Norton, *Catherine Parr*, Digital location 1349-1351.
14. Weir, *Six Wives*, p. 495.
15. Wilson, *The Queen and the Heretic*, Digital Location 1989.
16. Mueller, *Complete Works and Correspondence*, p. 153, n. 81.
17. Christopher Haigh, *English Reformation*, Oxford University Press, 1993. p. 160.
18. Janel Mueller, et. al., *The Cambridge History of Early Modern English Literature*, p. 90.
19. Norton, *Catherine Parr*, Digital Location 457.
20. Starkey, *Six Wives,* Digital Location 12216.
21. Porter, *Katherine the Queen*, pp. 167-168
22. Norton, *Catherine Parr*, Digital Location 1590-1591

23. Ibid., Digital Location 1630-1631
24. See James, *Catherine Parr*, Digital Location 2020
25. Mueller, *Complete Works and Correspondence*, p. 77
26. See Norton, *Catherine Parr*, Digital Location 1446.
27. James, *Catherine Parr*, Digital Location 3033.
28. Brandon G. Withrow, *Katherine Parr,* p. 37.
29. Haugaard, William P. "Katherine Parr: The Religious Convictions of a Renaissance Queen." *Renaissance Quarterly* 22, no. 4 (1969): 346-59
30. Mueller, *Complete Works and Correspondence*, p. 197, n.2.
31. Ibid., p. 220.
32. Ibid., p. 230
33. Ibid., p. 202
34. Porter, *Katherine. the Queen,* p. 202.
35. Mueller, *Complete Works & Correspondence*, p. 396.
36. Hoffman, C. Fenno, Jr. "Catherine Parr as Woman of Letters." *Huntington Library Quarterly* 23, no. 4 (1960): 349-67
37. James, *Katherine Parr*, Digital Location 3826.
38. Mueller, *Complete Works & Correspondence*, p. 406.
39. Ibid., p. 407.
40. Hoffman, C. Fenno, Jr. "Catherine Parr as Woman of Letters," pp. 349-67.
41. Ibid.
42. Randall Martin, *Women Writers in Renaissance England*: An Annotated Anthology, Routledge; 2010, p. 45
43. Wilson, *The Queen and the Heretic*, Digital Location 706.
44. Mueller, *Complete Works & Correspondence*, p. 370.
45. Porter, *Katherine the Queen*, pp. 134-135.
46. Ibid., p. 136.
47. Mueller, *Complete Works & Correspondence*, p. 46.
48. Porter, *Katherine the Queen*, p. 153
49. Wilson, *The Queen and the Heretic,* Digital Location, 1231.
50. Ibid., p. 129.
51. Ibid., p. 131.
52. Ibid., p. 133.
53. Starkey, *Six Wives*, Digital Location 12330
54. Norton, *Catherine Parr*, Digital location 1349-1351.
55. James, *Catherine Parr*, Digital Location 1737
56. Don Matzat, *The Lord Told Me...I Think,* Harvest House Publishers, 1996.

6. *Henry and Kate*

1. Strickland, *Queens of England*, Vol. 1., p. 433.
2. Wilson, *The Queen and the Heretic*, Digital Location 1304.
3. Porter, *Katherine the Queen*, p. 145.
4. Weir, *Six Wives*, p. 498.
5. Porter, *Katherine the Queen*, p. 147.
6. Starkey, *Six Wives*, Digital Location 12408.
7. Weir, *The Six Wives*, p. 499.
8. Strickland, *Queens of England*, Vol. 1. Pp. 434-435.
9. Norton, *Catherine Parr*, Digital Location 2236.
10. Porter, Katherine the Queen, p. 148.
11. Ibid., p. 147.
12. Ibid., p. 149.
13. Wilson, *The Queen and the Heretic*, Digital Location 1225.
14. Strickland, *Queens of England*, Vol. 1, p. 437
15. Porter, *Katherine the Queen*, p. 349
16. Ibid., p. 153.
17. James, *Catherine Parr*, Digital Location 1900.
18. Porter, *Katherine the Queen*, p. 154.
19. Norton, Catherine Parr, Digital Location 1468.
20. Porter, *Katherine the Queen*, p. 155.
21. James, *Catherine Parr*, Digital Location 2432.
22. Norton, *Catherine Parr*, Digital Location 1487-1489
23. 1 John 2:15
24. Parr, *The Lamentation of a Sinner*, pp. 36-37.
25. Norton, *Catherine Parr*, Digital Location 1514.
26. Ibid., Digital location 1516-1522.
27. Ibid., Digital Location 1568
28. Mueller, *Complete Works & Correspondence*, p. 49.
29. Norton, *Catherine Parr*, Digital Location 1870.
30. James. *Catherine Parr*, Digital Location 2549
31. Porter, *Katherine the Queen*, p, 202.
32. Ibid., p. 201.
33. Norton, *Catherine Parr*, Digital Location 1971.
34. Ibid., Digital Location 1881.
35. Porter, *Katherine the Queen*, p. 213.
36. Weir, *Six Wives*, p. 508.
37. Mueller, *Complete Works & Correspondence*, p. 63. (Edited for clarity)
38. Starkey, *Six Wives*, Digital Location 12812
39. Parr, *The Lamentation of a Sinner*, p. 42

40. William P. Haugaard, "Katherine Parr: The Religious Convictions of a Renaissance Queen." pp. 346-59.
41. Mueller, *Complete Works and Correspondence*, p. 70.

7. *One Happy Family*

1. Porter, *Katherine the Queen*, p. 66.
2. James, *Catherine Parr*, Digital Location 997.
3. Ibid., Digital Location 1956.
4. Erickson, *The First Elizabeth*, p. 55.
5. Porter, *Katherine the Queen*, p. 172.
6. Mueller, *Complete Works & Correspondence*, p. 82,
7. Ibid, p. 62.
8. This work, an 1897 edition, is available online at no charge. After a lengthy introduction by a Percy M. Ames, the remainder are facsimile pages in Elizabeth's own hand. While much of it is illegible due to the age of the paper and the nature of the old English, it is amazing to view the work of this eleven-year-old child.
9. Mueller, *Complete Works & Correspondence*, pp. 84-85.
10. Weir, *Six Wives*, p, 506
11. Mueller, *Complete Works & Correspondence*, p. 113
12. Ibid., p. 116
13. Ibid., p. 118. Janel Mueller identifies "Romans script" as writing in italics and "good literature" as Latin classics.
14. Ibid., p. 117. Janel Mueller identifies the "suitable messenger" as John Fowler, a page and later groom in Edward's household.
15. Ibid., p. 119.
16. Porter, *Katherine the Queen*, p. 306.
17. Ibid., p. 179.
18. Martienssen, *Queen Katherine Parr*, p. 220.

8. *From Opportunist to Reformer*

1. Weir, *Six Wives*, p. 495
2. Wilson, *The Queen and the Heretic*, Digital Location.706
3. James, *Catherine Parr*, Digital Location 3789
4. Ibid., Digital Location 3426
5. Ibid. Digital Location 3752.
6. James, Catherine Parr, Digital Location 3723.
7. Porter, *Katherine the Queen*, p. 229

8. Ibid., p. 248. Dr Linda Porter is the only biographer of Queen Katherine who includes this incident.

9. Elizabeth I, *Elizabeth I: Collected Works 1st Edition* (ed. Marcus, Mueller, Rose) University of Chicago Press, 2000, p. 10. I thank Dr Linda Porter for directing me to this source. In her *Katherine Parr: Complete Works and Correspondence,* Dr Janel Mueller does not include this correspondence.

10. John Calvin, *The Institutes of the Christian Religion,* Eerdmans, 1983, p. 39.

11. Parr, *The Lamentation of a Sinner,* p. 35

12. Porter, *Katherine the Queen,* pp. 246-247

13. A "chantry" was a trust fund for the purpose of employing one or more priests to sing a stipulated number of masses for the benefit of the soul of a specified deceased person in purgatory. Churches often had "chantry chapels" or specific altars where the supplications would take place.

14. James, *Catherine Parr,* Digital Location 4001-4003

15. Porter, *Katherine the Queen.,* p 115.

16. Mueller, *Complete Works & Correspondence,* p. 77

17. James, *Catherine Parr,* Digital Location 4386.

18. Martienssen, *Queen Katherine Parr,* pp. 190.191.

19. Wilson, *The Queen and the Heretic,* Digital Location 1452

20. Parr, *The Lamentation of a Sinner,* p. 73.

21. James, *Catherine Parr,* Digital Location 4415.

22. This encounter is found in John Foxe's *Acts and Monuments*. While it may be apocryphal, most accept it as true. It is recorded in most sources.

23. James, *Catherine Parr,* Digital Location 4592-4595,

24. Parr, *Lamentation of a Sinner,* pp. 61-62.

25. Porter, *Katherine the Queen,* p. 271.

9. *The Dowager Queen*

1. James. *Catherine Parr,* Digital Location 4837.

2. Mueller, *Complete Works & Correspondence,* p. 131.

3. Wilson, *The Queen and the Heretic,* Digital Location 3144.

4. Erickson, *The First Elizabeth,* p. 62.

5. Mueller, *Complete Works and Correspondence,* p. 133.

6. Ibid., p. 135.

7. Ibid., p. 146

8. Norton, *Catherine Parr,* Digital Location 3140.

9. Weir, *Six Wives,* Digital Location 5069-5074,

10. James, Catherine Parr, Digital Location 5065

11. Ibid., Digital Locations 5069-5074.

12. Norton, *Catherine Parr*, Digital Location 3284
13. Quoted in James, *Catherine Parr*, Digital Location 5222.
14. Norton, *Catherine Parr*, Digital Location 3504-3505.
15. John Strype, *Life of the Learned Sir John Cheke* (Oxford, 1821), p. 44.
16. Porter, *Katherine the Queen*, p. 298.
17. Mueller, *Complete Works & Correspondence*, p. 341.
18. Norton, *Catherine Parr*, Digital Location 3529
19. Quoted in Ibid., Digital Location 3275.
20. James, *Catherine Parr*, Digital Location 3787.
21. Norton, *Catherine Parr*, Digital Location 3506
22. Porter, *Katherine the Queen*. p. 348.
23. Ibid., p. 308.
24. Mueller, *Complete Works & Correspondence*, pp. 171-172.
25. Ibid., p. 174.
26. Ibid., pp. 177-178.
27. Wilson, *The Queen and the Heretic*, Digital Location 2919
28. Mueller, *Complete Works and Correspondence* p. 80
29. Erickson, *The First Elizabeth*, p. 79

10. *Katherine Parr Reprise*

1. Roland H. Bainton, "Catherine Parr." In *Women of the Reformation in France and England*, Digital Location 1619.
2. James McConica, *English Humanists and Reformation Politics*, Oxford at the Clarendon Press, 1965, p. 229.
3. Roland H. Bainton *Erasmus of Christendom,* Hendrickson Publishers, 1969, p. 294
4. Ibid.
5. Peter Marshall, *Heretics and Believers,* p. 124.
6. H.A. Enno Gelder, *The Two Reformations in the 16th Century*, Springer Netherlands, Digital Location 185.
7. Martienssen, *Katherine Parr*, pp. ix-x.
8. Gregory D. Dodds, *Exploiting Erasmus, The Erasmian Legacy and Religious Change in Early Modern England,* University of Toronto Press, 2009, p. 1.
9. Gregory D. Dodds, *Exploiting Erasmus:* p 6.
10. Mueller, *Complete Works and Correspondence*, p. 101
11. Marshall, *Heretics and Belivers,* p. 140
12. Mueller, *Complete Works and Correspondence*, p. 456, n. 52.
13. William P. Haugaard, *"Katherine Parr: The Religious Convictions of a Renaissance Queen."* Renaissance Quarterly 22, no. 4, 1969, pp. 346-59.
14. Mueller: *Complete Works and Correspondence.* p. 24.

15. J.I Packer and O.R. Johnston, *Martin Luther on the Bondage of the Will*, Fleming H. Revel, 1957. P. 69.

16. Mueller, Janel. "A Tudor Queen Finds Voice: Katherine Parr's Lamentations of a Sinner." In *The Historical Renaissance: New Essays on Tudor and Stuart Literature and Culture* edited by Heather Dubrow and Richard Strier, Chicago: The University of Chicago Press, 1988, pp. 15-47.

17. Ibid.

18. Porter, *Katherine the Queen*., p 115.

19. M. Luther, *Luther's Works*, vol. 49: Letters II Philadelphia: Fortress Press, p. 8.

20. Quoted in James, *Catherine Parr*, Digital Location 3776.

21. Wilson, *the Queen and the Heretic*, Digital Location 2983.

22. Mueller. *Complete Works and Correspondence*, p. 109.

23. Marshall, Peter. *Heretics and Believers: A History of the English Reformation*. Yale University Press, 2017. p 308

24. A.G. Dickens, *The English Reformation*, p. 67.

25. Packer and Johnson, *Martin Luther on the Bondage of the Will*, pp. 59-60.

26. Plass, *What Luther Says*, p. 964.

27. 1 Timothy 1:16.

28. Marshall, *Heretics and Believers*, p. 145.

29. Hoffman, C. Fenno, Jr. "Catherine Parr as Woman of Letters," pp. 349-67.

30. Parr, *Lamentation*, pp. 31-32.

31. Porter, *Katherine the Queen*, p. 299.

32. Parr, *Lamentation*, p. 83

33. Ibid., pp. 82-83.

34. Bainton. *Women of the Reformation: In France and England,* Digital Locations 2578-2580.

35. Ibid., Digital Location 2568.

36. Marshall, Heretics and Believers, p. 384.

37. Ibid., p. 423.

38. Bainton. *Women of the Reformation: In France and England*, Digital Location 2820.

11. *The Lamentation of a Sinner*

1. Chapter headings were not a part of the original 1547 edition but were added to the 1548 edition. I have included them to help distinguish the various themes presented by Queen Katherine.

2. Perhaps a reference to the Roman Catholic teaching of transubstantiation whereby the elements in the Sacrament are changed into the body and blood of Christ.

3. John 3:6
4. Luke 15:7
5. 1 John1:9
6. Psalm 37:5
7. Galatians 3:22
8. 1 Peter 2:24
9. Psalm 19:12
10. Luke 19:40
11. John 3:19
12. Romans 1:21-28
13. Luke 10:27
14. 1 Corinthians 2:2
15. 2 Corinthians12:2
16. Philippians 3:7
17. Romans 10:3
18. Luke 18:9-14
19. John 10:12
20. 1 Corinthians 1:30
21. Philippians 2:9
22. 1 John 2:2
23. Luke 5:31
24. Matthew 15:27
25. Psalm 51:11
26. 1 Corinthians 12:3
27. Romans 8:26
28. Matthew 11:28
29. Matthew 7:11
30. Hebrews 11:6
31. Luke 17:5
32. John 17:3
33. Romans 3:20
34. Galatians 2:21
35. Galatians 5:6
36. 1 John 4:8
37. 1 John 4:16
38. John 3:16
39. Ephesians 1:18
40. 1 John 2:15-17
41. 2 Corinthians 8:9
42. Romans 5:8

43. 1 Corinthians 1:20
44. Colossians 2:15
45. Ephesians 6:10
46. John 19:21
47. 1 Corinthians 15:56
48. Romans 7
49. Genesis 3:15
50. 1 John 3:8
51. 1 Corinthians 15:56
52. Roman 8:28
53. Romans 8:38-39
54. 1 Corinthians 3:19
55. Colossians 2:14
56. 1 Corinthians 15:56
57. 1 Corinthians 15:55
58. 1 Corinthians 15:24
59. Colossians 2:9
60. Colossians 2:3
61. John 4:14
62. Romans 8:1
63. Romans 5:10
64. Ephesians 4:5
65. It is evident that Katherine wrote this while King Henry was still alive even though it was published after his death.
66. Possible reference to transubstantiation.
67. Matthew 7:21
68. Matthew 15:8
69. John 4:4
70. Matthew 15:14
71. Titus 1:11: Money
72. 1 Corinthians 13
73. Ephesians 4:26
74. Galatians 5:17
75. 1 John 2:15-17
76. Romans 8:5-8
77. Matthew 10:17
78. Matthew 11:17
79. Matthew 16:23
80. Mark 7:2
81. John 12:5

82. John 2:15
83. Mark 3:1-6
84. John 4
85. Acts 8:9-24
86. Matthew 13:3-9
87. Luke 6:45
88. Matthew 21:31-32
89. When the Bible became available in English, it became evident that there were many doctrines taught by Rome that were not found in Scripture. These became known as "unwritten truths" that were only known to the educated clergy.
90. Ephesians 1:4
91. Romans 8:16
92. Romans 8:38-39
93. Ephesians 2:10
94. Ephesians 5:27
95. Colossians 2:8
96. Ephesians 4:5
97. 1 Peter 2:1
98. Luke 22:42
99. Ephesians 5:25-26
100. 1 Corinthians 14:34
101. Matthew 7:3
102. Matthew 25:34

12. *Textual Sources*

1. Derek Wilson, *The Queen and the Heretic*. Lion Hudson, 2018. Kindle Edition, Location 2971
2. Martienssen, *Queen Katherine* Parr, p. 201.
3. Janel Mueller, "A Tudor Queen Finds Voice: Katherine Parr's Lamentations of a Sinner." In *The Historical Renaissance: New Essays on Tudor and Stuart Literature and Culture,* edited by Heather Dubrow and Richard Strier, pp. 15-47. Chicago: The University of Chicago Press, 1988.
4. Marshall, *Heretics and Believers*, p.124.
5. Ibid. p. 125.
6. Porter, *Katherine the Queen*, p. 248.
7. Luther, M. *Luther's Works,* Vol. 25: Lectures on Romans, Saint Louis: Concordia Publishing House.
8. Luther, *Luther's Works*, Lectures on Romans, Saint Louis: Concordia Publishing House, Introduction.

9. In *Representing Women in Renaissance England*, edited by Claude J. Summers and Ted Larry Pebworth. Columbia: University of Missouri Press, 1997, pp. 24-41.

10. Mueller, *Complete Works and Correspondence*, p. 431.

11. Luther, *Luther's Works*, Vol. 42: Devotional Writings, Philadelphia: Fortress Press, pp. 7-15.

12. Porter, *Katherine the Queen*, pp. 241-2.

13. James, *Catherine Parr*, Digital Location, 3819

14. Wilson, *The Queen and the Heretic*, Digital Location 2391.

15. Mueller, *Complete Works and Correspondence*, pp. 429-430.

16. Tappert, *The Book of Concord,* The Augsburg Confession, Philadelphia: Fortress Press. 2, XX, 22

17. James 2:19

18. Romans 3:20

19. Galatians 2:21

20. Galatians 5:6

21. Theodore G. Tappert, *The Book of Concord*, Fortress Press, 1959, p. 113:48

22. Mueller, *Complete Works and Correspondence*, p.456, n. 51.

23. Ibid., 114:48

24. Ibid., 114:56.

25. Ibid., 116:64.

26. Ibid., 112:35

27. Roland Bainton, *Women of the Reformation: In France and England,* Digital Locations 1643-1644.

Appendix

1. Porter, *Katherine the Queen*, p. 242.

2. Ephesian 2:3

3. 1 Corinthians 2:14

4. Psalm 51:5

5. Genesis 8:21

6. Romans 7:18-21

7. Romans 3:23

8. Calvin, *Institutes*, Vol. 2, p. 78

9. Paul Tournier, *Guilt and Grace*, Harper and Row, 1959, pp. 159-160.

10. Werner Elert, *The Structure of Lutheranism*, Concordia Publishing House, 1962, p. 85

11. David E. Roberts, *Existentialism and Religious Belief* (New York: Oxford University Press, 1959) p. 99.

12. Calvin, *Institutes*, Vol. 1, p. 211.

13. Paul Tournier, *Guilt and Grace* (New York: Harper and Row, 1959), p. 81.

14. Martin Luther, *First Lectures on the Psalms* I: Psalms 1-75, Vol. 10, Concordia Publishing House, Psalm 2:9.

15. Psalm 139:23

16. Plass, *What Luther Says*, p. 1293.

17. Weir, *Six Wives*, p. 255

18. Plass, *What Luther Says*, p. 964.

19. Mueller, *Complete Works & Correspondence*, p. 230.

20. 1 Corinthians 12:3

21. Plass, *What Luther Says*, p. 1349

22. R.C. Sproul, *The Prayer of the Lord*, Reformation Trust Publishing, 2009, p. 101.

23. William Wilberforce, *Real Christianity*, Dreamscape Media, 2018, p. 6

24. Parr, *Lamentation*, p. 96.

25. Ibid. p. 115

26. 2 Peter 1:21

27. 2 Timothy 3:16

28. Romans 1:16

29. Calvin, *Institutes*, p. 475.

30. Romans 1:16

31. 1 Corinthians 2:7,10,14

32. William Wilberforce, *Real Christianity*, p. 73

33. Parr, *Lamentation*, p. 43

34. Ibid., p. 240.

35. Martin Luther often spoke of grace, faith, and the Holy Spirit as being "infused" into the heart. Controversy arose when the term was applied to justification, the word "infusion of righteousness" as opposed to Luther's "imputation of righteousness" was established by Rome at the Council of Trent.

36. 1 Corinthians 1:23.

37. John 3:16

38. Romans 1:18

39. Leviticus 17:11.

40. Hebrews 9:22.

41. Romans 3:25.

42. Ephesians 1:7-8.

43. *Luther's Small Catechism*, Concordia Publishing house, 1986, p. 14

44. Hebrews 9:12.

45. John 1:29.

46. Wilson, *The Queen and the Heretic*, Digital Location 2414,

47. Plass, *What Luther Says*, p. 703.

48. Calvin, *Institutes*, Vol. 2, p. 37.

49. Nicolaus Ludwig, Graf von Zinzendorf, translated by John Wesley.

50. Matthew 5:20

51. Matthew 5:48.

52. James 2:10.

53. Tappert, *The Apology of the Augsburg Confession*, I, VI, 45

54. According to Roman Catholic tradition, the Holy Stairs are the steps leading up to the praetorium of Pontius Pilate in Jerusalem on which Jesus Christ stepped on his way to trial during his Passion. The Stairs reputedly were brought to Rome by St. Helena in the fourth century. For centuries, the *Scala Sancta* has attracted Christian pilgrims who wish to honor the Passion of Jesus Christ by ascending the stairs on their knees.

55. David C. Steinmetz, *Luther in Context* (Grand Rapids: Baker, 2002), p. 2.

56. Roland Bainton, *Here I Stand* (Nashville: Abingdon Press, Reprint, 2013), p. 41.

57. In presenting his experience, Luther himself cites this date, but it is unrealistic. In his 1516 *Commentary on Romans* he already presents an enlightened understanding of justification as he also did in a letter to George Spenlein dated August 1516. In all probability, Luther got his dates mixed up.

58. Romans 1:16-17 (KJV)

59. Martin Luther, *Luther's Works* (Philadelphia: Fortress Press, 1999), Vol. 34, pgs. 336-337.

60. Philippians 3:4-9

61. 2 Corinthians 5:20.

62. Romans 5:1.

63. Porter, *Katherine the Queen*, p. 275.

64. Parr, *Lamentation*, p. 42

65. Romans 1:18-19.

66. James 2:9.

67. John Calvin, *Institutes*, Vol. 1, p. 477

68. *Luther's Works*, Commentary on Galatians, Vol. 27, p. 28.

69. Romans 10:14

70. Luther, M. *Luther's Works*, Vol. 50, Philadelphia: Fortress Press, Page 203.

71. Porter, *Katherine the Queen*, p. 255.

72. Luther, M., *Luther's Works*, Letters III, Vol. 50, Page 202.

73. Tappert, T. G., *The Book of Concord*. The Augsburg Confession: XX, 27-29.

74. Galatians 5:22-23.
75. Colossians 2:6-7.
76. Tappert, T. G. *The Book of Concord*, The Formula of Concord: 2, VI, 7.
77. John Calvin, *Institutes*, Vol. 2, p. 5
78. 1 John 1:8-9.
79. Ephesians 5:18-20.
80. Colossians 3:15-17.
81. Bainton, *Erasmus of Christianity*, p. 193.
82. Ibid., p. 200.
83. Plass, *What Luther Says*, p. 455.
84. Ibid., p. 454
85. Tappert, *Book of Concord*, The Formula of Concord, p. 495:5
86. Ibid., p. 629.

INDEX